HARDPRESS.NET
HOME OF HARD-TO-FIND BOOKS

A Journal During a Residence in France, from
the Beginning of August, to the Middle of
December, 1792
by John Moore

Address:
HardPress
8345 NW 66TH ST #2561
MIAMI FL 33166-2626
USA
Email: info@hardpress.net

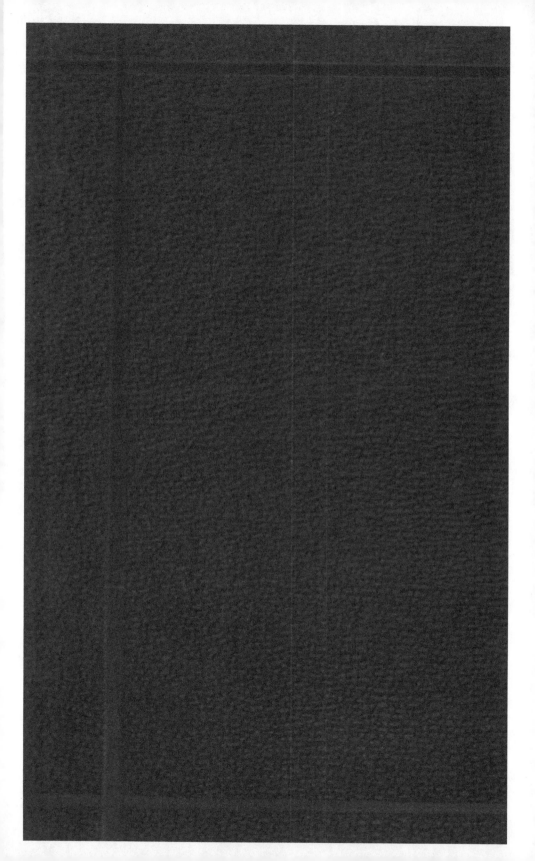

H May Poynter
Oxford

A

J O U R N A L

DURING A RESIDENCE IN FRANCE,

FROM THE

BEGINNING OF AUGUST,

TO THE

MIDDLE OF DECEMBER, 1792.

A

JOURNAL

DURING A RESIDENCE IN FRANCE,

FROM THE

BEGINNING OF AUGUST,

TO THE

MIDDLE OF DECEMBER, 1792.

TO WHICH IS ADDED,

AN ACCOUNT OF THE MOST REMARKABLE EVENTS
THAT HAPPENED AT PARIS FROM THAT TIME TO
THE DEATH OF THE LATE KING OF FRANCE.

BY JOHN MOORE, M.D.

IN TWO VOLUMES.
VOL. II.

Opus opimum casibus, atrox præliis, discors seditionibus, ipsa
etiam pace sævum.   Tacit.

LONDON:

PRINTED FOR G. G. AND J. ROBINSON,
PATERNOSTER-ROW.
1793.

...is place, and arrived juſt time enough to be admitted before the gates were ſhut;

B but

A

J O U R N A L, &c.

Aire, October 7.

WE left Calais this morning, and came to St. Omers in the expectation of receiving such information as would determine us whether it might be expedient to take Lille in our way to Paris: for at Calais the accounts were contradictory; according to some the siege was raised, according to others it still continued.

On arriving at St. Omers, we were assured that the Austrian army had retired from before Lille. We therefore set out directly for this place, and arrived just time enough to be admitted before the gates were shut;

but we had very great difficulty in finding lodgings: all the inns being full of people, particularly of women and children from Lille, we were obliged to drive about in the dark from inn to inn for a confiderable time before we could find one to receive us; and at laft were glad to be allowed to take fhelter in a miferable nafty houfe, with the fign of the Three Kings over the door. Nothing can be a ftronger proof of the neglected and defpifed ftate of this inn, than that a fign fo obnoxious is tolerated, or rather overlooked.

We were much difappointed on our arrival at Aire, to find the accounts of the retreat of the Auftrians from before Lille as uncertain and contradictory as thofe of Calais. Not trufting to the information I received at our own wretched inn, I went to a coffee-houfe in fearch of fome more to be depended on: I addreffed myfelf to a grave looking man who fmoked his pipe at the door; I

foon

foon found that he knew nothing of the matter, and was more difpofed to afk queftions
than to anfwer them. He faid he perceived
I was a ftranger, and afked where I lodged ;
I anfwered, *Aux Trois Rois.* " Aux Trois
Rois !" repeated he with a grimace, " ma
foi, Monfieur, vous avez choifi là des hôtes
qui ne font plus à la mode*."

Although none of the inhabitants of Aire,
with whom I converfed, could inform me
whether the Auftrians had left Lille or
not, they were all able and moft willing to
tell many ftories of their cruelties. Whether
they added *aught in malice* I know not, but
I am perfuaded they did *nothing extenuate.*
The maid of the inn, after giving a terrible
account of the devaftation and deftruction
occafioned by the pillaging in the villages,

---

* At the three Kings !—Truly, Sir, you have chofen
your lodgings with people who are not much in fafhion
at prefent.

faid

said it was not eafy to tell whether the Hulans or the red-hot bullets were the moft
mifchievous; but, continued fhe, " Ce qui eft
certain, Monfieur, eft, que le fang coule dans
ce pauvre Lille depuis huit jours comme
l'eau coule dans les rues d'Aire—ah ! Monfieur, cela déchire le cœur !*"

Having pronounced this with a fympa-
thifing accent, fhe went out of the room,
and I heard her finging a very gay tune as
fhe went down ftairs.

The road to Paris this way is much more
agreeable than that by Boulogne, the land
being more fertile, the fields better culti-
vated, the country better inhabited, and the
peafantry richer.   A great deal of tobacco
is raifed in the country around St. Omers,
and between that town and Aire : the leaves
are hung up to dry on the walls of the cot-

* What is quite certain, is, that blood flows in that
poor town of Lille, in as great abundance as water in
the ftreets of Aire.   It is enough to break one's heart.

tages,

tages, and on the fides of the ftacks of corn and of beans in the farm-yards.

We paffed long trains of waggons with grain for the army now affembling near Lille.

Arras, October 8.

Aire has the appearance of a very poor town, and it might be imagined that the number of women and children who have fled to it from Lille would render it alfo a very melancholy place : I could not help remarking, however, that the firft thing we heard laft night when we entered the town, was the tune of *ça ira;* and on quitting it this morning the fame tune was refounding through the ftreets, the paffengers, whether going to their work or to matins, moving their heads and fteps in cadence all the way.

As a great many poft-horfes are employed in the public fervice, it was with great difficulty that we got to Bethune. When we arrived at the poft-houfe, which is on the outfide of the fortifications, we were informed,

B 3

formed, that we could not get horses for the chaise in lefs than three or four hours, and none for the fervants even then.

We walked into the town, which is beautifully fituated on a rifing ground, with a delightful profpect of a rich country all around. It was market day, and the town was crowded with well dreffed cheerful looking peafants.

We entered into converfation with an officer of cavalry on the public fquare: he had left Lille three days before. He faid that the firing was violent when he came away, but there had been none heard fince Saturday night:—this is Monday. He had fince heard that the enemy had retired to the diftance of a league from the town; whether they meant to renew the bombardment or not, he did not know, but at any rate he was perfuaded they would not be able to take the town, as the inhabitants were refolved to be buried in the ruins rather than furrender.

Another perfon accofted me foon after,

as

as I was looking at the tree of Liberty which is planted in the market place; it was hung round with garlands of flowers, with emblems of freedom, and various inscriptions. He informed me that it was not yet certainly known whether the Austrians had entirely relinquished their attack on Lille; that at the worst they could only destroy the houses, but would never be able to take the town. On my asking if he thought we should be allowed to enter the town, in case we were to proceed by that route, he answered, that the town had never been entirely blockaded, and that even during the bombardment, which was made on the opposite side, the gate towards Bethune had been kept open for several hours every day; that as we were provided with passports we would be admitted as soon as we arrived, but, he added, that the roads were very much cut and destroyed, and he questioned whether we should find horses at the post-houses between Be-

thune

thune and Lille. On the whole, he said, we muft expect to meet with many obftacles, and therefore advifed us to go to Paris by Arras.—We determined to follow his advice. He then explained the allegoric figures that had been placed round the tree of Liberty two days before on account of fome public feaft or rejoicing : this led him on to fpeak of the revolution, to which he appeared to be a zealous friend. He profeffed a great efteem for the Englifh, becaufe they are the friends of freedom; and added, that although fome of his acquaintance had a ftrong perfuafion that the Britifh cabinet was watching for an opportunity of declaring againft France, when fhe was attacked and menaced by fo many other powers, yet he, for his part, could not believe that fo cowardly a policy would be adopted by fo brave a nation. The conduct of the French court towards Great Britain during the conteft with America occurred to me, but I did

I did not think it expedient to remind him of it. He continued to obferve, that France being now unanimous for a republic, all the efforts of their enemies to conquer the country, or dictate a government to the inhabitants, would prove vain ; they would be exterminated, rather than fubmit to foreign powers, or to their old oppreffors.—" We have been," added he with great warmth, " too long oppreffed by a race of weak luxurious princes, and trode upon by an infolent yet flavifh nobleffe; it is difficult to get rid *de toutes ces vermines,* but as they are now moftly gone, it will be our faults if we ever allow them to return."—Here I could not help reminding him, that many of the nobility had diftinguifhed themfelves as the friends of Liberty, and fome were actually at the head of the armies of the republic at that moment; I mentioned Cuftine, Biron, and Montefquieu. He acknowledged the merit of thofe I had named, and of fome others; " but as for the greater part of the reſt," added he, " the only ſervice they ever rendered their country was by running away from it : if they had all remained, the democrates would not have ſuch an eaſy game, and Heaven knows what might have happened ; but they are gone, and it is our buſineſs to keep them off: let them go and crouch to other kings, and domineer over other ſlaves, none are to be found in France.——This is the land of liberty and equality.——A camp is already formed at Douay, another is forming nearer Lille ; if thirty thouſand more men are required, they will be raiſed in this neighbourhood without difficulty : hardly a peaſant or tradeſman in France, but is zealous in the cauſe of freedom, and ready to ſhed his blood for his country."——The man talked with ſuch animation of voice and geſture as drew a crowd around us, who all ſeemed to ſympathiſe with what he ſaid: this was not unobſerved by the ſpeaker, who

who by the looks he threw on the furround-
ing circle, and by the elevation of voice,
fhewed that he was as folicitous to be heard
by it as by me.

. I was told, after he quitted me, that he was
not a citizen of Bethune, as I firft imagined,
but a Parifian. I underftand that there are
many fpies and emiffaries in the various towns
of France, hired by the executive power
for the exprefs purpofe of fpreading thofe
fentiments, and alfo to examine what are the
prevailing opinions. Whether this man is
one of thofe I know not, but he could not
have fhewn himfelf a more zealous republican had he been ever fo well paid for it.

When we returned to the poft-houfe, we
were informed that we might have horfes
for the chaifes, but there were no bidets for
the fervants, all of them being employed by
the couriers who were continually paffing
and repaffing on the public fervice. There
was a neceffity therefore to take the fervants
into

into the chaifes, and in this manner we were dragged through very bad roads to Arras.

We met a battalion of national guards on the way. The citizens of Amiens no fooner heard that Lille was invefted, than they raifed, clothed, and armed this battalion at their own expence. The men feem in high fpirits, and were marching with great ardour to Lille.

Robefpierre is a native of Arras; this great luminary of the revolution not only renders Arras more confpicuous, but has thrown a ray of light on his brother, who lived here in obfcurity, but is now chofen a deputy to the convention.

Cuvilly, October 9.

We left Arras at fix in the morning, and with much difficulty arrived at this wretched village a little after it was dark : we had been detained feveral hours at Peronne, waiting

for

for the return of poft-horfes, and afterwards till the poor animals were fed, and had in fome meafure recovered their fatigue.

Peronne is ftrongly fortified, but the only garrifon in it at prefent confifts of citizens; they are however well armed, and moft of the men, and all the officers, are in the uniform of the national guards.

A battalion of the Gens d'Armes of Paris are expected at Peronne this night. The quarter-mafter with fome other of the corps are already arrived.

I was witnefs to a fcene which will give fome idea of the kind of liberty which exifts in France at prefent.

I had joined three officers of the city guards, who were walking in the fquare oppofite to the poft-houfe. One of them, a very genteel and obliging man, was giving me what information I afked, when two men, in the uniform of the expected battalion, came up to us, and one of them in a

haughty

haughty and menacing manner, demanded how it happened that the fleurs de lis and other fymbols of royalty, to which he pointed, were not effaced from the fteeple and the front of the town-houfe.

The officer replied, that it was the bufi-nefs of the mayor, and he knew nothing about it. On which the other burft forth into many abufive expreffions againft the mayor, calling him rafcal and ariftocrate, and fwearing that when he met him, he would cut him in pieces : as he faid this, he drew his fabre and feemed difpofed to quarrel with all around him.

Another officer of the city guards, more advanced in years than the former, addreffed this furious fellow in a foothing manner, affuring him that the municipality had al-ready given orders that the emblems of which he complained fhould all be re-moved ; that the reafon of its not being al-ready done was becaufe the mayor, who was

a very

a very honeſt man, and of courſe no ariſtocrate, had been entirely occupied in ſending
neceſſaries to their diſtreſſed friends at Lille,
and in providing good quarters for the battalion of Pariſians which was expected.

This conciliatory language ſmoothed
the threatening brow of the man, who at
laſt ſheathed his ſword, and walked away
with his companion. Each of theſe fellows
had a brace of piſtols ſtuck in his belt, and
there was ſomething in their looks, as well
as their deportment, which gave me a ſuſpicion that they belonged to the aſſaſſinating
band of September.

For the firſt two poſts after leaving Peronne, we were continually meeting ſmall
bodies of the Gens d'Armes who were
haſtening to the relief of Lille : they march
in a very ſtraggling manner. The battalion
conſiſts of a thouſand men ; I do not ſup-
poſe there was above two hundred in a body,
with the colours. They cried as we paſſed,

2   Vive

Vive la nation ! vive la république ! and in
a manner that sufficiently denoted that it
was expected we should do the same, which
we did accordingly; but this ceremony becoming a little fatiguing, one of the servants
refrained from joining in the cry when he
was invited.——A soldier observing this, seized
the bridle of his horse, and ordered him to
repeat the words; with which as the man
did not immediately comply, another le-
velled his piece, and would probably have
fired, if Lord Lauderdale had not darted his
head out of the window of the carriage, calling out, that the man did not understand
their language, that he was un Anglois; on
which the soldier raised his musket, and a
young officer waving his hat and calling out
Vivent les Anglois! we passed on. Although there is no danger of a man's losing
his money by robbery on the high-way
when he travels in France, he is in considerable danger of losing his life, if he happens
not

not to be attentive and obedient to the word
of command on occasions like this.

It was fifty to one that this servant was
not shot through the head, or thrust through
with a bayonet for his tardiness in the
present instance; and if he had, some
one would have observed, as the man did
at Clermont, *C'est un homme de moins,* and
no farther notice would have been taken of
the incident.

The whole of this battalion consisted of
stout men, all well armed and well clothed, but
there seemed to be little subordination among
them; and I understand that, in general there
is less in those regiments which are formed
of Parisians than in the other corps.

When we arrived at the post-house, a
considerable number were carousing and
singing songs in honour of the revolution.
They seemed desirous to converse with us,
and one who was a good deal elevated with
wine, proclaimed aloud the exploits they

were to perform. "After driving *aes Gueux des Autrichiens*," said he, "from Lille, we shall follow them to Bruffels, and there pafs the winter." Another, addreffing Lord Lauderdale, said, " Je vois bien que vous êtes Anglais, Monfieur, mais j'efpere que vous n'êtes pas du chambre des pairs qui font tous de . . ." here he added a very grofs epithet, in too great ufe all over France.

They then proceeded on their march, vociferating certain fongs of the groffeft nature, and shamefully abufive of the King and Queen. Several were in a fituation which put it out of their power to march to Peronne that day. Their comrades, however, prepared a carriage for them, which at length drove away.

I afked the poft-mafter if thofe men were obedient to their officers : " Comme vous êtes à moi, Monfieur," anfwered he, " et peut-être pas même autant—comme je vais vous le prouver :"—this excited my curiofity—

fity—" For," continued the poft-mafter, as I am perfuaded that *Monfieur* is a man who liftens to reafon, you would par conféquence comply with what I required, provided it were juft and reafonable ; whereas thofe men never mind what their officers fay, whether it is reafonable or not."

There was fomething more precife and formal in this man's manner than is ufual with Frenchmen, which induced me to enquire a little about him of one of the poftillions ; who told me he had formerly been a fchool-mafter in a neighbouring village.

He gave us another proof of his power of reafoning; on his putting only two horfes to a chaife inftead of three, which is ufual, he advertifed us that he expected to be paid for three. I hinted that this did not feem quite reafonable : he immediately undertook to prove that it was highly reafonable in him to exact as much for two horfes as for three, or, if any difference were to be made, fome-

what

what more: we were all attention.——" I will have the honour, Gentlemen, refumed he with a folemn air, of making this as clear as day light. You muft all know that tra-vellers are often detained in the middle of their journey by an accident happening to one of the horfes in their carriage ; but there is a greater chance of this happening to one of three horfes than of two."——His argument was allowed to be irrefiftible, and he was paid his full demand. " All that I ever de-fire of any mortal," faid the poft-mafter as he received payment, " is that he will only hear me, and liften to the voice of reafon—but thofe men who are juft gone would do neither."

I underftood that while he was proving to them that his bill was very reafonable, they had cut him fhort in the middle of his argument, and paid him with half ; defiring him to recolleÆ that falt, which before the revolution coft fourteen fols the pound, was

now

now fold at two, and that the price of tobacco had been diminifhed in the fame proportion.

Paris, October 10th.

Having left our miferable quarters a little
after five this morning, we arrived at Paris
about four in the afternoon, paffing through
the lines which have been forming in the
plains of St. Denis. Military men laugh at
the idea of defending fuch a town as Paris
by any intrenchments which could be made
before the Pruffians come, if they come at
all; and which, if made, would require a
garrifon of a hundred thoufand men, and all
the cannon in France to protect. The Parifians, however, feem pleafed with thefe
intrenchments; particularly the women, of
whom we obferved great numbers, with their
ufual gaiety, intermingled with the work-
men.

Having written to an acquaintance to in-

form

form him about what time we expected to be
at Paris, we drove to the Hotel des Tuileries, where he had engaged lodgings, which
were preferred on account of their vicinity
to the Conventional Affembly, ·

It will not be improper to mention here
fome things which took place in the Convention during our abfence from Paris, but
of which I did not know the particulars till
my return.

One moft important object, and which
demanded the early attention of the Convention, was to vindicate, as far as is poffible, the
French nation from the foul ftain of the late
maffacres, by bringing the real authors of
them to punifhment. To this the Convention was invoked by juftice, and prompted
by every feeling of our nature.——In an affembly in which there are fome clergymen,
many lawyers, and, as I am told, a confiderable number of philofophers, it was not to be
fuppofed that a meafure fo neceffary and becoming

coming would be long delayed. But it is somewhat extraordinary, that a seaman was the first who fixed the attention of the Assembly upon it.

" Il est temps," said Kersaint, " d'élever des échafauds pour ceux qui commettent les assassinats, et pour ceux qui les provoquent, &c. . . . Il y a peut-être plus de courage qu'on ne pense à s'élever contre les assassins, mais dussai-je tomber sous leurs coups, je serai digne de la confiance de mes concitoyens*."

He then moved that four commissioners should be immediately appointed to propose the most effectual measures for the preventing and punishing assassination, and that

* It is full time to erect scaffolds for those who commit assassinations, or prompt others to commit them, &c. . . . Perhaps it requires more courage than might be imagined to speak against assassins, but should I fall the victim of their vengeance, I will shew myself worthy of the confidence of my fellow-citizens.

their

their plan fhould be prefented to the Convention the next day.

It could hardly be fuppofed that fuch a meafure would be oppofed.—Strange as this appears, however, it met with oppofition.

Bazire obferved, that France was ftill in the crifis of a revolution, and *very vigorous meafures* were neceffary.—It was true, he added, that many fufpected perfons had been arrefted and punifhed; thofe perfons had been endeavouring to raife a civil war; but, continued he, there are not four men to be found in all France capable to give a plan which can, in the prefent moment, reconcile the public intereft with the rights of the citizens.

Tallien (he who was fecretary to the Council of the Community on the 2d of September,) faid, that the exifting laws againft affaffination were fufficient for the fafety of the

the citizens, and propofed the order of the day to Kerfaint's motion.

Others afked for its adjournment.

To demand the adjournment of fuch a motion, cried Vergniaud, is to demand impunity for affaffins, to propofe the order of the day is to propofe anarchy—There are men, added he, who call themfelves republicans, and are, in reality, the flaves of tyrants; they fpread fufpicions, hatred and vengeance among the citizens—they wifh to excite the French people, like the foldiers of Cadmus, to cut one another's throats inftead of fighting the common enemy.

He ended an eloquent fpeech by fupporting Kerfaint's motion.

Collot d' Herbois and others faid, that this motion was intended for eftablifhing *a law of blood*, and that there were men in office who would ufe it for the deftruction of the moft diftinguifhed patriots.

Some of thofe whom Collot d' Herbois meant by the moft diftinguifhed patriots are

ftrongly

strongly suspected of being the planners of the massacres—Collot d'Herbois himself is not clear of this suspicion, which accounts for the opposition to Kersaint's motion.

Merlin of Thionville opposed the motion, and went so far as to assert, that the baker who was murdered by the mob some months before, on a suspicion of engrossing grain to raise the price of bread, had been murdered on purpose to furnish a pretext for proclaiming martial law, and by that means to justify the troops for firing on the people, which was then intended, and afterwards performed in the Champ de Mars. The Queen, from motives of humanity, had shewn kindness and generosity to this man's widow;——in consequence of which the ridiculous falsehood, now mentioned by Merlin, was invented and propagated.

Kersaint spoke with energy against those absurd imputations; and Buzot, with strong and perspicuous reasoning, shewed

that

that the propofed law was not to fhed blood,
but to prevent blood from being fhed ; and
in addition propofed, that a guard fhould be
formed from all the 83 departments for the
immediate protection of the Convention,
that each department might have the conviction that its deputies could fpeak and
vote freely, and were not influenced by fear
either of the people in the galleries, or of
the Council General of the Community of
Paris, which had ufurped fo much power,
and had exercifed it with fo much tyranny.

It was at laft decreed, that fix commiffioners fhould be appointed to form a law
againft the inciters to murder and affaffination, and alfo to give in a plan for the for-
mation of a guard to be at the difpofal of
the Convention, which was to be drawn
from all the 83 departments, to prevent the
Convention from being domineered over by
the

the General Council of the Commune of Paris as the Legiflative Affembly had been.

This General Council exercifes its ufurped power in a dreadful manner : citizens are ftill arrefted and imprifoned by orders iffued by its members.

Two commiffioners from this council, declared at the election of the deputy at Auxerre, that the Commune of Paris poffeffed the whole power of the State ; that thofe chofen as deputies fhould put their confidence in the Commune, and not in the National Affembly, the minifters, or the generals.

Commiffioners from the fame council advifed the inhabitants of Douay to erect fcaffolds on the ramparts, and to execute all who were of a different opinion from them, as ariftocrats and traitors.

And two other commiffioners from that community raifed fuch a fpirit of infurrec-

6   tion

tion at the Electoral Assembly of Seine and Marne that fourteen persons were murdered in the tower of Meaux.——Those facts were announced by different members of the Convention.

Nothing therefore can be more urgent than to deprive this Community of its usurped power; and for this purpose it seems absolutely necessary that the Convention should have guards, and such executive force at its command as will overbalance and keep in awe the rabble of the suburbs, who are at any time to be put in action by the influence of Santerre, and the money of another person who has a great deal at his command, which he is said to lavish among the sans-culottes of the suburbs, when any measure is to be carried for the interest of the party.

Some time after this a most extraordinary scene was exhibited in the Conventional Assembly:——Merlin de Thionville, a man far more distinguished for zeal than prudence, declared

declared that La Source had in private conversation said, that there was a faction in the Convention for establishing a dictator, and he called on La Source to announce who this intended dictator was, that he might be instantly poniarded.

La Source, who must have been somewhat surprised to hear a private, perhaps a confidential remark, published in this manner, explained what he had said differently. He said that he had complained of the tyranny of certain men, who flatter and deceive the citizens of Paris, and who point out the best friends of the people as victims to the rage of assassins : that such men were already dictators; that there was the greatest necessity for an armed force to secure the independence of the Convention, and prevent it from being dictated to by those who had usurped illegal influence.——" Let those men of blood, he added, tremble, and know that the same power which hurled Lewis from

from his throne, will not long suffer the despotism of others."

But in the course of the debate Rebecqui, one of the deputies for Marseilles, in direct terms, accused the partizans of Robespierre of a design of raising him to the dictatorship.

Danton, dreading that this might draw on a discussion and produce an investigation which he wished to prevent, endeavoured with some address to turn the attention of the Assembly to a different object. He moved that the pains of death should be decreed on any person who should attempt to destroy the unity of France, by dividing it into different commonwealths, bound together by a federative bond, like the United Provinces and the Cantons of Switzerland. Danton knew that Buzot, Vergniaud, Guadet, and others who were eager for the punishment of all who had been directly or indirectly concerned in promoting the murder of the prisoners, were accused of inclining

2 to

to this plan of federative republics, which is by no means the wish of the majority of the Convention——he therefore intended to intimidate them from profecuting the affaffins, by holding up the dread of being accufed themfelves.

Buzot, fenfible of his intention, boldly oppofed the infinuation. " Who is it," he exclaimed, "that thinks of difuniting France? I propofe that a guard for the Conventional Affembly fhall be furnifhed by the 83 departments, with a view to union, and thereby to fignify that the Convention is equally under the care of them all ; thofe who oppofe this meafure appear rather to wifh for difunion."

He put this in fo clear a light, that Robefpierre thought the only means to prevent its evidence from being apparent to the moft fhort-fighted of the Affembly, was by overwhelming the argument with a torrent of words, and obfcuring it in a mift of fophiftry,

phiftry, both of which this popular orator has at his command.

He began by expatiating on his own patriotifm, on his incorruptibility, and the fervices he had rendered the ftate while he fat in the conftituent affembly.——The theme was attractive, but becoming lefs pleafing to the audience than to the orator himfelf, one of the members called out, " *Robefpierre veux tu bien terminer cette longue kyrielle*; declare nous franchement en quatre mots tes fentimens et non ta vie paffée*." This, however, did not bring him to give any explicit anfwer to the accufation; he dwelt for an hour longer on the favourite fubject with which he began, then launched into proteftations of his love for his country, and of the incredibility of his ever forming any fcheme againft that freedom for which he had fo

---

* Pray put an end to your tedious harangue, and inform us, in two words, of your fentiments on the point in queftion, and not of all your paft life.

D long

long struggled; and finished by declaring his suspicions that there were among their body, those who watched an opportunity of dividing France, and then combining it into federate states; and therefore he seconded Danton's motion.

Barbaroux, a young man, and deputy from Marseilles, in support of what his colleague Rebecqui had asserted, declared, that on his arrival at Paris, it had been insinuated to him by certain intimates of Robespierre, and particularly by Panis, that in the present emergency there was a necessity for uniting under some person of great popularity, in whom a power equal to that of the Roman dictators should be placed for a certain time; and that Robespierre, from his known patriotism and popularity, was the properest person they could fix upon for that office.

Panis endeavoured to defend himself by saying that Barbaroux had assuredly either mistaken his words or meaning.—" Is it possible," poffible," added he, wifhing to conciliate his accufer, " that Barbaroux, whom I love, becaufe I know him to be a good patriot, can believe I ever meant fuch a thing ?"

This manner of denying fuch a charge forms a ftrong prefumption of its truth ; for a man would hardly fpeak in fuch terms of another, who accufed him falfely of fo dangerous an offence.

Barbaroux, however, was not to be foftened, but perfifted in the charge. " Who, befides yourfelf," cried Panis, " can witnefs that I ever made fuch a propofal ?"

" I can, cried Rebecqui," " for I heard you." This feemed to difconcert both Panis and Robefpierre, and to filence and confound the whole party, till Marat, thinking the exigency worthy of his intrepidity of countenance, afcended the tribune. He no fooner appeared than murmurs and execrations arofe in every corner of the Affembly.

" It would appear," faid he, without

D 2

any

any mark of emotion, " that fome in this Affembly are my perfonal enemies."

" All! all ! we are all your enemies !" refounded from every quarter.

He lamented the general delufion with the accent of regret, and then affuming an air of courage, with a full fwell of voice, he declared that he, and he only, had conceived the idea of appointing a dictator ; that he had mentioned it to feveral, fome of whom may have repeated it, but that the thought was originally his own. That, convinced as he had long been of the plots of a perfidious court, and as he ftill was of the treafons of many citizens, he thought the exigency of the times required that the direction of the public affairs fhould be placed in the hands of an honeft and determined man, an enlightened patriot, who, without fear or refpect of perfons, would *apply the axe of juftice to the necks of the guilty.*——"Such is my own opinion," continued he ; " I have publifhed it, it, and if your ideas have not foared to the height of mine, fo much the worfe for you."

Such an inflated declaration iffuing from a little dirty mortal, whofe murky vifage fcarce overlooked the tribune, turned the indignation of the Affembly into mirth, and many of the members burft into laughter.

But Vergniaud reftored the gravity of the Affembly, by bringing forward a very extra-ordinary circumftance, which points out pretty plainly thofe to whom the maffacres of the prifoners, not only in Paris, but in every other part of France where they took place, are to be attributed.

He then read a letter figned by certain members of the council of the Commune de Paris, which had been tranfmitted to all the municipalities of France, immediately after the flaughter of the prifoners at Paris in the beginning of September.

This letter is of fo very fingular a nature,

D 3

that

that I think it proper to tranfcribe the whole.

Freres et amis, un affreux complôt tramé par la Cour pour égorger tous les Patriotes de l'empire François, complôt dans lequel un grand nombre de membres de l'Affemblée Nationale font compromis, ayant réduit, le 9 du mois dernier, la Commune de Paris à la cruelle néceffité de fe fervir de la puiffance du peuple pour fauver la Nation, elle n'a rien négligé pour bien mériter de la patrie.

Aprés les témoignages que l'Affemblée Nationale venoit de lui donner elle-meme, eut on penfé que des-lors des nouveaux complôts fe tramoient dans le filence, et qu'ils eclatoient dans le moment même, ou l'Affemblée Nationale, oubliant qu'elle venoit de déclarer que la Commune de Paris avoit fauvé la patrie, s'empreffoit de la deftituer, pour prix de fon brûlant civifme ?

Fière de jouir de toute la plénitude de la confiance

confiance nationale qu'elle s'efforcera de mériter de plus en plus, placée au foyer de toutes
les confpirations, et déterminée à perir pour
le falut public, elle ne fe glorifiera d'avoir
rempli pleinement fes devoirs que lorfqu'elle
aura obtenu votre approbation, qui eft l'objet
de tous fes vœux et dont elle ne fera certaine
qu'aprés que tous les départemens *auront
fanctionné fes mefures pour le falut de la chofe
publique* ; et profeffant les principes de la plus
parfaite egalité, n'ambitionnant d'autre pri-
vilége que celui de fe préfenter la premiére
á la breche, elle s'empreffera de fe remettre
au niveau de la Commune la moins nom-
breufe de l'empire, dès qu'il n'y aura plus
rien à redouter.

Prévenue que des hordes des barbares
s'avancent contre elle, la Commune de Paris
fe hâte d'informer fes freres de tous les départemens, qu'une partie des confpirateurs
féroces, détenus dans les prifons, a été mife à
mort par le peuple, *actes de juftice qui lui ont paru*

D 4   *indifpenfables*

indifpenfables pour retenir par la terreur les legions de traitres cachés dans fes murs, au moment ou il alloit marcher à l'ennemi ; *et fans doute la nation*, aprés la longue fuite de trahifons qui l'a conduite fur les bords de l'abyme, *s'empreffera d'adopter ce moyen fi utile et fi néceffaire*, et tous les François fe diront, comme les Parifiens : Marchons à l'en-nemi, *mais ne laiffons par derriére nous ces bri-gands pour égorger nos femmes et nos enfans.*

Signed PIERRE DUPLAIN, JOURDEUIL, PANIS, SERGENT, L'ENFANT, MARAT L'AMI DU PEUPLE, LE CLERC, DUFORTRE &c. &c. Adminiftrators of the Committee of the Public Safety. *

The

* Brethren and friends, a horrid plot, planned by the Court, to murder all the patriots of the French em-pire ; a plot in which a great number of the National Affembly were engaged, having, on the ninth of laft month, forced the Commune de Paris to the cruel ne-ceffity of making ufe of the power of the people to
fave

The moral of this virtuous epiſtle is evident—If you have any regard for your country,

ſave the nation, the Commune has neglected nothing
for the ſervice of the country.

After the approbation which the National Aſſembly
itſelf beſtowed on the Commune, could it have been
imagined that new plots were projecting in ſilence, which
broke forth at the moment when the National Aſſembly, forgetting that ſhe had declared that the Commune
de Paris had ſaved the country, haſtened to diſſolve
that very Community as a recompence for all its faithful ſervices.

Proud of poſſeſſing the full confidence of the Nation,
which we are reſolved to deſerve more and more; placed
in the centre of all the conſpiracies, and determined to
periſh in defence of the public, we cannot boaſt of having entirely fulfilled our duty till we ſhall obtain your
approbation, which is the object of all our wiſhes, and of
which we cannot be certain till all the Departments
have *ſanctioned our meaſures for the public ſafety.* Profeſſ-
ing principles of the moſt perfect equality, wiſhing no
other privilege but that of preſenting ourſelves the firſt
at the breach, we will put ourſelves on a level with the
ſmalleſt

try, or any tenderneſs for your wives and children, you will cut the throats of all your priſoners as ſoon as you conveniently can.

What an infernal letter! and what renders it ſtill more atrocious, is its being deliberately written by men in the character of magiſtrates.

ſmalleſt municipality in the Nation, as ſoon as the dangers which now threaten the country are paſt.

Informed that bands of barbarians are advancing, the Commune de Paris haſtens to acquaint all the departments, that part of thoſe furious conſpirators detained in the priſons of Paris have been put to death by the people; *an act of juſtice which ſeemed indiſpenſable to ſtrike terror* into the breaſts of thoſe legions of traitors hid within her walls, at the time when the citizens were about to march againſt the enemy. And no doubt the Nation, after that long ſucceſſion of treaſons which have brought her to the brink of ruin, will haſten to adopt a meaſure ſo uſeful and neceſſary; and all the inhabitants of France will ſay, like the Pariſians: Let us march againſt the enemy, but let us not *leave behind us a band of villains to murder our wives and children.*

It

It might naturally be expected that the reading of this invitation to murder should have filled the Assembly with so much indignation, that a decree of accusation would have been immediately passed against Panis and the rest. It produced however only new clamours and confusion, with an outcry from one part of the hall for the order of the day.—At last *Couthon* proposed that they should turn their attention from accusations against individuals to the more important exigencies of the state: this was supported by all those who dreaded any inquiry or investigation respecting the promoters of the massacres ; and those who had been at first inclined to that measure being fatigued, or perhaps afraid to persist, the order of the day was agreed to—On which Marat, who remained in the tribune, pulled a pistol from his pocket, which having held to his head, he said, " I now declare to you, citizens, that if the fury which has been displayed on this

4   occasion

occasion had carried you the length of a decree of accusation against me, I should have blown my brains out before your faces." What he meant by this I know not, unless it was to vex the Assembly on being disappointed of so desirable an event.

Next to the disorderly conduct of some of the members themselves, nothing disgraces the National Assembly so much as the insolence of the audience in the galleries—How could any court or any assembly of men support dignity, if it was exposed to be applauded or hooted according to the opinions or caprice of those admitted to hear their debates ? There is, it is true, a decree against all noises and signs of approbation or disapprobation; but notwithstanding its being broken every day, nobody has ever been punished on that account.

The majority of the Convention have a great desire that a strict investigation should be made into the massacres, that the promo-

2   ters

ters of them may be punished in the most exemplary manner; and the same majority are equally solicitous to have an armed force at the command of the Convention decreed and established. But I imagine they have thrown a great obstacle in the way of obtaining the last of these objects, by manifesting a design to pursue the first. They would have shewn more policy if they had said nothing of the one till they had secured the other. A considerable number of members of the Convention itself are supposed to be conscious of being directly or indirectly involved in that horrid business; they see their own ruin in such an investigation, and therefore will oppose it by every means in their power. What means have they in their power since a majority of the Convention is for the measure? They cannot object to a law against assassination, and for the punishment of murder; but, knowing what use is immediately to be made of the armed force, they

will

will raife objections to that being eftablifhed;
and till fuch a force is eftablifhed, their friends
in the fuburbs will be able to protect the authors of the maffacres. In fhort, the minority
in the Convention, at the head of which are
Danton and Robefpierre, already have an
armed force at their command, in the active
citizens of the fuburbs; and will in all probability ufe every means, and they are not
fuppofed to be fo fcrupulous as their rivals
in the means they employ, to prevent any
other armed force from being eftablifhed.

The fituation of the generals who command the armies of France at prefent is difagreeable in many refpects; but particularly
in their being under the control, and expofed to the cenfure of men who are no
judges of their military abilities, and ex-
tremely liable to prejudice and fufpicion.——
Nothing can be more detrimental to the intereft of the ftate, than that thofe men who
are rifquing their lives in the public fervice,

and

and peforming their duty with fidelity to their country, fhould be expofed to calumny, and furrounded with fufpicion, the tendency of which muft be to difcourage their minds, cool their zeal, and difturb all their operations.

Talien, a young man who was fecretary to the municipality of Paris, and is now a member of the Convention, made an attack lately, in that Affembly, on General Montefquiou, who commands the army in Savoy. —He accufed him of being tainted with ariftocracy, and added, which was a pretty bold affertion for a man who was bred a clerk, that, *in his opinion*, the general was deficient in military abilities, and therefore he moved that he fhould be deprived of his command.

It is not to be imagined that much attention would have been paid to Talien's judgment of the abilities of a general officer, had he not been a creature of Danton's, and

fuppofed

supposed to act under his direction—His proposal, therefore, was supported by others, who were for passing a decree that General Montesquiou had lost the confidence of the nation.

La Riviere observed, that as it might occasion disquietude to other generals, if one of their brethren was to be cashiered with so little ceremony, it might be reasonable to appoint a committee to examine a little into Montesquiou's conduct in the first place, and defer the punishment till it should appear that he deserved it.

This observation in favour of the general was made in such very guarded terms, that one would hardly think it could have given offence even to his bitterest enemy.—Billaud de Varennes, however, said in reply, that it was not surprising that the same person should defend Montesquiou, who had formerly defended the conduct of La Fayette. In the present circumstances, this insinuation might

might have been very hurtful to La Riviere; he therefore afcended the tribune with pre-cipitation, and declared that he was one of the 224 members of the Legiflative Affem-bly who had on the 8th of Auguft voted againft La Fayette ; that what Billaud had faid was falfe and calumnious, and required that he fhould be called to order, and cen-fured as a calumniator by the prefident.

" Called to order ! for what ?" cried Danton. " In the fenate of Rome Brutus and Cato boldly fpoke out thofe plain truths which we from the pufillanimity of our manners evade as perfonalities ; for my part I am refolved to accufe, without circumlo-cution, every perfon whofe conduct I think fufpicious."

Although it may be granted that Billaud and Danton have as great a refemblance to Brutus and Cato as the Convention has to the Roman fenate, yet ftill there is a dif-ference between the bold truths of the latter, and the bold falfehoods of the former ; the comparifon therefore is not quite appofite.

Danton however infifted upon General Montefquiou's being deprived of his command, for which he urged two additional reafons ; one, that when the public fafety is in danger, it is fufficient that a general is fufpected : the other, added he, is, " qu'il faut nous montrer terribles ; c'eft du caractere qu'il faut pour foutenir la liberté *."

This is certainly the character that Danton has uniformly fupported fince the 10th of Auguft, which tends to ftrengthen fome fufpicions of a terrible nature, indeed, which are harboured againft him.

The propofed decree was paffed, that General Montefquiou fhould be deprived of his command.

What renders Montefquiou obnoxious to fome leading members in the Convention,

* That we may appear terrible ; fuch is the character requifite for fupporting the caufe of liberty.

doe⒮

does him honour in the eyes of impartial people—he ſtrenuouſly oppoſed the petitions for the dechéance of the King, and was for ſupporting him in the exerciſe of the veto which the conſtitution gave him. He was alſo accuſed by Bazire of having ſaid at the extraordinary commiſſion, that if they ſuſpended the King's authority, they ran the riſk of being abandoned by the army; it is alſo imagined that he wiſhes to behave with more mildneſs to the Genevois than is agreeable to certain people in power. But what will prove more injurious to Monteſquiou than all theſe charges, is, that Danton is his enemy.

It muſt have been very mortifying to Danton, and the other enemies of this gentleman, when the news arrived a little after their decree, that he had already entered Savoy, and was proceeding with the moſt triumphant ſucceſs.—He concludes his letter to the miniſter of war with the following words. " Je vous rends grace, Monſieur,

de

de m'avoir procuré cette maniere de re-
pondre, à la calomme ; c'eft ainſi que j'aime-
rai toujours à la repouſſer *."

The friends of General Monteſquiou
feized this opportunity of moving that the
decree againſt him ſhould be recalled.

His enemies oppoſed this.

Manuel feconded the motion which was
firſt made by Lacroix, adding, that he hoped
they would recal this decree without loſs of
time, left Monteſquiou, by gaining a new
victory, ſhould put them ſtill more in the
wrong. Danton, perceiving the tide flowing
in favour of Monteſquiou, and being unable to turn it entirely againſt him, propoſed that the Affembly ſhould extend the
power of the commiſſioners that were ſent
to his army, by leaving it to their judgment
to deprive the general of his command, or

* I return you thanks, Sir, for having put it in my
power to make this kind of anſwer to calumry; I
ſhould wiſh to repel her attacks alway in the ſame
manner.

to continue him in it, as they might think expedient. Danton had before given a more extensive commiffion to an officer of Montefquiou's army, namely, to watch the conduct of the general, and, if he fhould make one retrograde movement, to fhoot him through the head.

Genfonné, with much reafon, fhewed the impropriety of the Affembly's allowing the execution of their decrees to depend on the judgment of any but themfelves; and it was obferved by Couthon, that the nation had given to the Convention the right of making decrees, but not the power of delegating that right to others. On which Danton, pufhing prejudice and want of candour as far as poffible, exclaimed: " They fay that Montefquiou has gained a victory, but I beg leave to obferve, that victories are not gained by a fingle man—the victory was gained by the French army."

This argument certainly does prove that Montefquiou has no better title to his vic-

tory

tory in Savoy, than Hannibal had to that at Cannæ, or Cæſar to the victory at Pharſalia.

Danton perſiſted in his motion; although, he added, that it was poſſible that an old courtier, like Monteſquiou, ſeeing the ſucceſs which attended the army of the republic in all quarters, might at laſt reſolve to adhere to it.

It was decided, however, according to the propoſal of Genſonné, that the execution of the laſt decree againſt Monteſquiou ſhould be ſuſpended.

I know not whether the continued ſucceſs which attends General Monteſquiou, will finally overcome the envy and malice of his enemies; but, in a third letter, which came ſoon after the ſecond, he announces the reduction of all Savoy, from the Lake of Geneva to Mount Cenis : the progreſs of his troops, he ſays, reſembles a triumphant proceſſion more than the march of an army; the inhabitants of towns and villages flock to him with congratulations, and the three-coloured

coloured ribbon in their hats; and adds, that the minds of the people feem difpofed to a revolution like that of France; and that the propofal had been already made of form- ing Savoy into an 84th department of France.

On tranfmitting Montefquiou's letter to the Convention, Servan, the war minifter, wrote to the prefident, that, as the expedi- tion into Savoy had rendered that country free, it was worthy of the French Repub- lic to folemnife fo happy an event by or- dering the hymn of the Marfeillois to be performed in the Square of the Revolution, with the utmoft magnificence, by vocal and inftrumental mufic. He adds, " que ce chant patriotique, expreffion fidelle des fentimens François, retentiffe dans tout l' empire, que nos voifins l' entendent, et qu'il devienne à jamais, l'efpoir des peuples, et la terreur des tyrans *."

After

* Let that patriotic fong, the faithful expreffion of the fentiments of France, refound all over the nation;

may

After General Kellermann had given the firſt check to the Pruſſians on the 20th of September, he wrote to Servan for liberty to celebrate a *Te Deum* in his camp, on account of that important affair.——" The ſong of the Marſeillois," replied the miniſter, " is the *Te Deum* of the French republic ; let it be performed by the muſic of your army, and ſung by the ſoldiers."

In both inſtances Servan's propoſal was adopted.

To ſubſtitute a profane ſong in preference to a religious rite, it might be imagined, would give great offence : ſuch a propoſal from the parliament to their army in the time of the Engliſh republic, would have produced a mutiny and have ſhocked the whole nation. It had no ſuch effect in the preſent inſtance in France, where religious zeal is wonderfully extinguiſhed ; and an enthuſi-

may it be heard by all the neighbouring countries ; and may it become the hope of the people, and the terror of tyrants !

aſm

aſm of another kind glows in its ſtead, the enthuſiaſm of Liberty, what they call Ci-viſme, in which an attachment to the pre-ſent government, and an abhorrence of mo-narchy, are included.

This is profeſſed with as much oſtentation and apparent zeal as ever the Roman Ca-tholic religion was, in the moſt ſuperſtitious times; for, although the puniſhment with which a want of civiſme is attended, is not ſo durable as that pronounced againſt the irreligious, it is more immediate; which, on the generality of mankind, has full as great an effect. Civiſme, like religion, produces both enthuſiaſts and hypocrites: the former deteſt and abominate a king and nobility, as much as their zealous forefathers, two cen-turies ago, abominated the devil and his an-gels; and they are as zealous perſecutors of every deviation from the orthodox creed of civiſme, as their predeceſſors were of hereſy. The enthuſiaſts are chiefiy among the poor; the hypocrites among the rich: many of
whom

whom are juſt ſuch republicans in France, as the Jews are Chriſtians in Portugal.

Immediately after Monteſquiou's letter had been read in the convention, Bancal, one of the deputies for the department du Puy-de-Dome, put the Convention in mind, that the Conſtituent Aſſembly had by a ſolemn decree renounced every idea of conqueſt; and therefore he very wiſely moved that the Convention, faithful to that ſacred principle, ought to reject the propoſal of erecting Savoy into an 84th department of France, and ſhould order it to be proclaimed all over Savoy, that France renounces conqueſt, and deſires no extenſion of territory.

This motion, equally juſt and politic, was oppoſed: it was ſaid, France has not given a temporary freedom to a country, that it may again fall under the yoke of its former tyrant. She ought to agree to the generous wiſhes of the people ſhe has freed, by accepting their union, and extending the empire of Liberty as far as poſſible. " All

8   Europe,"

Europe," faid a member, " will gradually join you, and all Europe will be like one family.——The people of every nation will be your friends, and you will have no enemies but kings——you cannot furely refufe fuch a fublime idea."

A flourifh of this kind might be applauded in a difputing club, or might perhaps be admired in a vifionary declaimer on politics ; but it was hardly to be imagined that fuch fentiments would make any impreffion on an affembly of legiflators, where practical knowledge and fober good fenfe prefided. It was hardly to be expected that thofe fine words would not be conftrued by all Europe into an abfolute renunciation of the decree againft conqueft, and really meant that the new republic intended, under a pretence of fpreading liberty, to overturn every government, and fubdue every nation around.

Jean Baptifte Louvet, notwithftanding the applaufe which was very liberally beftowed on the fentiments above mentioned, had the firmnefs

firmnefs and good fenfe to declare, that, without renouncing one of the wifeft decrees of the conftituent affembly, they could not interfere in the government of any other country : that they could not, without infringing the moft facred right of the people of Savoy, prefs upon them the conftitution which France might affume for herfelf. How did they know that the conftitution which was expedient for France, was alfo expedient for Savoy? and if expedient, how did they know that the Savoyards at the bottom of their hearts chofe it ?——" That which is effentially juft," Louvet continued, " is for the moft part found policy. Let it be folemnly declared to all the people who fhall be, I will not fay fubdued, but freed by your arms, that they may choofe to themfelves what form of government they pleafe, that their laws fhall be of their own making, that you not only wifh to give them freedom, but freedom in the mode which they themfelves prefer.——" I am convinced,"

convinced," added he, " that in Brabant, whither your armies intend to march, there exist strong prejudices against some of your laws, and your constitution in general; prejudices which it will require many years to eradicate, and which will render you more odious in their eyes than their present master, if you attempt to force your constitution upon them. It is as expedient, therefore, as equitable, to declare the complete independence of every country into which you carry freedom."

Danton, in answer to this, said, that they had assuredly the right to declare to every such country, that it should never more be governed by a king: that if the people were so absurd as to desire a government contrary to their interest, it should not be allowed: that the National Convention of France should be *a committee of insurrection against all the kings in the universe.*

Nothing can be imagined more mad than

this

this propofition, the tendency of which is to force all the monarchs in Europe, in felf-defence to make war on the Republic : what private view Danton has in this, I do not know, but it evidently goes to the ruin of France.

The Affembly, however, becoming impatient to clofe the difcuffion, ordered General Montefquiou's letter to be printed, and referred the propofition refpecting Savoy to the confideration of the diplomatic and the war committees.

Notwithftanding the prudent conduct and brilliant fuccefs of Montefquiou, I am informed that there is no great probability of his being continued in his command. His enemies are of a difpofition not to forgive him for having reduced Savoy at the very time that they were afferting he would never enter it, or to forget the injuftice they have already done him. Befide thefe and the motives of diflike previoufly mentioned, they

they have another ground of hatred towards him, namely, his being a nobleman, and of a very ancient family. This appears equally unjuft and abfurd :——unjuft, becaufe a man of noble birth, who from a love of general freedom has adhered to the revolution, has more merit than they can boaft who had no fuch facrifice to make——and it is abfurd, becaufe, inftead of giving no importance to the accidental circumftance of birth, it is giving a great importance to it, which operates againft the poffeffor. But if a man's nobility is not allowed, independent of perfonal merit, to be of fervice to him, neither ought it to be allowed, independent of demerit, to injure him.

Accounts are arrived that Dumourier, having left a fufficient force to harafs the retreating army of Pruffia, has quitted his own camp, and is foon expected in Paris.

October 11.

I was prefent this day for the firft time at the

the Conventional Affembly, where a virulent attack was made on Dillon, one of the generals employed againft the German army, and who, from the lateft accounts, is now preffing upon their rear at Verdun.

As it elucidates what immediately follows, I fhall here infert a fhort account of Dumourier's memorable campaign, from the time he was appointed to the command till he left the army, although I was not acquainted with all the particulars till fome time after this date.

General Arthur Dillon commanded the French army on the frontiers of Flanders, when he heard of the infurrection of the 10th of Auguft.

Dumourier, being at that time fubordinate to him, commanded in the camp of Maulde. From the accounts which Dillon received of that affair, he conceived it to be a rafh infurrection which would be difapproved of by the nation, and that it would foon end in the

the ruin of all concerned in it. He therefore gave out an order to the army on the 13th, in which he said, that the conftitution had been violated by men who were the enemies of liberty; that he determined to remain faithful to the nation, to the law, to the king, and to the conftitution framed by the affembly in the years 1789, 1790, and 1791, to which they had all fworn.

He tranfmitted this order from Pont-fur-Sambre, where he was with his army, to the camp of Maulde, with a letter to General Dumourier, directing him to publifh it there.

Dumourier had a different idea of the tranfactions of the 10th. He faw that the public opinion went in favour of the fuccefsful party; that it would be very difficult to wreft the government out of the hands which had feized it; that an attempt of that kind by the army would immediately produce a civil war, and expofe the country to foreign invasion; and that he himself would remain subordinate to Luckner, La Fayette and Dillon. Dumourier was nearer to Paris than Dillon, and had received earlier and, as is supposed, more distinct information from his friend Gensonné, of the state of affairs. In his answer to Dillon's letter, he regretted that general's precipitancy, assured him that he would not publish the order in his camp, and advised Dillon to retract it without loss of time.

He sent at the same time an account of what he had done, and was disposed to do, to his friends at Paris; and when the three commissioners from the National Assembly arrived, he not only took the oath of Equality himself, but persuaded Dillon to do the same. That officer found no difficulty in explaining his conduct to the commissioners, assuring them, that it had proceeded from the misrepresentation which had been made to him of the affair of the 10th, but that he was

2

zealous

zealous to serve the French nation, whatever form of government they should think proper to adopt.

The National Assembly were so much pleased with this conduct of Dumourier, that they gave him the supreme command of the army formerly under M. de la Fayette, placing Dillon, who is an elder officer, under him. Having no pretext for putting Dumourier above Luckner, and desirous at the same time that the former should be the efficient commander, they ordered Luckner to Chalons, to form an army there of the men who were marching from all parts to that place, where they were to be clothed, armed and sent in detachments wherever the exigencies of the state required. Kellermann was, at Dumourier's recommendation, ordered to replace Luckner as commander of the army in Lorraine; Biron and Custine commanded the army on the Rhine, and Montesquiou that which was ordered against

Savoy:

Savoy : all thefe officers took the oaths required by the Affembly, and made the armies under their orders take them alfo.

Dumourier fent Dillon to command the army of the Ardennes, which comprehended all the troops placed in that part of the frontiers of France, between Rocroy and Montmedy. The two generals afterwards met at the town of Sedan, with a view to fix on future meafures.

The enemy had already entered France, was in poffeffion of Longwy, the firft fortified town on the frontier next to the dutchy of Luxembourg, and feemed at once to threaten Montmedy, Verdun and Thionville.

The Duke of Brunfwick's army was above 50,000 ftrong : General Clairfait had joined him with 15,000 Auftrians, befide a confiderable body of Heffians and French emigrants, amounting in all to 90,000 men.

After leaving the frontier towns tolerably garrifoned,

garrifoned, Dumourier had not above 17,000 men to act immediately againft this immenfe force ; and thefe 17,000 had been ufelefsly encamped between Sedan and Stenay, the Meufe being fordable in numberlefs places between Stenay and Verdun, where the enemy had no oppofition.

On comparing the ftrength of the invading army with the weaknefs of that which was to oppofe it, it was at one time imagined that all direct oppofition would be vain, and that the moft effectual meafures would be, by a fudden irruption into Auftrian Flanders, to endeavour to divert the enemy from advancing againft Paris : but the fmall probability there was that fuch an expedition, however fuccefsfully conducted, would have the defired effect, foon made that fcheme be laid afide; and Dumourier, infpired by an immenfe defire of renown, and trufting to the refources of his own genius, and the enthufiafm which animated his

F 3

country-

countrymen, refolved, by the defending of pofts, and every other poffible means, to attempt to check and retard the progrefs of the enemy, till he fhould be reinforced by the army of Kellermann from Lorraine confifting of 20,000 men, by that which Bournonville was leading from Flanders which amounted to 13,000, and what Luckner had fent to him of the new levies which were affembling at Chalons.

Small as Dumourier's force was, he had the courage, on the 29th of Auguft, to detach from it two battalions of infantry, under the command of M. Galbaud, an excellent officer, who had orders to throw himfelf into Verdun, and affift in the defence of that town.

Dumourier gave the command of the advanced guard of his army to Dillon; it confifted of five battalions of infantry, with fourteen fquadrons of light horfe. Dillon was ordered to march to Stenay, where Dumourier

Dumourier intended to join him on the first of September, and difpute the paffage of the Meufe with the enemy.

Dillon, with a thoufand horfe, pufhed on before the reft of his troops, to Stenay, and was making arrangements for the defence of the place, when the advanced guard of the Auftrian army, four thoufand ftrong, with feveral pieces of cannon, appeared. Convinced of the impoffibility of defending the town without infantry, and without cannon, he evacuated Stenay, croffed the Meufe, and drew up his troops upon the oppofite fhore of that river, fending notice to his infantry, who were advancing, to return to the camp at Mouzon. When he himfelf retired to join them there, his rear was attacked by the Auftrian cavalry, who were repulfed with confiderable lofs, and Dillon arrived in fafety at Mouzon in the middle of the night *.

* Compte rendu au miniftre de la guerre, par le Lieut. General A. Dillon.

Dumourier

Dumourier advanced with his fmall army to Mouzon on the firft of September, and then marched on to Beaumont en Argonne, where Dillon had previoufly traced out a camp.

Finding that it was now too late to difpute the paffage of the Meufe, Dumourier determined to make himfelf mafter of the various ftraits in the foreft of Argonne. This foreft extends from the Chene le Populeux to Paffavent, a fpace of about forty miles; the German army, in marching to Paris, was under the neceffity of going by fome of thefe ftraits, or making a confiderable circuit by bad roads, and turning the foreft. Dumourier detached Dillon with fix thoufand men, to feize upon the very important pafs of Biefme, near the Grandes Iflettes, in the foreft of Argonne. It is about feven or eight miles from Verdun, on the direct road from that city to Paris by Chalons. He had at this time heard nothing from Galbaud, and had no doubt

of

of Verdun's holding out a much longer time than would be neceſſary for Dillon to perform this ſervice. But Verdun ſurrendered by capitulation on the ſecond of September, without having made any reſiſtanee, and Dillon would in all probability have arrived too late, had it not been for the ſagacity of M. Galbaud. When that officer came near to Verdun, he found it ſo completely inveſted by the Pruſſians, that it was impoſſible to execute the orders of Dumourier. He conſidered, in the next place, how he could employ the two battalions under his command moſt effectually for the public ſervice; and, anticipating the intentions of his commander, he marched them to Biefme, and immediately ſent a meſſenger to Dumourier, to inform him of what he had done, and to demand a reinforcement. The army at Verdun, in advancing to Paris, were now under the neceſſity of forcing this poſt, or making a

circuit

circuit of forty miles, by Varennes and Grand Pré on the north, or one still larger by Bar-le-duc on the south. Dumourier thought the former the most probable, for he posted himself with the body of his army at Grand Pré. This is also a pass in the forest of Argonne, requiring however a much greater force to defend it than that of Biefme; to which Dillon marched with redoubled efforts, in the dread that Galbaud, who he had heard was in possession of it, should be forced before he arrived *.

While Dumourier remained at Grand Pré, he detached General Miranda with a body of two thousand cavalry, to protect a convoy he expected, and also to reconnoitre the Prussian army, whose movements at this time seemed equivocal. Miranda performed this service with ability and success; an advanced guard of Prussians, consisting

* Compte rendu au ministre de la guerre, par le Lieut. General A. Dillon.

of four thousand, were posted in such a manner that they must have intercepted the convoy—He attacked and defeated them, and the convoy arrived in safety at Dumourier's camp *.

The march of Dillon from Mouzon to Biesme, through a forest exceedingly difficult to traverse, and so near to a superior army, required military skill in the commander, and steadiness in the troops, especially as they were assured by the municipal officers of a village through which they passed, that Galbaud, discouraged by the terror spread among his troops by those who came from Verdun, had quitted Biesme, and fallen back towards Chalons, and that the town of Sainte-Menehould was in the possession of the enemy. Dillon, however, having sent couriers to all quarters to ascer-

* Rapport des Commissaires de la Convention aux Armées reünies.

tain

tain thofe facts, foon difcovered that they were not true, and on the afternoon of the fifth of September effected his junction with Galbaud.

The troops were immediately employed in fortifying, by all the refources of art, the natural ftrength of this poft, which was done fo effectually that, when the King of Pruffia in perfon, with the Duke of Brunf-wick, reconnoitred the place from the heights near Clermont, they thought it too ftrong to be forced.

Some people have ventured to cenfure the Duke of Brunfwick for neglecting to attack this poft of Biefme before Galbaud was reinforced by Dillon, or for not order-ing Dillon to be oppofed in his march from Mouzon to it.

It belongs to military men only, and fuch as are acquainted intimately with the fitua-tion of the country, and the circumftances

6   in

in which the German army was at that
time, to decide on this point; but any one
may naturally conclude, that a general of so
high a reputation as the Duke of Brunfwick
muſt have had ſufficient reaſons for acting
as he did.

M. Gobert, adjutant general of Dumourier's army, and probably better qualified
to judge of the conduct of the Duke of
Brunfwick than moſt who have cenſured
it, obſerves, that Galbaud was in poſſeſſion
of the paſs on the 31ſt of Auguſt, that the
garriſon of Verdun had joined him on the
ſecond of September, and that the Duke
of Brunfwick might naturally believe that
many peaſants from the neighbouring villages would immediately reſort to Galbaud,
and affiſt in defending the paſs, this being a
kind of ſervice in which new troops might
be as uſeful as veterans.

Whatever were the Duke's reaſons for
waving

waving the attack of this poſt, the poſſeſſion of it enabled Dillon to afford protection to a number of villages ſituated on the river Aire, and put the Pruſſians to the neceſſity of long and moſt fatiguing marches, by Grand Pré to the camp of La Lune near St. Menehould, inſtead of going directly through Bieſme.

Dumourier was in poſſeſſion of the defiles of Grand Pré for ſome time before he was diſturbed, and at laſt became perſuaded that the Duke of Brunſwick meant to avoid the foreſt of Argonne altogether, and march to Chalons by Bar-le-duc. Under this conviction he wrote to Dillon that he was preparing with a ſtrong advanced guard to haraſs the rear of the enemy's army, who, he underſtood, were endeavouring to paſs by Dillon's right to Chalons. He directs him to leave 2000 men to guard the paſs; and then to aſſemble all the troops, and order them to

St. Mene-

St. Menehould, where he would endeavour to join him, and, with their united force, afterwards form a junction with Kellermann. He concludes his letter in these words :

" Faites rassembler, par le tocsin, tous les paysans pour aller border les abattis : portez-vous tout-à-fait à votre droite, et dirigez-y tout ce qui se rassemble à St. Menehould. Après notre jonction, nous nous arrangerons ensemble pour couvrir cette place et pour suivre le mouvement sur Chalons. Faites sonner le tocsin sur toute votre route, j'en ferai autant, et cela deconcertera un peu la marche des Prussiens. Je commencerai mon mouvement à minuit *.

DUMOURIER.

Le Général en Chef de l'Armée du Nord."

It

---

* Assemble all the peasants by the alarm bell, that they may line the abatis †. Direct your march to the

† An abatis is formed by trees cut down and arranged with their branches towards the enemy, so as to form a kind of fortification.

right,

It is probable that the Duke of Brunswick had made some movements which indicated an intention of marching by Bar-le-duc to Chalons; or had otherwise contrived to spread this impression, on purpose to conceal his real design, which was to force the defiles of Grand Pré.

Kellermann and Luckner were both deceived in this point. The former was so much convinced that the Duke's movement was a feint, that he had thoughts of marching from Sainte Dizier, where he then was, to Chalons, so as to arrive before the enemy.

right, and order all the troops who shall assemble at St. Menchould to move in the same direction. After our junction we will fix upon measures for covering that place, and attending the march of the enemy to Chalons. Order the alarm bells to be rung during your march, I will do the same; this will somewhat disconcert the march of the enemy. I will begin my march at midnight.

(Signed)   DUMOURIER.

Luckner

Luckner had fent reinforcements to the army of Kellermann where they were not needed, inftead of fending them to Dumourier at Grand-Pré, by a fhort route which Dillon had indicated.

Dumourier was foon convinced of his miftake, and wrote the following letter to Dillon.

Grand-Pré le 12 Sept. l'an 4me de la Liberté.

LES enemies vous ont abandonné, mon cher Général, pour fe porter fur moi; ils me font une attaque dans le moment; je ne fais pas encore fi c'eft la véritable, je crois que ce n'eft qu'une feinte pour attaquer la Trouée du Chêne-le-Populeux *, ou je porte du renfort. Envoyez moi du

---

* This is a poft on the north end of the Foreft of Argonne, which Dumourier meant to defend. By the Trouée de Clermont he means the Straits of Biefme.

G   fecours,

of the 13th, without fuccefs ; and he adds,
" Je fais qu' hier le Duc de Brunfwick furieux a dit au Roi de Pruffe—Je perdrai
bien du monde, mais j'y pafferai *."

The Duke of Brunfwick was as good as
his word—On the 14th of September the
attack of the Pruffians was irrefiftible. During the time that Dumourier was himfelf
attacked, he was informed that a poft called
La Croix aux Bois, which General Chazot
defended, was forced. Dumourier therefore
was obliged entirely to abandon the paffes of
of Grand-Pré, and to direct his march to
Sainte-Ménehould, where he had previoufly
traced a camp in a very ftrong pofition.—
On his march, his army was fo violently
preffed by the advanced cavalry of the
Pruffians, that it was thrown into confufion, and part fled in a fhameful man-

* I know that the Duke of Brunfwick faid to the
King of Pruffia yefterday in a violent paffion—I fhall
lofe a great many men, but I am refolved to pafs.

ner,

ner, quite to the town of St. Menehould, which they entered, crying, " All is loft !" and fpreading difmay on all fides. Dumourier, in the account which he fent to the Convention, feems to think that if the Pruffians had pufhed on with vigour during this panic, his army might have been difperfed.

Dillon happened to be at St. Menehould when the fugitives arrived—he did every thing in his power to prevent the terrour from fpreading—he fent detachments of horfe to the neighbouring villages to ftop thofe who fled, and prevent the alarm reaching Chalons, where it might have had the worft effect on the new levies affembling under Luckner.

By Dillon's exertions, and the animating prefence of Dumourier, the army regained order, fpirit, and confidence in their officers.

Thofe who had diftinguifhed themfelves in this fhameful manner were fent in dif-

grace

grace from the army, which on the morning of the 15th entered the camp at St. Menehould, and began with all diligence to fortify it, in the perfuafion that it would very foon be attacked. Bournenville, at the head of a body of 13,000 men, joined Dumourier on the 17th. The Duke of Brunfwick knew that Kellermann was near at hand with a greater force, and formed the plan of attacking him before he could join Dumourier. Kellermann, by forced marches, gained the heights of Valmy on the evening of the 19th. Valmy is within lefs than a mile of other heights, on which was the ftrong camp of Dumourier. Kellermann received intelligence of the march of the Pruffians during the night, which convinced him that he would be attacked the following morning. He made his difpofitions accordingly, and ufed every poffible means of encouraging his foldiers. He walked through the lines with fome of the most

most popular officers, to animate them by their difcourfe. The army anfwered them by huzzas, and the cry of Vive la nation ! Kellermann's army extended from a village called Dammartin la Planchette, along the heights of Valmy. A free communication was kept up between his army and that of Dumourier, who fent 8000 men to his affiftance during the cannonade, which lafted the whole day. The Pruffians manœuvred with their ufual coolnefs and addrefs, fometimes forming into columns, as if their intention had been to attack with the bayonet, and fometimes moving with an intention to furround Kellermann, and cut off his communication with Dumourier. The firmnefs of the French, under the fkilful direction of their Generals, prevented the Pruffians from accomplifhing either. Dumourier was in perfon at the batteries during feveral hours of the cannonade, and at the head of

his

his own troops to oppofe the Pruffians when they attempted to furround Kellermann. The fuperior addrefs of the French cannoneers was apparent during the whole action; and the army in general fhewed a degree of fteadinefs which difciplined troops alone have been fuppofed to poffefs, and rivalled the Pruffians in fteadinefs and obedience to their officers, while their natural vivacity appeared in fongs and cries of Vive la nation! amidft the carnage of the cannonade. In Kellermann's army there were above four hundred killed, and between five and fix hundred wounded. The General himfelf narrowly efcaped, his horfe being killed under him. It is faid, and it is moft probable, that the lofs of the Pruffians was confiderably greater. What military men peculiarly admire in the conduct of Kellermann, was the fkill he difplayed that evening in changing his pofition in the prefence of the

the enemy, to one still more advantageous; by which his right wing touched the army of Dumourier, his left was protected by heights easily defended, while in his front was a rivulet greatly swelled by the recent rains *. That he was not attacked during this manœuvre is not only a proof of the ability with which it was performed, but also forms a strong presumption of the great loss which the Prussians had sustained, and of their being discouraged by this unsuccessful attack.

At the same time that the attack was made on the army of Kellermann, the 20,000 men which had been left at Clermont made an attempt on Dillon's camp at Biesme.—— The Duke of Brunswick had been under the necessity of leaving this strong party

* Observations sur la Compagne de 1792, par Gobert, Adjutant Général.

behind,

behind, otherwise Dillon would have intercepted all his convoys; so that Dillon, with about five or six thousand men, had detained 20,000 from the Prussian army when it marched against Dumourier and Kellermann. Those 20,000 now marched to the attack of Biesme; they were so confident of their own success, and that Dumourier would be routed by the Prussians, that they made their whole equipage and baggage of every kind follow them, in the expectation that after they had forced the post of Biesme, they would be ordered to join the Prussians and accompany them to Paris. Dillon's defence, however, was attended with the same success, as Kellermann's—the Austrians and Hessians were repulsed and obliged to retire in great disorder.

After these unsuccessful attacks, the Duke of Brunswick encamped his army at La Lune, near the army of Dumourier,

and

and between St. Menehould and Chalons. Here the Pruſſians, who had already ſuffered by ſickneſs, were greatly dif-
treſſed from a want of proviſions. Bournonville, detached with a body of 4000 men
by Dumourier, had intercepted ſeveral convoys that were advancing from their magazines at Grand-Pré. He intercepted in particular ſeveral droves of cattle going to the
Pruſſians, and ordered them to be ſlaughtered for the uſe of his own army: for this
laſt exploit, joined to his courage and
ſtrength, he was called the French Ajax.——
Nothing could bribe the French peaſants
to carry any kind of neceſſaries to the
Germans, while they flocked with ſupplies
to the camp of Dumourier. It alſo was
difficult and moſt expenſive for the Duke of
Brunſwick, or any officer who commanded
his detached parties, to procure intelligence,
as they were ſurrounded with ſpies, who
informed Dumourier of all their movements.

ments. As the Pruffians could procure no provifions but from their own magazines, the fcarcity was increafed by the exceffive rains which fell at this time, and rendered the roads uncommonly deep, and in fome places almoft impaffable ; in the mean time, the Pruffians were more expofed to the inclemency of the weather, and fuffered more from cold, moifture, and want of provifions, than the French, who were protected in fome degree from thofe evils by the care and attention of their countrymen. To thefe diftreffes were added the vexation and difcouragement which the Pruffians muft have felt at finding the whole country united againft them, inftead of a great proportion being difpofed to join them, as they had been made to expect.

There are profeffions in which men fometimes acquire great reputation with little merit; this may happen either from the public being no judges of the merit of thofe

thofe particular profeffions, or becaufe fuccefs in the profeffion may arife from the
merit of others who direct the meafures of
the individual who acquires the reputation.

This is often the cafe in the military profeffion, at the top of which men are placed
from the circumftances of birth, independent of all idea of merit, and frequently in
fpite of the moft glaring proofs of incapa-
city. In this profeffion, likewife, men have
acquired fame from fucceffes that have been
entirely owing to the fuperiour valour of
their troops, and the fuperiour fkill of fome
fubordinate officer.

But if the commanders of armies may on
fome occafions acquire fame without de-
ferving it, no fet of men are more expofed
to cenfure on account of finifter events,
which no fagacity could forefee, and no
human power could prevent.

Few men have experienced this more
than the Duke of Brunfwick, who has

I   been

been blamed for not marching directly to Chalons, or Rheims, as soon as he found himself between those cities and Damou-rier's army. Those who make this cri-ticifm do not think of the danger and dif-ficulty of marching with an enemy hanging on the rear, and intercepting the convoys of the advancing army.

But without taking farther notice of such random cenfures, it is the opinion of many of the military profeffion, that inftead of remaining inactive at his camp at La Lune after the cannonade of the 20th of Sep-tember, he ought to have attacked Du-mourier at St. Menehould. Those who hold this opinion fay, that from the fu-periority of the Pruffians over the raw troops of France, he had a great probability of beating and difperfing them, which would have fpread fuch an alarm that the levies which were marching againft the Duke would have joined in the flight; and in-

5   ftead

ſtead of enemies, he would have met only friends on his way to Paris; for nothing is ſo efficacious as a victory, in converting enemies into friends.

I have been aſſured, that this meaſure was propoſed by the Marechal de Caſtries, in a Council of War held at La Lune; and his opinion was ſupported by that of M. de Poilly, a General Officer in the French army, who had reſided in that province, and had an accurate knowledge of the country; and that this attack of the camp of Menehould was alſo greatly deſired by the whole corps of French Emigrants.

Without any pretenſions to military knowledge, it is not difficult to conjecture what may have determined the Duke of Brunſwick againſt riſking ſuch a meaſure.

He certainly had entered France with a perſuaſion that he would be favoured by a great part of the country who diſliked the conſtitution : he had reaſon to believe
that

the events of the 10th of Auguft, and the third of September, would render the people more averfe to the new government, and more favourable to his expedition. The eafy conqueft of Longwy and Verdun tended to confirm him in thofe fentiments. He found no very great difficulty in forcing the Straits of Grand-Pré.

Thus far therefore every thing rather had a tendency to encourage the Duke to proceed; but the action of the 20th of September, and the difpofition in which he found the country, muft have had a very different effect on his mind. By the former he had the proofs of a firmnefs in the French army, and a fkill in the General which he did not expect; and in the country, fo far from any favourable difpofition towards his enterprize, every appearance was hoftile in the higheft degree. At his camp at La Lune his convoys were fometimes intercepted; he could obtain no pro-

vifions

visions from the inhabitants, and his army was suffering under the complicated distress of want, and a dangerous epidemic; it is said there were near ten thousand sick in his camp, and at Grand-Pré. In such circumstances an attack on Dumourier's army, now 70,000 strong, and whose strength he had already experienced, was not very promising of success; and if unsuccessful, would have been attended with the entire ruin of his own. But even upon the supposition that he had been victorious, the remains of the French army after a defeat, with the troops at Chalons, Rheims, Soissons, and in every part of the country, would have rendered the retreat of his army, diminished by victory and enfeebled by sickness, very dangerous if he had marched much farther into France.

As soon as it was evident that the country was against him, the Duke of Brunswick's enterprize might have been considered as having failed. He had nothing

H

to think of but to effect a retreat, which he finally conducted with a skill equal to the higheft reputation.

But he firft propofed a truce; during this a conference took place between the chiefs of the oppofite armies. It has been faid, that Dumourier agreed to this with a view to promote defertion among the German foldiers, by diftributing the decree of the National Affembly for the encouragement of deferters, and alfo in the hopes of inducing the King of Pruffia to break with the Auftrians, at this moment of indignation and difappointment; and it has been afferted that Dumourier proved himfelf a much better politician than the Duke of Brunfwick on this occafion. The reverfe of this however feems to be the truth; for if what is mentioned above were really Dumourier's objects in agreeing to the truce, he failed in both. There was *no* defertion from the Pruffian army, and the

King

King did *not* break with the Emperor; but it was of infinite importance to the Duke of Brunſwick, who had already determined on a retreat, to have a few days of truce, which he employed in conveying his artillery and heavy baggage undiſturbed from the camp of La Lune to Grand-Pré.

Nothing can be more uncandid and inconſiſtent than the manner in which the Duke of Brunſwick's conduct has been criticiſed——It is aſſerted in the firſt place, that he inconſiderately led his army into a ſituation ſo deſperate, that if they advanced, they muſt be all either killed or taken priſoners; if they retreated, one half muſt be cut in pieces; and if they remained where they were, they muſt be ſtarved.——Taking this account to be the true ſtate of the caſe, one would imagine that he ſhould be allowed ſome credit for having extricated his army from ſo perilous a ſituation——inſtead of which, we are told, that even in this, he ſhewed

leſs

lefs addrefs than the enemy, from whom
he delivered them.

In confirmation however of my own
opinion on this fubject, I fhall only add,
that it was the Duke of Brunfwick who firft
propofed the truce, and not Dumourier—
that during the whole time it continued,
his artillery and baggage were moving to
Grand-Pré, and that as foon as he knew
they were fafe there, he renewed his original manifefto, which he muft have known
would put an end to the truce. All thofe
circumftances render it probable that, however acute and able Dumourier may be, the
truce was more advantageous to the Duke
of Brunfwick than to him.

On the thirtieth of September the Duke
raifed his camp at La Lune, and retreated with
his whole army by Grand-Pré to Bufancy.
The Auftrians, under the command of General Clairfait, feparated from the Pruffians,
and paffed the Meufe at Stenay, and took the
neareft

neareſt way to the county of Luxembourg; while the Pruſſians paſſed at Dun, and purſued the courſe of the river to Verdun. Their march was ſlow, on account of the number of their ſick, as well as of the badneſs of the roads; but in ſuch order, that although purſued by numerous detachments of French, no conſiderable advantage was gained over them during this whole march.

When Dumourier ſaw the enemy in full retreat, and that they could attempt nothing of importance in that quarter this ſeaſon, he determined to go to Paris. He wiſhed to ſettle with the Executive Power a plan of operations for an immediate expedition into Auſtrian Flanders, whither he has ordered a great part of his army, and where he expects to gather freſh laurels. What gives a high idea of Dumourier's vigour of mind is, that in adhering to the plan of operations which he

had

had traced out for the défence of France, he refisted the injunctions which he frequently received from the adminiftration at Paris— and took the whole refponfibility upon himfelf. At Paris there was fo great an alarm, on hearing that fome German irregulars had been near Rheims, that they wifhed him to fall back. And Servan, the war minifter, has the following expreffions in a letter to Dumourier, dated the 27th of September.

" J'efpere toujours, mon cher Général, que vous refterez convaincu, ainfi que nous, que vous n'avez plus un moment à perdre pour vous rapprocher de la Marne, afin de couvrir par la Chalons, Rheims, et les fuperbes campagnes du Soiffonnois et de la Brie : que nous import actuellement que l'ennemi occupe les plaines arides de la Champagne?" —And he ends the fame letter with thefe words, " Perfonne ne vous voit tranquillement à Sainte Menehould tandis que les houlans

houlans viennent infulter les fauxbourgs de Rheims*."

When we reflect on the character of the people Dumourier was accountable to for his conduct, and how little they are difpofed to forgive what they confider as reprehenfible, we muft the more admire his fteadinefs. It is now generally faid, that if he had fallen back to Chalons and Rheims, the enemy might have got poffeffion of a plentiful country, and perhaps wintered in France. He left Bournonville to harrafs the Pruffians during their retreat. That General

---

* I hope, my dear General, that you are as much convinced as we, that you ought, without a moment's delay, to move towards the department of La Marne, on purpofe to protect Chalons, Rheims, and the fertile fields of the Soifonnois and La Brie. Of what importance is it to us that the enemy are in poffeffion of the barren plains of Champaigne ?

We cannot with patience think of your remaining at St. Menehould, while the Hulans are infulting the fuburbs of Rheims.

followed

followed them as far as Bufancy; and then being ordered to the army intended againft Flanders, he was replaced by the Generals Kellermann and Valence, who, with all their zeal and activity, were not able to gain any advantage over this retreating and fickly army.

Dillon, on his part, followed that body of Auftrians and Heffians who had attacked his poft at Biefme, and were now retreating by another route towards Verdun.

He had about 16,000 men with him, and the army he purfued was more numerous, and confifted of well difciplined troops. Having heard that the Auftrians and Heffians were irritated againft each other, and having been informed that the Landgrave himfelf had fpoken with anger againft the conduct of the Auftrians, he wrote a letter from Domballe to that Prince, which he fent by M. Gobert his Adjutant General, at the fame time that he difmiffed M. Lindau,

dau, an Heffian officer, who had been taken prifoner. In this letter, after fome general reflections refpecting the right of nations to change their governments, which it is not probable the Landgrave will think conclufive, Dillon affures him that he is furrounded in fuch a manner that it will be very difficult for him to efcape; but that if he will fet out the following morning for his own country, and entirely evacuate the French territories with his troops, that he will be allowed to pafs undifturbed by certain pofts which were at that time occupied by the French.

Dillon faw, that it was not in his power with 16,000 men to prevent the retreat of 20,000; but he thought if he could perfuade the Heffians to feparate from the Auftrians, he might cut off the latter.—It was not very likely indeed that the Landgrave would be fo far deceived as to accept of Dillon's offer; but whatever may be

thought

thought of the depth of the ftratagem, it is evident that Dillon meant to ferve, not to injure France; for he fhewed the letter to General Galbaud before he fent it, and he alfo gave a copy of it, with the Landgrave's anfwer, to Sillery, Carra, and Prieur, the Commiffioners of the National Convention *.

But what puts Dillon's intentions out of all queftion is, that on the 4th of October he intercepted a letter from the Director of the diftrict of Etain, to the Landgrave of Heffe, dated the firft of October, by which it appeared that the Landgrave was expected to take his head quarters at Etain; on which Dillon fent a courier from his camp at Sivry-la-Parche to General Favart at Metz, to inform him, that he intended to attack the enemy on their retreat, and that they were to retreat by Etain; to prove which he tranfmitted the intercepted letter to Favart, and defired

* Rapport des Commiffaires de la Convention.

him

him to fend, a detachment from the garrifon
of Metz to co-operate in haraffing them.

He adds, " Faites avertir tous les villages,
que tous les citoyens reprennent de la confiance, que l'on fonne le tocfin par-tout,
toutes les armes feront bonnes pour harceler
l'ennemi, et tomber dans cháque defilé
fur fes equipages. Faites proclamer que tous
ceux que lui fourniront une livre de pain,
font traitres à leur pays. Je le purfuivrai
fans rélache s'ils fe retirent ; je les com-
battrai s'ils reftent," &c.*

General Dillon's letter to the Landgrave
of Heffe Caffel, and the Landgrave's anfwer,

---

* " Let this be proclaimed in all the villages, that
the citizens may recover their fpirits ; let the alarm be
founded every where : all forts of arms will ferve to harrafs the enemy, and to affift in attacking their carriages
in every defile. Let it be proclaimed, that all who
furnifh them with a fingle pound of bread will be confidered as traitors to their country. I will purfue them
without relaxation if they fly—I am determined to fight
them if they remain," &c.

were

were tranfmitted to the Convention without any commentary. They were read in the Affembly, and, inftead of appearing meritorious or innocent, they had the moft malignant and moft unnatural copftruction put on them by fome of the members. Merlin of Thionville exclaimed, that this letter was a complete proof of Dillon's being a traitor.——This Merlin is a moft zealous accufer; he feems to think that by murdering the reputation of others, he fhall accumulate a vaft ftock of fame to himfelf, as the Indian imagines that he becomes the immediate poffeffor of all the courage and dexterity of the enemy he kills. Merlin, not fatisfied with the interpretation he had given to this letter to the Landgrave, reverted to Dillon's proclamation at Pont-fur-Sambre and other parts of his conduct previous to the 10th of Auguft; on all which he put the moft malignant conftruction, and

and finished by proposing a decree of accusation against him.

"One general officer," said Kerfaint, "has already answered your decree of accusation by a victory—How do you know that Dillon was not obeying the orders of Dumourier when he wrote the letter in question?"

Couthon, in answer to Kerfaint, declared that no decree of accusation could be better founded than that now proposed against Arthur Dillon—He said, he would not take into consideration any thing laid to his charge before his letter to the Landgrave, but in the same breath he recapitulated whatever was most likely to injure him in the mind of the Convention respecting his conduct long before that time, and immediately after the tenth of August.

Couthon labours under a disease which renders him unable to walk, or even to stand; and which seems to have communicated its malignity to his disposition.
He

He is always brought in the arms of his
servant from his carriage into the Assembly, and is indulged in the liberty of
speaking without rising from his seat—He
has the reputation of being a man of acute
parts; there is a mildness in his countenance that is not found in his opinions,
which are generally violent and severe.
His speech rendered the enemies of Dillon
more furious—One member said that he
seemed inclined to make no other use of
the army committed to his charge but as
a safe-guard to conduct the enemies of
France out of the country; another observed, that it was highly expedient that the
Convention should charge the Executive
Power to take particular care that Dillon
did not make his escape. And a third ascended the tribune and made a motion
which terminated the climax of intem-
perance and injustice—He proposed that
the three Commissioners should be immediately

diately arrested as traitors for not having
suspended Dillon from his command, the
moment he shewed them a copy of the
letter he had written to the Landgrave.
Nothing could be more uncandid and cap-
tious than the spirit shewn by those men on
this occasion; they must have known that
Dillon had pursued the Hessians and Austrians with indefatigable activity to Verdun, and that it was in consequence of the
batteries which he lost no time in erecting
against that town, that it soon after sur-
rendered, but they could not forget Dillon's
conduct on his first receiving the accounts
of the proceedings at Paris on the 10th of
August. Prudence and good policy indicate a different conduct; the best way
surely to conciliate men to a revolution, is
to present them with greater advantages
under the new government than they enjoyed under the old.——But these furious
reformers, whilst they declaim against the

2   tyranny

tyranny of the ancient government, prefent nothing in fupport of the new, but accufations, poniards and guillotines. With much difficulty, inftead of an immediate accufation, they at laft came to a refolution, that the Executive Council fhould to-morrow ftate to the affembly all the circumftances relative to General Dillon's conduct to the Landgrave of Heffe Caffel, before they made any decree refpecting him

October 13.

I went this morning to the Conventional Affembly, and was admitted into the box where, on the 11th of Auguft, I had feen the unfortunate family, now prifoners in the temple, feated.

The hall and galleries were uncommonly crowded, becaufe Dumourier, who arrived in Paris laft night, was expected to come to the Affembly this day.

The forenoon was fpent in debates, in which

which Buzot, Vergniaud, and fome other of the moft diftinguifhed members of the Convention took part. About one o'clock I faw one of the huiffiers go to the Prefident, and I heard him acquaint him, that Dumourier attended in the adjoining room.

The Prefident, however, did not interrupt the debate, which continued for at leaft an hour after this information was given. It was known to fome in the Affembly, that Dumourier was waiting to be called in; feveral members thinking the Prefident was ignorant of that circumftance, went up and whifpered him—he fignified by a nod that he already knew it, and allowed the debate to continue.

It ftruck me as fingular, that a General who in fuch critical circumftances had rendered the moft important fervices to his country, and was juft returned victorious, fhould be treated with fuch coolnefs.—I have no doubt it was done on purpofe, and;

in the republican fpirit, intended as a hint to the General not to overvalue his importance.

At laft, however, the Prefident read a letter from General Dumourier, in which he informs the Convention, that he defires to pay his duty to them, and waits their orders. A member moved that he fhould be admitted directly; and the General, attended by feveral officers, appeared at the bar, amidft the applaufe of the Affembly, and the acclamations of the galleries.——He is confiderably below the middle fize, of a fharp and intelligent countenance, and feems rather above 50 years of age. He pronounced the following difcourfe, throwing his eyes occafionally on a paper which he held in his hand.

" Citoyens Legiflateurs——La liberté triomphe par tout : guidée par la philofophie, elle parcourra l'univers, et s'affeoira fur tous les trônes, aprés avoir écrafé le defpotifme,

I

potifme, aprés avoir eclairé les peuples.
Les loix conftitutionelles auxquelles vous
allez travailler, feront la bafe du bonheur
et de la fraternité des nations. Cette
guerre-ci fera la derniére ; et les tyrans et
les privilégiés, trompés dans leurs criminels
calculs, feront les feules victimes de cette
lutte du pouvoir arbitraire contre la raifon.

" L'armée, dont la confiance de la nation
m'avoit donné la conduite, a bien merité de
la patrie: réduite, lorfque je l'ai jointe le 28
Août, à 17,000 hommes, déforganifée par
des traitres que le châtiment et la honte
pourfuivent par tout, elle n'a été effrayée
ni du nombre, ni de la difcipline, ni des
menaces, ni de la barbarie, ni des premiers
fuccés de 80,000 fatellites du defpotifme.
Les defilés de la forêt d'Argonne ont été les
Thermopyles, où cette poignée de foldats de
la liberté a prefenté, pendant quinze jours, à
cette formidable armée une refiftance im-
pofante. Plus heureux que les Spartiates,
nous avons été fecourus par deux armées

I 2   animées

animées du même esprit que nous. Nous nous sommes rejoints dans le camp inexpugnable de Sainte Menehould. Les ennemis, au désespoir, ont voulu tenter une attaque, qui ajoute une victoire à la carrière militaire de mon collégue, et mon ami, Kellermann.

" Dans le camp de Sainte Menehould, les soldats de la liberté ont deployé d'autres vertus militaires, sans lesquelles le courage même peut être nuisible : la confiance en leurs chefs, l'obéissance, la patience et la persévérance. Cette partie de l'empire Français presente un sol aride, sans eau et sans bois, les Allemands s'en souviendront : leur sang impur fécondera, peut être, cette terre ingrate qui en est abreuvée. La saison étoit très pluvieuse et très froide : nos soldats étoient mal habillés, sans paille pour se coucher, sans couvertures, quelquefois deux jours sans pain, parceque la position de l'ennemi obligeoit les convois à de longs detours,,

detours, par des chemins de traverse très *mauvais* en tout tems, et *gatés* par des pluies continuelles ; car je dois rend re jus-tice aux regiffeurs des vivres et des four-rages, qui, malgré tous les obftacles des mauvais chemins, de la faifon pluvieufe, des mouvemens imprévus, ou que j'etois obligé de cacher, ont entretenu l'abondance autant qu'il leur à été poffible ; et je fuis bien aife de publier que c'eft à leurs foins qu'on doit la bonne fanté des foldats. Ja-mais je ne les ai vus murmurer. Les chants et la joie auroient fait prendre ce camp ter-rible pour un de ces camps de plaifance, ou le luxe des rois raffembloit autrefois des au-tomates enrégimentés pour l'amufement de leurs maitreffes ou de leurs enfans.

" L'efpoir de vaincre foutenoit les foldats de la liberté; leurs fatigues, leurs privations, ont été récompenfées : l'ennemi a fuccom-bé fous la faim, la mifére et les maladies; cette armée formidable fut diminuée de moitié ; les cadavres et les chevaux morts ja-

I 3

lonnent

lonnent la route; Kellermann les pourfuit avec plus de 40,000 hommes, pendant qu'avec un pareil nombre je marche au fécours du département du Nord, et des malheureux et eftimables Belges et Liégeois.

" Je ne fuis venu paffer quatre jours ici que pour arranger avec le Confeil les details cette campagne d'hiver. J'en profite pour vous prefenter mes hommages. Je ne vous ferai point de nouveaux fermens; je me montrerai digne de commander aux enfans de la liberté, et de foutenir les loix que le peuple fouverain va fe faire à lui même par votre organe *."

The

---

* Citizen Legiflators—Liberty is every where triumphant; directed by philofophy, fhe will pervade the world, fhe will crufh defpotifm, open the eyes of mankind, and feat herfelf on the throne of the univerfe. Thofe conftitutional laws which you are about to frame will ferve as a bafis for the union and happinefs of nations. The prefent war will be the laft of wars, and the tyrants of the world, deceived in their crimi-

nal

The loud applaufe of all the deputies and fpectators was renewed feveral times after

mal calculations, will be the fole victims of this contention between arbitrary power and reafon.

The army entrufted to my command by the public confidence has deferved well of their country : reduced, when I joined it, to 17,000, and weakened by the machinations of fhamelefs traitors, who I hope will one day meet the punifhment they deferve, it was never intimidated by the numbers, the threats, the barbarity, or even by the firft fuccefs of 80,000 flaves of defpotifm. The ftraits of the foreft of Argonne was the Thermopylæ in which that handful of the foldiers of liberty, for fifteen fucceffive days, prefented a refiftance which kept that formidable army in awe. More fortunate than the Spartans, we were fuccoured by two armies animated by the fame fpirit with ourfelves; they joined us at the impregnable camp of Saint Menehould. The enemy, prompted by defpair, hazarded an attack, which adds a victory to the military career of my friend and colleague Kellermann.

At St. Menehould the foldiers of freedom difplayed other military virtues, without which valour itfelf may become hurtful, namely confidence in their officers,

I 4   obedience,

after Dumourier had concluded, before the President could make a reply, which he did at

obedience, patience and perseverance. That part of France is barren, and destitute of wood and water. The Germans will remember it. Their slavish blood with which it is drenched, may perhaps render it more fertile. The weather was uncommonly wet and cold, our soldiers were ill clothed, they had neither straw to lie upon, nor blankets to cover them, and sometimes they were for two entire days without bread; for such was the position of the enemy that our convoys were obliged to make a circuit, by cross roads, at all times bad, but then rendered worse by the late excessive rains. Here I must do justice to the commissaries of stores and forage: notwithstanding all the obstacles of bad roads, bad weather, and of sudden movements, which I could not always foresee, and, when I did, was often obliged to conceal, they supplied us as well as possibly could have been expected. And it is with pleasure I take this opportunity of declaring, that the health of your army is owing to their extraordinary care and diligence. Amidst all the difficulties I have stated, the soldiers were never heard to murmur: on hearing the songs of joy which resounded from every corner of our warlike camp, it might have been mistaken for one of these

at length in the following terms—" Citoyen
General—L'accueil que vous venez de re-
cevoir de la Convention Nationale, exprime

thofe camps of pleafure in which luxurious monarchs
formerly affembled regimented automatons to manœuvre for the amufement of their children and miftreffes.

The hope of victory fupported the foldiers of liberty.
Their fatigues and hardfhips have been fully compenfated. The enemy funk under fatigue, famine and
difeafe. That formidable army was diminifhed one
half; directed by the dead bodies of men and horfes,
Kellermann purfues them at the head of forty thoufand
men.

I purpofe to march immediately with the fame number to fuccour the department of the North, and to the
relief of our efteemed and unfortunate friends, the inhabitants of Brabant and Liege.

I am come hither, for four days, to fettle with the
council the plan of our winter campaign—I avail myfelf
of the opportunity to pay my duty to you. I bind myfelf by no new oaths; but I will fhew myfelf worthy of
commanding the fons of liberty, and faithful in fupport
of thofe laws which the fovereign people are now about
to frame through you.

mieux

mieux que je ne le pourrois faire fa fatif-
faction de vos fervices, et la haute opinion
qu'elle a conçue de vos talens et de votre
patriotifme. Continuez, Citoyen General,
continuez à diriger les foldats de la liberté
dans le chemin de la victoire ; continuez a
vous couvrir de lauriers ; continuez a bien
fervir la patrie, et vous acquirerez de nouveaux droits a la reconnoiffance de la république.

"-La Convention Nationale vous invite,
ainfi que vos fréres d'armes à la feance *."

One of the deputies then moved, that the

---

* Citizen General—The reception you have met
with from the National Convention is a ftronger teftimony than any expreffion of mine could be, of their
approbation of your conduct, and of their high opinion
of your talents and patriotifm. Citizen General, continue to lead the foldiers of liberty in the road of victory—continue to gather laurels—perfift in ferving your
country, and you will acquire new claims to the gratitude of the republic.

Con-

Convention fhould authorize the Prefident to demand of General Dumourier what he thought refpecting the affair of Dillon.

This was done accordingly, and Dumourier readily anfwered, that he had read a copy of the letter in queftion; that he confidered it merely as a bravado on the part of Dillon, and of little importance, efpecially as General Dillon had foon after purfued the Heffians with the utmoft vigour.

Having faid this, Dumourier, with the officers who accompanied him, entered the hall—Many of the deputies rofe and faluted him, after which he feated himfelf among them.

Two officers then appeared at the bar, one of whom addreffing the Affembly faid, "Legiflators, the Adjutant General of the army of the North prefents you with a ftandard taken in the midft of fireand flaughter from the French emigrants; as foon as it was feen by the foldiers of liberty, they

they broke through the fquadrons of thofe traitors, and tore it from them."

The Prefident having made a fuitable anfwer, Vergniaud obferved, that feveral ftandards which had been won from defpotifm were already hanging in the hall ; that as thofe were honourable trophies of the victories of the republic, they were worthy of being expofed to the view of the citizens :——but as for this, he added, around which the enemies of their native country, a fet of affaffins whom you have deftined to the fcaffold fought ;——this odious flag ought not to fhock your fight ; I move, therefore, that it be delivered into the hands of the executioner, and publicly committed to the flames.

This propofal was applauded and adopted. Dumourier remained in the Affembly till it broke up. He was dreffed in the uniform of a General Officer, blue and gold lace ; he is faid to be a great deal lefs

5

attentive

attentive to drefs than is ufual in France ; but in any drefs I fhould know him to be a Frenchman. He poffeffes the peculiar vivacity of air and manner that diftinguifhes the natives of this country. I underftand that he is remarkably entertaining and agreeable in converfation ; that though he has indulged in pleafure, and yielded to diffipation, yet he is capable of the moft indefatigable exertion, both of body and mind, when the importance of the object requires it; that he has always been fonder of pleafure than of money, and ever ready to facrifice both for renown. His enemies, who allow that he poffeffes great acutenefs of mind, and the moft unfhaken courage, throw doubts upon his fteadinefs in other refpects. His military talents have been fufficiently evinced in the courfe of the laft memorable campaign : without the fingular circumftances which raifed him to command, and drew them into action, the

man

man who with inferior force baffled the attempts of the moſt renowned Generals of the age, would have remained undiſtin-guiſhed and ſubordinate to thoſe on whom birth without talents, or age which has not profited by experience, ſo often devolves the command of armies.

Paris, October 13.

The minds of the Pariſians are greatly elevated by the wonderful ſucceſs of the French arms. The repulſe of the Auſtrians at Lille, the fortunate expedition of General Anſelme into the county of Nice, the reduction of Savoy, the rapid progreſs of Cuſtine on the Rhine, and above all, the retreat of the Pruſſians, are events of a nature to have raiſed the national vanity of a people leſs ſuſceptible of its influence than the French.

They ſeem convinced that their arms are irreſiſtible, and they begin to indulge the moſt

moſt romantic ideas. Of all failings to which mankind are liable, vanity is the moſt comfortable; and perhaps it may be fortunate for a people entangled in circum—stances rather vexatious, to have this for a compenſation. But ſhould the Convention be affected in the ſame way, it may be at-tended with afflicting conſequences to the country. I heard ſome things this day in the Aſſembly, and alſo from one of the de-puties, with whom I had ſome converſation, ſince, that give reaſon to ſuſpect that the romantic notions above alluded to are not confined to the people without doors.

The late ſucceſſes are imputed, beſide the valour of the troops, to the ſuperiour dex-terity, ſagacity, and natural quickneſs of the French cannoniers over thoſe of all other nations.

It has been propoſed to erect a monument in the town of Varennes in commemora-
tion

tion of the flight of two kings, meaning Lewis XVI. who fled to that town, and the King of Pruffia, who lately retired through it; thofe who make the propofal give this infcription for the monument, *Regibus fugatis;* and add this refle&ion, *Dans peu, chaque état aura fa Varennes.*

Every ftroke of fatire dire&ed againft kings is fure of being well received by the Convention.

The War - Minifter feems fenfible of this—He tranfmitted to it lately an intercepted letter, which he pretends is from fome perfon at Berlin, addreffed to the Pruffian Minifter, Bifchofswerder, in which the writer afferts, that the people are highly difpleafed at the part their fovereign has taken againft the French nation, and that the following epigram on that fubje& is read with delight——" Un jour Dieu voulut épargner une ville a caufe d'un jufte qui y étoit;

y étoit; aujourd'hui un prince Allemand veut faire périr toute la France pour un imbécille couronné qui s'y trouve."

But in the midst of this exaltation on account of their success against external enemies, and of all this severity against kings, the representatives of the people seem not to have it in their power to punish the insolence of certain persons within the city of Paris.

The Convention decreed, that the election of the municipal officers of Paris should be by ballot. Certain turbulent people, who wish the electors to be overawed by the mob, disapproved of this, and prevailed on the section of the Theatre François to proceed according to the old method of voting aloud.——For this act of disobedience and contempt the President and Secretary of the section were ordered to appear at the bar of the Assembly.——Being questioned by the President, they answered in a style that by no means indicated repentance; yet as they did not avow an intention of persisting in their disobedience, a very slight apology was accepted, and the two culprits were admitted to the honours of the sitting—of course this feeble attempt to maintain authority will encourage disobedience. Buzot took this occasion to urge the necessity of adopting the measure of having a body of troops at the command of the Convention, to ensure obedience to its decrees, and protect the persons of the deputies.

There are certain members of the Assembly, who, deriving their importance entirely from the favour of the rabble, are prepared to oppose this measure; but as the majority approve of it, their opposition, it is thought, will be soon overcome.

October 14.

I was sitting this morning in the Conventional Assembly, when suddenly the

8. firing

firing of cannon was heard—This produced some signs of emotion among the deputies, who, like me, were ignorant of the cause.

Having been accustomed to such sounds on account of victories, or some other occasion of public rejoicing, a noise of this nature was formerly apt to excite chearful and agreeable ideas only. The impression I had in the present instance was of a very different nature. The firing which took place when the Royal Family were sitting in the same box on the 10th of August, instantly sprang up in my mind; an idea closely linked with that of the execrable second of September, and the dreadful peal which was the harbinger of three continued days and nights of blood and slaughter.

Those unpleasant reflections were removed when I was informed that the firing in the present case was on account of the festival which had been decreed for the

success

fuccefs of the arms of the Republic in Savoy.

I immediately left the Aſſembly, and went through the gardens of the Tuileries to the Place de Louis XV. now called the Place de la Revolution.

A ſtatue, with the emblems of Liberty, was placed on the pedeſtal on which the equeſtrian ſtatue of Lewis XV. formerly ſtood. On the eaſt and weſt ſide of the pedeſtal was inſcribed, République Françoiſe, 1792 : on the ſouth ſide, Entrée de Montefquiou à Chambéry, Capitale du Duché de Savoye; on the north, Entrée d'Anſelme, dans le Comté de Nice et Mont-alban.

A large body of the national guards, with a number of armed citizens from all the different ſections of Paris, with diſplayed banners, marched in proceſſion to the place.

A deputation from the National Convention,

tion, and another from the Municipality of Paris, attended at an amphitheatre erected for the purpose, near the statue of Liberty. A great number of Savoyards of both sexes and all conditions, holding each other by the hand, and with every appearance of joy, preceded by a band of music, marched between two long ranks of men armed with pikes, to the square, and were received by the acclamations of an immense number of spectators. All the colours and banners of the different regiments assembled in the square were arranged around the statue of Liberty. A numerous band of music then performed the hymn of the Marseillois, and that favourite song was sung by some chosen singers of the band; and most of the people with whom this vast and magnificent square was crowded joined in the chorus. After which the cannon were repeatedly fired, and in the intervals

K 3

the

the fky refounded with universal fhouts of Vive la République!

The hymn of the Marseillois is called for every evening at every theatre in Paris, and nothing can exceed the enthusiasm with which it is heard.

I went laft night to a new musical piece called the Ephesian Matron. The house was pretty full, but the appearance of the audience was very different from what I recollect to have been usual on such occasions before the Revolution.

The women still display fancy and some degree of elegance in their drefs, but the men are universally dreffed with the utmost simplicity. I fat in the parquet next to a remarkably tall man wrapt in a drab coloured great coat, who feemed between fixty and feventy years of age. On his withdrawing, I was told that this was Admiral d'Eftaign, who commanded the
French

Freneh fleet and army in America and the West Indies in the laſt war.

The conduct of the Count d'Eſtaign was more univerſally approved of during the late war, than ſince the Revolution.

He was Commander of the national guards of Verſailles in October 1789, when a mob from Paris broke into the palace, murdered ſome of the guards, and committed many ſhameful exceſſes.

M. d'Eſtaign appeared to be at once a friend to the principles of the Revolution, and an aſſiduous courtier.

In a nation whoſe conſtitution is mellowed by time, and where the ſubjects have experienced the bleſſing of that liberty which the ſpirit of their anceſtors obtained, united to the tranquillity ariſing from the monarchical form of their government; a love of freedom not only is compatible with attachment to the monarch,

K 4

but,

but, as long as he governs according to the principles of the conftitution, thofe fentiments mutually ftrengthen each other.

But, in a nation on whofe government the fcions of freedom are but newly engrafted, at the expence of the monarch, and without having hitherto produced any palatable fruit, the cafe is different. The ftruggles and animofities between thofe who produced the alteration, and thofe who oppofed it, are too recent; mutual fufpicion and a fenfe of mutual accufations are ftill exifting; and he who attempts to be the friend of both parties, is trufted by neither.

M. d'Eftaign has taken no part in the lateft tranfactions; he feems to defire to live unnoticed, and hitherto he has been undifturbed.

October 15.

The emigration of the nobleffe has been fo very extenfive, that it is rare to meet with any perfon of name within the walls of Paris, particularly any who have ever

been

been employed or entrufted with the ancient government. Yet thofe of this defcription, who venture to remain in France, are perhaps in lefs danger in Paris than in a provincial town; becaufe in the capital there is always a fufficient force to fupprefs *partial* and *incidental* tumults, provided the magiftrates are difpofed to call it forth, and make ufe of it; whereas in the villages and provincial towns a tumult may be excited, which the magiftrates, were they ever fo much inclined, are unable to quell.

A groundlefs fufpicion, or a calumny invented and propagated by an enemy, may kindle the fury of a few fanatics, and the head of the perfon who is the object of it, may be fixed on a pike before the magiftrate can affemble force to protect him.

His innocence is made apparent when it is too late; every body laments his fate: the murderers however are excufed, becaufe they were mifled (*egaré* is the palliative
word

word used on such occasions) by the no-
blest of all errors, too much zeal for their
country's good ; and tranquillity is restored
only till fresh suspicions and calumnies excite new murders.

I heard a petition read in the Convention from the widow of a sword-cutler of
Charleville. A report had been spread
that he furnished arms to the enemy : this
immediately roused the people, and in the
first fury of their civisme, as it is called,
they cut off his head. Very soon after it
appeared that the report was false, and that
the 'unfortunate sword-cutler had always
been a zealous patriot. Some of the deputies seemed very much shocked at this ; but
I heard one observe, with great coolness,
that he was sorry for what the people of
Charleville had done ; and then added, with
an air of sagacity, " but the best people in
the world are liable to be mistaken."

However ready the French are to accuse
individuals,

individuals, the inhabitants of the moſt deſpotic country are not more afraid of ſpeaking treaſon, than the French are of ſaying any thing to the diſadvantage of the *people*: no nation was ever more indulgent to the caprices of its tyrant, than France is at preſent, to that moſt capricious and bloody of all tyrants, Le Peuple Souverain.

Some of the battalions which have been lately raiſed at Paris, though retained in tolerable ſubordination while they continued within the capital and ſurrounded with the national guards of all the ſections, have been guilty of great exceſſes ſince they left it——The firſt diviſion of the gendarmes à pied de Paris, on entering lately into the town of Cambray, broke open the priſon, and ſet all the priſoners at liberty except one man, whom they, in their wiſdom, thought juſtly confined.——On theſe troops leaving the town, all the priſoners whom they had ſet free were again confined by order

order of the magiſtrates ; but the ſecond diviſion paſſing through the ſame town the day following, threw open the priſons once more, and beheaded the unfortunate perſon whom their companions had kept in confinement when they gave freedom to all the other priſoners. They murdered, in the ſame manner, ſeveral of their officers, who were endeavouring to prevent their exceſſes, and bring them to order. An official account of thoſe alarming tranſactions has been read to the Convention, and was immediately referred to the war committee ; but what makes it doubtful whether any effectual meaſures will be taken to puniſh thoſe aſſaſſins, is, that Marat continues to palliate, and almoſt to juſtify every crime of this nature that is committed, whether by the populace or ſoldiers : until the Aſſembly are able and willing to ſuppreſs his Journal, and puniſh the Author, what hope is there that they will have it in their power to remedy

or

or prevent that blood-fhed and anarchy to
which the fpeeches and writings of this
man fo greatly contribute?

October 16.

The committee appointed to fuperintend
the camp and entrenchments forming near
Paris, made fome propofitions yefterday to
the Convention. They were not agreed to:
one member faid, that the pitiful farce of *la
precautione inutile* had been acted too long,
and propofed that an immediate ftop fhould
be put to that work, which, after fome debate, was decreed.

All ideas of defence are now thought ufe-
lefs.——Nothing but attack, and taking vengeance on the enemies, and maintaining the
dignity of the Republic, is now fpoken of.

If, however, there be dignity in affuming
fome degree of loftinefs in tranfacting with
the powerful Potentates who invaded the
country, there furely is none in affecting a
dictatorial tone with the weakeft of their
neighbours.

neighbours. This domineering spirit however appears too much in the conduct of the Convention towards Geneva, the comfortable condition of whose citizens for a series of years has sufficiently proved that the happiness of the subject does not depend on the extent of the State's territories. Geneva has been considered as the nursery of freedom, and has long maintained, by the prudence of her councils, that independency which was obtained by the valour of her citizens, whose prudent conduct the French would do well to imitate, if they wish the Republic of France to be as durable as that of Geneva.

Some members of the Convention have taken offence, because Geneva lately thought proper to demand those succours from the cantons of Berne and Zurick, to which they are intitled on emergencies like the present by existing treaties.

Although France had not invaded Savoy, the

the state of disorder in which the former has
been, the excesses which have been committed by the French army in various parts
of the country, in spite of the decrees of
the Convention at Paris, rendered it highly
expedient for the Republic of Geneva to
take every measure in her power to secure
the town from a sudden attack. For, however well disposed the Convention might
be, who could say that a band of patriots,
some independent portion of the peuple
souverain, would not, without consulting
the Convention, seize on Geneva? But measures of precaution became still more necessary when France declared war against the
King of Sardinia, and when a French army
was ready to invade Savoy; for, as the possession of the city of Geneva might be advantageous to either of the armies, in order to
preserve a strict neutrality, it was necessary
to guard it from both. The Republic therefore received within the walls of Geneva
1600

1600 men of the militia of Zurick and Berne; a force which, joined to that of the citizens, might secure the town from being seized by a sudden assault, but could not be considered as an act of hostility against France, even although there had been no previous treaty between Geneva and the Swiss cantons by which she was entitled to claim this succour.

Geneva is acknowledged by all the powers of Europe as an independent state: it seems contradictory to acknowledge sovereignty and independency in a state, and then complain of so natural an exercise of it as the calling in the aid of neutral powers to enable it to maintain strict neutrality.

The Convention seems, however, to have been guilty of this contradiction, and at the same time displayed unbecoming pride in superciliously passing to the order of the day at the meeting of yesterday, after hearing the explanations from the council of

4   Geneva

neva read, and in approving of the haughty conduct of their commiffioners towards that ftate. This ill accords with the prudent and pacific tenor of the declarations which the National Affembly formerly made, and ftamps credit on the affertions of the enemies of the Revolution, that the treatment which Geneva now receives from the new Republic is a fpecimen of what all the neighbouring States may expect.

Although it may be thought natural that a monarch, particularly an arbitrary one; fhould, from motives of vanity, avarice, or ambition, endeavour to extend his dominions by war and conqueft ; yet the vanity or avarice of a private citizen of Paris, Lyons, Marfeilles, or any other part of France, can be little gratified by the acceffion of new provinces. France, therefore, being now a Republic, the ambitious and reftlefs fpirit of her kings, that fatal fource to which the other States of Europe have imputed almoſt all the wars of the two laſt centuries, being now dried up, long peace and tranquillity is to be expected when this new form is acknowledged and eſtabliſhed.

This reaſoning ſeems plauſible *a priori* :—— it is unfortunate, however, that the hiſtory of the world ſhews that Republican States have been inſpired with as violent a deſire of conqueſt, and as reſtleſs an ambition, as any monarch from the age of Alexander to that of Lewis XIV. And the ſpirit which the new Republic of France begins already to manifeſt, gives no reaſon to expect that the philoſophy from which ſhe boaſts her origin, has taught her more moderation than her predeceſſors.

Independent of the diſlike one naturally feels of an act of power unſupported by juſtice, I confeſs I could not ſee my old friends, the citizens of Geneva, treated in this manner without indignation.

When the Convention is conſidered as
main—

maintaining the independency of their
country againſt a powerful league, and un-
diſmayed by the idea that all the powers of
Europe may join in the combination, it is
impoſſible not to reſpect their firmneſs. But
when they are ſeen behaving with haughty
injuſtice to a neighbouring people devoid of
the power of reſiſtance or retaliation, and
reſpectable from their talents and virtues
only, the conduct of the Convention excites a very different ſentiment.

October 16.

The Convention ſhewed more moderation this day in their conduct towards the
Republic of Genoa, than they had manifeſted towards Geneva ; although for many
obvious reaſons it might have been expected
they would have been partial rather to the
latter.

The miniſter for foreign affairs informed
them, that in a quarrel which had happened

in the port of Genoa, between fome Venetian foldiers and the crew of the French frigate Juno, the flag of the frigate had been pulled down and torn in pieces; in confequence of which the Venetians had been imprifoned, and condemned, by a decree of the Senate of Genoa, to provide the frigate in a new flag before they fhould be fet at liberty. The minifter gave it as his opinion, that as he underftood the French failors were the aggreffors, no farther notice fhould be taken of this affair, but that the Convention fhould remain fatisfied with the decifion of the Senate of Genoa.

Several of the members differed in opinion from the minifter. One deputy faid, that the decifion of the Senate of Genoa would have been confidered as fufficiently fatisfactory under the ancient government, becaufe then fhips of war were given by the favour of princes, of their miftreffes, and of their valets; and thofe appointed to command

mand them were of as frivolous characters as thofe by whofe influence the appointments were obtained. But France being now formed into a Republic, where talents, exertion, and the manly virtues alone can lead to promotion, or fituations of confidence, and above all, at this time, when the caufe of freedom is triumphant, more ample redrefs fhould be infifted on.

I perceive that many people expect a great improvement, both in the army and navy, in all effential points, from the new order of things which began in France on the 20th of laft September.

It will foon be put to trial whether the rough Republican qualities will render men better officers than that gallant fpirit and delicate fenfe of honour, which, in fpite of effeminacy and corruption, always formed part of the character of the French nobleffe.

I have had frequent converfations with deputies who are fuppofed to have con-

fiderable

fiderable weight in the Convention, concerning the probable fate of the King: they feem
to be perfuaded that the majority of the Affembly, including the moft refpectable members, are inclined to banifhment, and are endeavouring to poftpone every motion tending to bring on the trial till the people have
cooled fo far as to be fatisfied with fuch a
fentence, which they fear is not the cafe at
prefent. A remark made by one of the deputies, it is thought, had great effect on the
Convention: the remark was, " Charles I.
eut des fucceffeurs, les Tarquins n'en eu-
rent point *."

It is a dreadful thing to think that a judi-
cial or leg flative affembly, fuppofed to be fupreme, and which ought to be influenced
by no confiderations but thofe of juftice
and public good, fhould, in a matter of this

* Charles the Firft had fucceffors, the Tarquins had
none.

moment

moment to their country, and to their own confciences, be under any kind of conftraint.

As far as I can perceive however, the real citizens, or bourgeoife of Paris, by no means defire the death of the King; and if by the people is underftood the profligate idle rabble of the fuburbs, and the wretches who are hired to clamour in the public places, what probability is there that they will ever cool, or be fatisfied with any decifion except what thofe who hire them, or their own favage difpofitions, fuggeft?

This very day, in the Convention, I had an opportunity of judging how little the hopes given by the deputies above mention-ed are to be relied on. For at a time when there was no queftion regarding the King, a member afcended the tribune and faid, " He was going to remind the Convention of a part of their duty to their country, of the higheft importance, namely, the procefs of

L 4

Lewis

Lewis Capet (this is the name they generally give the King), which had been too long poftponed; he therefore demanded that a day might be fixed for his trial, that the wrongs of the nation might be avenged by the blood of that traitor."

By trial it is evident he meant execution. I underftand his name is Hardy, deputy of the department de Seine Inferieure.—He is a well-looking young man; but the harfhnefs of his fentiment formed a ftrong con‑traft with his countenance. This gave rife to many intemperate and foolifh ex‑preffions from other members who fup‑ported the motion for the trial, which they alfo ufed as fynonimous with execution. One talked of the martyrs of Liberty who had fallen before the palace on the 10th of Auguft, whofe ghofts called for vengeance on the perjured Lewis. And when another fuggefted that " the papers refpecting the King's treachery fhould be printed and de‑
livered

livered to the members, and that it would require a confiderable time before judgment could be pronounced; a third afferted, that "Lewis Capet could not be confidered as King, becaufe royalty was abolifhed in France—What is he then? why, a fimple individual, in a ftate of confinement for trial: but the law, continued he, exprefsly fays, that every perfon confined for a crime fhall be brought to his trial within the fpace of 24 hours of his being arrefted; the affaffin Lewis has been too long confined, and ought to be brought to trial and punifhed as foon as poffible."

On this, as on other occafions, I obferved that the people in the galleries redoubled their applaufe as often as cruel things were faid, and violent meafures propofed. This feemed to become a motive with thofe who wifhed to ingratiate themfelves with the multitude, to proceed in making new propofals; the laft always more violent than the

2   former.

former. Yet the difcuffion was not preme-
ditated, at leaft it feemed to me to arife accidentally.

Ruhl, one of the members for the department of the Lower Rhine juft arrived
from Strafbourg, informed the Convention,
that he had on the road paffed a party of
dragoons who were conducting thirteen
Emigrants to Paris, who had been taken in
arms on the frontiers——He was afraid that
thofe unhappy men were in danger of being
deftroyed by the populace as foon as they
fhould arrive, and thought it his duty to
acquaint the Convention that meafures
might be taken for their fafety until they
fhould be legally tried. Whether Ruhl
introduced the Emigrants with an intention to divert the Convention from the trial
of the King, I know not ; but for fome time
it had that effect, the debate turned to the
fubject of the Emigrants——But one member feemed difpleafed with this, and abruptly
exclaimed

exclaimed, There are others more guilty than all thefe Emigrants, and whofe trial is more preffing. " Je veux parler de Louis XVI. je demande que fon procés commence."

The debate recommenced refpecting the trial, and foon became as intemperate as at firft. From the hard unfeeling things that were uttered, one might have thought that the hearts of the difputants were of flint: they ftruck fire from each other fo faft, and wrought themfelves into fuch heat, that I expected fome violent refolution would have been taken directly.

Téte â téte, or in a very fmall circle, the French are nearly as calm, and generally more ingenious, than moft of their neighbours; but a numerous affembly of Frenchmen almoft always become turbulent.

Barbaroux of Marfeilles then rofe, and had the addrefs to put an end to the debate: the argument which proved effectual, did

little

little honour to thofe on whom it had influence. He began by afferting the right of the Convention, in confequence of the power tranfmitted by the people, to judge the King.——After having expatiated on this topic at fome length, he added, " But it is expected by all Europe that you will proceed in a bufinefs of that important nature with all poffible prudence and deliberation :" [Here fomething of a murmur was heard in the gallery]——becaufe, added he raifing his voice, perhaps Lewis and Marie Antoinette are not the only criminals whom the fword of juftice has to ftrike."

He no fooner uttered this, than the incipient murmur ended in acclamations of applaufe.——The certainty which this implied not only that the king and queen would be tried, but condemned and executed, and that feveral others would meet with the fame fate, feemed to pleafe them fo much, that they were fatisfied with a delay, which

perhaps

perhaps would not have otherwife been carried, and which was all that the moderate part of the Convention (who were convinced of the injuftice and imprudence of proceeding 'againft the King) durft at that time propofe, or had reafon to expect.

October 17.

General Dumourier fet out early this morning to take the command of the army deftined againft Auftrian Brabant. Some nights ago, accompanied with fome of his officers, he attended the meeting of the Jacobins: it is good policy in the General of a French army to pay this piece of refpect to a fociety which has fo great and fuch extenfive influence.——He addreffed them to this purpofe: " Citizens, you have torn the hiftory of defpotifm, you have faved France, your efforts in the caufe of Freedom are engraved by the hand of Liberty on the hearts of all good Frenchmen:

we

we are going to finifh what we have begun, and we will fulfil your expectations, or perifh in the attempt."——Danton, who was prefident, anfwered him to the following effect: " Citizen General, when La Fayette took flight, you did not defpair of the fafety of the Republic; you rallied our troops weakened by treachery and divifion; you repelled with a few foldiers the numerous armies of tyrants; you have deferved well of your country:——under your direction the republican pike fhall break the regal fcep-tre, and the cap of liberty fhall annihilate the diadem——We are your brethren and your friends, and your name fhall make a fhining figure in our hiftory." Other members fpoke in praife of Dumourier, who at length retired amid the applaufe of the fociety.

I went this evening to the fociety of the Jacobins, and was witnefs of a fcene of a different kind, and which was little to be

5   expected

expected so soon after what is above described.

It will be proper to mention here an affair
which happened about eight days before the
General's arrival at Paris.

Dumourier had written a letter to the Convention, informing them, that the Parisian
battalions of Mauconseil and Republicain had
committed a crime which threw dishonour
on the French nation, by massacring four
Prussian deserters in the town of Rethel, in
the department of Ardennes. The particulars of this shocking affair he transmitted
to the minister of war, and they appear in a
letter from General Chazot to Dumourier,
which was read in the Convention. The
four men in question were dragoons, who
deserted from the Prussians to Rethel, where
they inlisted in the French army. Some
soldiers of the battalions above mentioned,
having met the four deserters in a tavern,
picked a quarrel with them, abused them as
traitors to their country, dragged them into
the

the ſtreets, and threatened to behead them.
Chazot, who was in the town, hearing of this,
ſent orders to protect the men; but the
greateſt part of the ſoldiers of both battalions
being now joined, formed too ſtrong a body
for any force the General had to uſe againſt
them : all that his meſſengers could obtain
of thoſe mutineers therefore was, that they
ſhould carry the deſerters before the General,
which was done accordingly. He uſed every
argument and every perſuaſion (for no other
means were in his power) to prevail on
theſe mutinous madmen to uſe no violence
to the deſerters: ſo far from ſucceeding, ſome
of the wretches cried out, *Si le Général s'oppoſe
à nos deſirs, il faut l'expédier* *.

Chazot, finding that his remonſtrances
only rendered them more furious, puſhed
through the crowd, and with difficulty eſcap-
ed to his horſe and rode away. He was no

---

* If the General oppoſes our wiſhes, he muſt be
cut off.

sooner gone than the wretched deserters were cut in pieces.

The abfurdity of this abominable deed almoſt equals its barbarity, and this remark may be made with juſtice on many tranfactions in this country ſince the 10th of Auguſt. Common prudence might have prevented ſome of the moſt unjuſtifiable, without the fuggeſtions of humanity, and humanity would have prevented them, even where prudence did not exiſt. This atrocious deed deſtroyed the hope of weakening the Pruſſian army by defertion, which had been ſo great an object with the Convention, that a penſion of 100 livres had been decreed to every ſoldier who ſhould defert from the Pruſſian army to the French; and while it put an end to every expectation of this kind, it alſo deſtroyed every hope of quarter, or mercy, when any of themſelves fell into the hands of the Pruſſians *.

To

* I have heard it afferted ſince my return to England,

To expiate this guilt, and vindicate the character of his army, Dumourier had given orders to General Bournonville to march a body of troops with fome pieces of artillery againft the two battalions, who were ordered to ground their arms, and fubmit, on pain of being immediately put to death. They fubmitted accordingly, their colours were fent to their Sections, their arms and uniforms taken from them, and the men themfelves ordered in that difgraceful ftate to Paris, there to wait the pleafure of the Convention.

It afterwards appeared that the unfortu-

land, that there was a confiderable defertion from the Pruffians to the French at the Camp of St. Menehould, and that a fear of its increafing was the chief reafon of the Duke of Brunfwick's retreat; which reafon he took great pains to conceal. But as the Duke's retreat is fufficiently accounted for independent of that, I have allowed the account of it to remain as it was in my Journal, according to the intelligence I received at Paris.

nate

tiste men who had been thus murdered, were not native Pruffians, but Frenchmen, who had enlifted in the Pruffian army before the Revolution, and had feized the firft opportunity of returning to their countrymen.

Marat having heard of this circumftance, publifhed in his journal, and pofted on the walls, accufations againft the General, and vindications of the affaffins. The former he defcribes as a debauchee, as an old valet of the court, and, which includes every thing that is wicked, as an ariftocrate. The latter he reprefents as worthy men, full of patriotifm, which prompted them to anticipate by a few hours the blow of the executioner on the necks of four traitors. He afferts, that Dumourier, Chazot, and others, calumniate thofe innocent battalions, on purpofe to render the citizens of Paris, and particularly the General Council of the Commune, *to whom France owes the revolu-*

M 2

tion

tion of the tenth of August, odious to the country; that the four deserters were not Prussians, as had been perfidiously published by Dumourier, but French Emigrants, taken in arms, and therefore deservedly put to death by the patriotic battalions.

He likewise accuses Dumourier of having connived at the escape of the Prussians out of France, when he might have forced their camp, and obliged them to lay down their arms; and also for having quitted his own army at this critical time, on purpose to carouse with drunkards and opera girls.

I never was more surprised in my life than when Marat, having ascended the tribune at the Jacobins, began to repeat these assertions. The man's audacity is equal to any thing, but what I thought full as wonderful was the degree of patience, and even approbation, with which he was heard. The house was crowded, and it contains a very numerous numeróus audience. When Marat is in the tribune, he holds his head as high as he can, and endeavours to affume an air of dignity——He can make nothing of that; but amidſt all the exclamations and figns of hatred and difguſt which I have feen manifeſted againſt him, the look of felf approbation which he wears is wonderful——fo far from ever having the appearance of fear, or of deference, he feems to me always to contemplate the Affembly from the tribune, either with the eyes of menace, or contempt.

He fpeaks in a hollow croaking voice, with affected folemnity, which in fuch a diminutive figure would often produce laughter, were it not fuppreffed by horror at the character and fentiments of the man.

After having infifted for fome time on the guilt of the murdered, the innocence of the murderers, and the cruelty of Dumourier, he informed the fociety, that he had

M 3   thought

thought it his duty to queſtion the General in perſon, that he might learn from himſelf what he had to ſay in defence of his conduct towards thoſe two meritorious battalions. Marat then gave a very circumſtantial account of his having called on Dumourier the night before he left Paris; that he had been accompanied by two members of the National Convention, one of them I think he called Bentoble, the name of the other I do not recollect. At Dumourier's they were informed, that the General was at the Theatre des Variétés, and was not to ſup at home. " A number of carriages, and brilliant illuminations," continued Marat, " indicated to us where this ſon of Mars was ſupping with the ſons and daughters of Thalia; we found ſoldiers within and without: after traverſing ſome chambers filled with pikemen, muſketeers, dragoons, huſſars, the warlike ſuite of the General, we came to a ſpacious room full of company, at the door

of

of which was Santerre, commander of the
Parifian guards, performing the functions
of a lackey, or an ufher. He announced me
aloud, which I was forry for, becaufe it
might have made thofe perfons difappear
whom I fhould have wifhed to have feen ;
but I *did* fee fome, whom it is of ufe to
mention for the better comprehending the
operations of the ruling party in the Convention, and letting the public know who
are the ftate jugglers with whom the commander of our armies is moft connected.
To pafs over the officers of the national
guards, the aid-de-camps, and others, who
paid their court to the great Dumourier,
continued he, I faw in this auguft company
the minifters Roland and Le Brun, attended
by Kerfaint and La Source. As my name
had thrown the company into confufion, I
probably did not remark all who were prefent, I only remember thefe confpirators
whom I have named ; but it was early, and
M 4   it

it is probable that Vergniaud, Buzot, Rabaud, Lacroix, Guadet, Genfonnet, and Barbaroux, were alfo at this entertainment; for they all belong to the fame gang. At fight of me, continued Marat, looking very fierce, Dumourier was appalled."

At this a number of the fociety of Jacobins burft into laughter; and one perfon near me faid, " That is what he was not at the fight of the Pruffian army."

When the laugh was over, Marat, with an unaltered countenance, refumed, " At fight of me Dumourier was appalled; which is not to be wondered at," continued he, erecting his head, ftanding on his tiptoes, and looking very fierce, " fince I am known te be the terror of all the enemies of my country." He proceeded to inform the fociety, that he had defired to fpeak with Dumourier in another room; and being there, had afked an account of all the particulars relative to the four deferters : that the General

had

had told him he had already sent those particulars to the War Minister, and to the Convention, and had no other account to give." Marat concluded by saying, " that he had put other questions to the General, which disconcerted him so much that, instead of attempting to answer them, he was forced to sneak away abruptly with affected disdain; and so, having made it clear that he could not justify his conduct, I left this assemblage of generals, and actors, and ministers, and mountebanks, to pass the night together.

Marat endeavoured to enliven this recital with a few jokes, which excited laughter in the Jacobin Society, but had not that effect on me.—Marat attempting pleasantry, increases the horror which his appearance creates ; it gives something of the sensation which I imagine I should have, if a murderer, after cutting a man's throat by a

dexterous

dextorous ſtroke of a knife, ſhould ſmile in my face, and tip me the wink.

October 18.

When I went to the Convention this morning, the firſt thing that ſtruck me was the murky figure of Marat ſtanding on the ſteps which lead to the tribune, watching an opportunity of entering it: there was a great unwillingneſs to hear him, and he waited near two hours before he obtained the right to ſpeak, ſome other member being always pointed to by the Preſident.

Marat often exclaimed againſt this to no purpoſe, and ſeizing a moment when the tribune was empty, he began to addreſs the Aſſembly without the Preſident's permiſſion; but his voice was drowned in the outcry againſt him from all corners.— At length I heard De la Croix, the preſident, ſay to thoſe near him, " Je crois qu'il vaudroit mieux laiſſer parler ce gueux là ;" and

and raising his voice, he added, "Marat je vous donne la parole, mais je ne vous promets pas de vous la maintenir *.

Marat then entered the tribune, and began the same invective against Dumourier that I heard him pronounce laft night at the Jacobins.—He was interrupted by cries of indignation from all fides: one member addreffed the Prefident to filence him, and not permit a man who was a difgrace to the Affembly to calumniate citizens of the greateft worth: another added, that his calumnies were praife; all feemed to hold him in execration.

During the uproar, Marat ftood with an undifturbed air, looking down on the Affembly. When the clamour abated fo that his voice could be heard, he faid, with an air of irony, and in a tone of forrow,

* I believe we had beft allow the fellow to fpeak.
Marat, I give you the right to fpeak, but I cannot promife to maintain it with you long.

"I am

" I am really grieved to behold such indecent behaviour in the Affembly—Is it not
fingular that the perfon whom you try to
overwhelm with unjuft clamours, fhould be
more concerned for your honour than you
are yourfelves? Is it not extraordinary that
you fhould be fo much prejudiced againft
a man animated with patriotifm?"—Here
there was an univerfal laugh; but when he
attempted to refume his invectives againft
Dumourier and Chazot, the clamour recommenced, and the Affembly fhewed the
utmoft impatience.

Kerfaint then informed the Affembly
that the foldiers of the battalion called Republicain, fenfible of their error, had of
themfelves delivered up the traitors who
had excited them to mutiny and murder,
and had promifed to their general to efface
the memory of their crime by their conduct againft the enemy.

Marat, feeing that every body rejoiced
in

in the punifhment of the ringleaders, had
the boldnefs to affert that he never had
juftified the conduct of the battalions. The
cry in contradiction of this affertion was
fo univerfal that he could not·proceed, and
a member immediately exclaimed: " A man,
whofe name it is difagreeable to pronounce,
dares to affert, from that tribune, that he
never juftified the affaffins of the unfortunate
deferters ; in contradiction of which, I do
now affert, that laft night, at the Jacobins,
he faid that they merited a civic crown.——
Citizens, you may judge of the character
of this man from what I have told you.
Since he has been chofen as a deputy by
the people, and fince we are doomed fometimes to hear him, I now move, that as
often as he comes out of that tribune, it
may be purified before another member enters it."

After this, the Affembly paffed to the
order of the day. Marat defcended, and
ftrutted

ftrutted through the hall, affecting to
despise the murmurs which arose againft
him.

It feems extraordinary that a man fo
odious, and whose acquaintance every body
feems to fhun, fhould venture to attack,
in fuch an abufive manner, a popular and
fuccefsful general. Yet the difference between the manner in which Marat was
heard in the Jacobin Society, and in the
Conventional Affembly, is remarkable; and
I fee people who are perfuaded that Marat is
fupported in fecret by thofe who in public
difavow any connection with him.——The
fame people have alfo obferved, that the
prevailing opinion in the Jacobin Club
always becomes fooner or later the prevailing opinion in the National Affembly, and
that thofe fufpicions which Marat endeavours to raife againft Dumourier, are fpread
at the inftigation of one who has very
great influence in that fociety. That perfon,

fon, however, would do well to remember
the words of Orofmane in Zayre:

" Quiconque eft foupçonneux invite à le trahir."

The prefidency of De la Croix ended
this day; and Guadet, of the department of
the Gironde, was elected by a great majority.
Guadet feems to me one of the moft acute
men in the Convention; his fpeeches are
always perfpicuous and correct, and fometimes finifhed with an epigrammatic neat-
nefs.

October 19.

Two days ago a letter was read in the
Convention from the commiffioners to
the army of the North, acquainting the
Affembly, that a great number of volunteers
had applied for liberty to retire at the end
of the campaign.

Some members had reprefented the
danger of permitting this in the prefent
circumftances, and propofed a decree againft
it.

it. But this meafure having been thought harfh to men who had, as volunteers, rifked their lives in defence of their country, in a time of great danger; inftead of a decree, it was moved, that the Convention fhould fend an addrefs to all their armies, inviting the volunteers to prolong their fervice until the country was declared to be out of danger.——A committee of four, namely, Condorcet, Danton, Hercault de Sechelles, and Vergniaud, had been accordingly appointed to draw up the addrefs; and I heard Danton read it to the Convention this morning. It was rather too long; and although applauded by a few, it was very evident that the generality of the Affembly did not much relifh it.

A member then rofe, and, taking a paper from his pocket, faid, that he had compofed an addrefs, which he begged leave to read.——This furprifed me a good deal; but I did not obferve that it produced the

fame

fame effect on any member of the Convention :—it feemed to me a ftriking inftance
of that eafe with which the natives of France
do certain things which would mightily difconcert fome of their neighbours.   I hardly
think, that, in any public affembly in England, after a committee had been appointed
to draw up an addrefs, any individual of
the affembly would offer to read a compofition of his own, as preferable to that of
four of the moft diftinguifhed members in
it.—This gentleman, however, afcended
the tribune, and read his performance
without embarraffment.   It had the fate
of moft productions which are read by
their authors, whether in public or private
affemblies ; it gave far more fatisfaction to
the reader than to the audience ; with this
difference, that here the audience did not
take the trouble of pretending to admire.

The air of indifference with which this
was heard did not difcourage another member from offering a third addrefs.——By the

ſtyle of this performance, and the ſolemn manner in which it was read, it was evident that the author wiſhed to be conſidered as a man of depth and learning : he pronounced ſome ſentences with a warmth, which he, no doubt, thought would prove victorious : the warmth with which they were delivered, however, was ſurpaſſed by the coldneſs of their reception. --Towards the concluſion, reſuming his addreſs to the volunteers, he ſaid, Enſin ſoldats *philoſofhes*.

This unexpected epithet raiſed a laugh that overpowered a yawn which had been gaining very faſt on the audience for ſome conſiderable time.

I fully expected that ſo many unfortunate attempts would have prevented any new ſpecimens from being offered, and conſequently, that the addreſs of the committee would have been adopted. I was miſtaken in both conjectures, for the Aſſembly had no ſooner recovered their gravity, than

2   *Faure*,

Faure, deputy from the department of Lower Seine, defired leave to read one of his compofition. He is a man of about fixty years of age, very plain in his drefs, and devoid of affectation in his manner.— His addrefs was in the following words :

Citoyens Soldats,

La loi vous permet de vous retirer: le cri de la patrie vous le defend. Les Romains ont-ils abandonné leurs armes quand Porfenna étoit encore aux portes de Rome? L'ennemi a-t-il paffé le Rhin? Longwi eft-il repris? Le fang François, dont il a arrofé la terre de la liberté, eft-il vengé? Ses ravages et fa barbarie font-ils punis? A-t-il reconnu la majefté de la République et la fouveraineté du Peuple? Soldats, voila le terme de vos travaux : c'eft en dire affez aux braves defenfeurs de la patrie. La Convention Nationale fe borne à vous recommander l'honneur François, l'interêt

de

ce ia République, et les foins de votre propre gloire *.

The laconic energy of fome expreffions in this addrefs, pleafed the Convention; it was adopted, ordered to be printed, and tranfmitted to the armies.

October 20.

This was a day of exultation in the Na-

* Citizen Soldiers,

The law allows you, but the voice of your country forbids you, to retire. Did the Romans quit their arms, when Porfenna was ftill at the gates of Rome? Has the enemy yet repaffed the Rhine? Is Longwy retaken? Has the blood of your countrymen, with which the enemy has bedewed this land of liberty, been avenged? Have his ravages and his barbarities been punifhed? Has he acknowledged the Majefty of the Republic, and the fovereignty of the People?

Soldiers, thefe are the end of your labours: nothing more need be faid to the brave defenders of their country. The National Convention has only to recommend to your care, the honour of the French Nation, the intereft of the Republic, and your own perfonal glory.

tional

tional Affembly.—Letters were read from
their commiffioners, giving an account of
the retaking of the town of Longwy, and
that the Germans were now entirely driven
out of France. Flattering accounts alfo
came from the army of Cuftine, and that of
the South : and a paper entitled, " Addreffe
de la Societé des Amis de la Liberté, et de
l'Egalité féante à Chamberri," was read.—
It begins with this expreffion—"Legiflateurs
du Monde * :"—and, in the middle of the
addrefs to the Affembly, the King of Sardinia is apoftrophized in the following
terms : " O Roi de Jérufalem et de Chypre
affez long-temps tes fatellites ont appefanti
fur nos têtes ton joug de fer !—il eft tombé,
nous l'avons foulé aux pieds, &c. &c †."

* Legiflators of the World.

† O King of Jerufalem and Cyprus, too long have
thy fatellites oppreffed our necks with thy yoke of iron
—it is fallen at laft, and we have fpurned it under our
feet !

N 3

It

It is much in the fame ftrain throughout; and what will appear more extraordinary, this piece of bombaft was ordered by the Affembly to be printed in French, Spanifh, and German, and tranfmitted to the departments and to the armies.

But a fcene took place in the Convention yefterday, after I left it, which forebodes more, mifery to the country than can be compenfated by the moft brilliant fuccefs. An addrefs was read by deputies from the 48 fections of Paris, againft the armed force which was fome time fince propofed, and the modification of which is now under the deliberation of a committee. By this addrefs the Convention is told, " That it would be putting the members on a footing with tyrants, to furround them with guards—Pretorian guards.——That Paris made the Revolution of the tenth of Auguft—and that Paris would maintain it." They alfo admonifhed the Convention, that there are

thofe

thofe prefent who contemplate their conduct, and weigh their decifions ; and finally,
that the fections of Paris confider the project of a guard to the Affembly as dangerous
and odious.

The anfwer of Guadet, the Prefident,
was fenfible and fpirited. He faid, that the
exercife of the fovereignty of the French
people, and all the rights of the Republic,
refided in the Convention, which knew
how to defend them, and which, though
always willing to receive counfel from
good citizens, would receive orders from the
nation only.

But, in afferting that the Convention
can defend the rights of the Republic, he
afferts more than is true :—that an addrefs,
in fuch infolent terms, fhould be allowed to
be read, is a proof not only that the Convention has *not* that power, but that the
authors of the addrefs know this, and are
determined to do all they can to prevent

N 4   its

its ever having it, and for that reason oppose the establishment of the guard in question. yet nothing can be more evident than that, until the Convention has the power of imposing silence on the galleries, of protecting the persons of the deputies, and of enforcing its decrees, there can be neither wisdom nor stability in their government.——For, were we to suppose that a few members of the Convention, of distinguished capacity, were supported by a majority in measures of wisdom and moderation; yet if they are liable to be insulted by a mob, those deputies who support them one day from conviction, will desert them another through fear, and produce that confusion, and those contradictory measures which have of late occurred, and which, if not remedied, will end in complete anarchy and ruin.

A sufficient body of guards, under the entire disposal of the Convention, would prevent this.——But it appears by this address

dress from all the sections, that those who oppose the establishing any guard for the Convention, have not only the direction of the General Council of the Commune, but also of all the sections of Paris. It is true that the majority of the other departments of France, and of course the majority of the deputies, are for this guard; but I sometimes converse with those who are able to form a much juster notion of what is likely to be the consequence than I can—who are of opinion, that Paris will carry the point against all the other departments; and that whatever the *opinion* of the deputies may continue to be, the majority of their *votes* will, in a short time, be against the armed force.

Indeed it is evident, that, although all the departments of France are, in theory, allowed to have an equal share in the government, yet, in fact, the single department of Paris has the whole power of the govern-

government; the other departments govern by reprefentation—Paris rules in perfon. The Majefty of Le Peuple Souverain refides in the capital, and by dint of infurrection, which is always in the power of certain leading perfons here, Paris gives the law to the Convention and to all France, and will continue to do fo till an armed force is eftablifhed, and placed entirely under the command of the National Convention.

October 21.

The city of Marfeilles, on hearing of the danger to which the Convention is expofed from the mob, and the people in the galleries, raifed a battalion, which was ordered to march to Paris for its protection. The intrepid and decifive behaviour of the Fédérés from that city, on the tenth of Auguft, have made a ftrong impreffion on the minds of the Parifians; and a body of feven or eight hundred men from Mar-

feilles

feilles are confidered as equivalent to a much greater number raifed elfewhere. As this battalion comes for the exprefs purpofe of protecting the Convention, its approach has given difquietude to that party who wifh the Affembly to be overawed by the people in the galleries: endeavours have been ufed, therefore, to create a prejudice againft the Marfeillois in the minds of the populace of Paris—and particularly in the patriotic Sans Culottes of St. Antoine and St. Marcelle.—It is circulated that they are brought to the capital for fome purpofe of ariftocracy. The name of Marfeillois is in fuch high eftimation, that this infinuation has hitherto had little effect.

The battalion is arrived, and this day fent a deputation to the Convention. A member of the deputation pronounced a fpeech full of energy at the bar.—"We fet out," faid he, "from the fhore of the Mediterranean, to offer our lives in defence of of our brethren of Paris, then threatened by the foldiers of defpotifm, but that danger is over, and the only enemies which remain for us to fight, are thofe who defire to erect a *tribunitial* or *dictatorial* power in France.——Legiflators, you are delegated by the eighty-three departments, we have as great an intereft in you, therefore, as the citizens of Paris——We know that certain men tell the Parifians that the Convention has a defign of eftablifhing pretorian guards around them for the purpofes of tyranny——one word is a fufficient refutation of that calumny.——*We* fhall belong to thofe guards.

Reprefentatives, the children of Marfeilles how to obey, as they know how to fight, they hate *dictators* as they hate kings, and you may count upon them for the maintenance of your laws, and of your authority."

Another perfon came afterwards to the bar of the Affembly and accufed Marat in the

the fevereft terms.—" That blood-thirfty man," faid he, " after having preached murder and carnage within the city of Paris, now difperfes his journals among the armies, to excite the foldiers to mutiny. The electors of Paris have difhonoured themfelves in choofing fuch a perfon, and you will partake of that difhonour; you will cover yourfelves with the blood which Marat has caufed to be fhed, if you do not expel him from among you, and punifh him for his crimes."

Some members endeavoured to interrupt the fpeaker, and the Prefident reminded him that he ought to fpeak with refpect of a reprefentative of the people.

" It is not Marat, the reprefentative of the people, I attack," refumed the fpeaker; " it is Marat the journalift, the incendiary, againft whom the French Republic, and human nature, calls for vengeance."

A member faid, that this petition againft Marat

Marat was not in due form; that before the accusation could be sent to the Committee of General Safety, they ought to collect all the proofs that were against him.—— " If you insist upon *all*, they must be brought in a waggon," said another.

The protectors of Marat, for it is evident that this man has protectors in the Convention, said every thing they could to persuade the Assembly to pass to the order of the day, without further notice of this petition, or accusation; but in spite of all their efforts it was ordered to be transmitted to the Committee of General Safety.

The address from the Sections of Paris against the armed force, is a manœuvre of Danton and his friends, and their having the influence to obtain it, gives a higher idea of their strength than has been hitherto entertained.

The deputation of the Marseillois is considered as a measure of Roland and the Girondists,

Girondifts, to give the Convention an idea of the protection it has to expect, till such time as a more regular armed force shall be decreed.

October 22.

A very short time after the 10th of Auguft, thofe who had been united againft the court divided, and became hoftile to each other. Roland had been chofen minifter for the home department. He has the appearance of a man of fincerity, and, whether he deferves it or not, he has the reputation of a man of probity, is fupported by a great number, who are confidered as the beft intentioned in the Affembly, and alfo by fome who are diftinguifhed for their talents; among the latter are, Vergniaud, Guadet, Buzot, Briffot, Rabaut de St. Etienne, Jean Baptifte Louvet, La Source, Kerfaint, Petion, Lanjuinais, and Barbaroux.

Roland was likewife intimately connected with Claviere, Servan, and Le Brun; the two firft had formerly been in the adminiftration

ftration with him, and Le Brun was placed as Minifter for Foreign Affairs, after the 10th of Auguft.

The confidence which the people, and the majority of the Affembly put in the integrity of Roland, and the fupport he had from fo many men of the beft abilities in the Affembly, excited the jealoufy of certain members, particularly of Danton, who could not bear to fee a man, whom he confidered as far inferior in underftanding to himfelf, in poffeffion of fo much credit.

It is imagined that Danton had formed a plan for preventing Roland from continuing in adminiftration, and which, if it had fully fucceeded, would alfo have excluded him from being of the Convention.

It is even believed by fome that he was elected a deputy to the Convention without his own application or knowledge; according to the Conftitution, no member of the National Affembly can hold the office of minifter, it it was imagined that Roland would refign the fituation of minifter, that he might be of the Convention; and it has fince appeared, that there were certain flaws in his election as a deputy, which, as is fuppofed, were known to thofe who had brought it about, and which would have rendered it void : and thus, had he refigned his office of minifter, as Danton did, he might afterwards have found himfelf precluded from the Conventional Affembly. But before this could be brought to trial, it was propofed in the Convention that Roland fhould be *invited* by the Affembly to remain in adminiftration. This propofal had not been forefeen by Danton; he oppofed it with all his might, and in this he was joined by all his friends. The good qualities of Roland having been enumerated by thofe who were for the invitation, that very circumftance, with the popularity of the man, were laid hold of, as grounds of jealoufy, and reafons againft his being invited.

vited. One deputy put them in mind, that a Greek, in the fenate of Athens, had declared that he would not give his vote for Ariftides, becaufe he was tired of hearing him called *the juft* : another deputy faid, that as often as he heard any member of the Affembly greatly applauded, he trembled for his liberty.

If thefe reafons were ufed as pretexts, and in the expectation that they would have the effect to prejudice the Affembly againft Roland, thofe who urged them muft have a poor opinion of the underftanding of their audience.——If, on the contrary, they really thought that a man's being confidered as a juft man, rendered him dangerous as a minifter, their audience had a right to think meanly of theirs.——I perceive an affectation in the Convention to adopt maxims and ufages from antiquity, which, however juft and applicable they might be at a former age, and in a different counfry, are by no

means

means suitable to France in the present circumstances. This disposition of misapplying
general maxims, very often renders the
weak the dupes of the worthless.

Notwithstanding the opposition, however,
the Convention was on the point of decreeing, that Roland should be invited to
remain in administration; which Danton
perceiving, he could no longer restrain his
ill humour, but peevishly said, " If you are
determined on this measure, I move that
the invitation be extended to Madame Roland, who is known to assist her husband
with her counsel *."

This illiberal sally was heard with disapprobation by the Assembly, and would have
had no effect in preventing the invitation
which had been proposed, had not Cambon
spoken against it : he observed, that to *invite*
a minister to continue in office, was in some

---

* Madame Roland has the reputation of being a most
accomplished and amiable woman.

degree

degree to weaken his refponfibility; and
Buzot declaring that this obfervation had fo
much weight with him as to make him
alter his opinion, the invitation was no
more infifted on.

The day following, Roland, in a letter to
the Convention, expreffed his concurrence
in fentiment with thofe who thought that
to invite a minifter to continue, would be
derogatory of the rigorous principles of republicanifm, and tended befides to render
him lefs refponfible than he ought to be:
that, however, the Convention having even
deliberated on fuch a meafure, he confidered
as highly honourable to him, and a motive
to engage him to retain his office of minifter, and to wave that of deputy: that the
danger which he plainly perceived would
attend him in the firft fituation, was another
inducement for his retaining it; but that
his chief motive, however fuch a declaration might be conftrued by his enemies,

8   was,

was, that he thought his continuing minifter would, in the prefent circumftances,
be advantageous for his country.

Perhaps nothing but confcious integrity
could induce a man of fenfe to hold fuch
language : but certainly nothing but a ftrong
conviction of its truth on the mind of the
Convention, and a fentiment of high efteem
for the perfon who ufed it, could prevent it
from being thought prefumptuous. Roland's
letter excited no fuch fenfation.——The inftant it was perceived that he had refolved to
continue in office, the greateft joy appeared
in the Affembly, and his letter was ordered
to be printed, and fent to all the departments.

Roland has continued minifter for the
home department ever fince. I have feen
him frequently in the place appointed for
the minifters, which is immediately within
the bar, and oppofite to the Prefident.
None of them ever come to the Affembly

O 3

unlefs

unlefs they have been fent for, or when they have fomething to ftate, on which they wifh to have the inftructions of the Convention—and they withdraw as foon as they have made their report, without taking any part in the debate.

On fuch occafions I have feen fome of them obliged to remain feveral hours before they were heard. For, if a debate is already begun when a minifter enters, he is generally allowed to fit unnoticed in his place till it be finifhed. Some of Roland's addreffes to the Convention are diftinguifhed for correctnefs and elegance. It is faid, that they owe the latter to his wife : this report is founded entirely on prefumption, Mrs. Roland being a woman of tafte and literature ; and it is circulated not fo much with a view to add to her reputation, as to detract from that of her hufband.

When he enters, there is generally a whifper

whisper of approbation in the Assembly,
and, while he is speaking, I have often
heard the deputies near me say, with fer-
vour—*Ah le digne homme ! le brave ministre!*
What proves that he and those connected
with him enjoy the confidence of the majority of the Convention, is, that the President and the secretaries have hitherto been
chosen from among his friends.

Roland was the popular minister, whose
dismission raised so great a clamour against
the Court. One of the pretexts for the
shameful irruption of the populace into the
King's palace, on the 20th of June, was to
present a petition for his recall : if Roland,
himself had any hand in promoting that
insurrection, he has little claim to the
epithet which was applied to Aristides.
Those who wish to succeed him and his
friends in their offices, represent them to
the people as in all points as dangerous to
liberty as ever the Court was : so that it

O 4   is

is not improbable but that Roland and his friends may fall the victims of the example given on the 20th of June, of over-awing the legiflative power, and attacking the executive, by a mob.

The duke of Rochefoucauld was at that time Prefident of the Department of Paris, and was zealous to bring the authors of that infurrection to punifhment—the zeal he fhewed upon that occafion was thought to be the remote caufe of his murder.

The affaffinations formerly mentioned, that were committed at Clermont, at Cambray, at Charleville, by the volunteers as they paffed through thefe places, feem to have proceeded from want of difcipline and from the caprice, prejudice, and cruelty, which are fo apt to gain upon vulgar and uninftructed men, affembled in great numbers, and under no controul. Great pains have been taken to fpread the opinion, that fome other murders which have been

committed

committed in the provinces, were entirely owing to a fudden, unpremeditated commotion of the people — particularly the horrid affaffination of the Duke of Rochefoucauld. It is generally believed, however, that the murder of this nobleman originated in more diftant caufes, and more concealed promoters. ,

M. de la Rochefoucauld was a man of humanity and candour. Unfeduced by the advantages enjoyed by thofe of his own rank, he felt with generous fympathy for the diftreffed fituation of others : he beheld with fatisfaction the overthrow of the old arbitrary fyftem of government, in the hopes of feeing one more agreeable to juftice erected in its ftead—A friend to monarchy as well as freedom, M. de la Rochefoucauld had in his contemplation a monarchy of milder afpect than his country had ever enjoyed—more limited in its nature, but with fufficient power in the

Prince

Prince to defend his prerogatives, and sufficient means in the people to resist tyranny ; more agreeable to humanity, more conducive to the general happiness, not only of the people, which is infinitely the most important object, but also of the Monarch himself, if he happens to be a man of sense.

The Duke of Rochefoucauld was President of the Department of Paris on the 20th of June 1792, and did all in his power in the first place to prevent, and afterwards to discover and bring to punishment, the instigators of the scandalous irruption of an armed multitude into the King's palace.

Having made frequent allusions to the transactions of that day, I shall here give a short account of them.

For several days before the 20th of June it was known all over Paris, that the inhabitants of the Fauxbourgs of St. Antoine and St. Marcelle

St. Marcelle intended to march in arms to the Tuileries, on pretence of prefenting a petition to the King—but in reality with the defign of intimidating and forcing him to fanction two decrees of the National Affembly, which he had hitherto refufed.

The council of the department of Paris, of which M. de Rochefoucald was Prefident, did every thing in their power to prevent an attempt of a nature fo unjuftifiable, fo contrary to the principles of the conftitution, and which might be attended with the moft fatal confequences.

This council made reprefentations to the Mayor of Paris, to the Procureur of the Commune, and to Santerre, who at that time was commander of the battalion of Les Enfans-trouvés.

But unfortunately thofe to whom the council of the department made thefe reprefentations, and whofe peculiar duty it was to prevent the intended proceffion, were

were the very people who had planned it, and were secretly promoting it with all their influence.

The inhabitants of the two suburbs began to affemble in arms, on the morning of the 20th of June, at the place where the Baftile formerly ftood. As accounts of this came from all quarters, to thefe fecret inftigators, fome of whom were magiftrates, they could not decently avoid making a fhew of oppofing it. When the multitude were at the height of enthufiafm, and ready to march, thofe magiftrates appeared in their municipal fcarfs, and gravely *admonifhed* the people to depart peaceably home, lay up their arms, and go to bed. "You have acted *your* part," faid one of the rabble; "move out of the way, and let us act ours." The proceffion began at nine in the morning; the battalion of St. Antoine marched firft: between it and that of St. Marcelle banners were carried, fufficiently expreffive of the defign of this ceremony.

mony, if it had been at all doubtful. On one was infcribed thefe words,

Tyrans, tremblez, ou foyez juftes,
Et refpectez la liberté du peuple *.

On another,

Louis, le peuple eft las de fouffrir †.

On a third,

Tremblez tyran, ta derniere heure eft venue ‡.

On a fourth,

Le rappel des miniftres, la fanction ou la mort §.

Other banners were carried, ornamented with vile allegorical figures, and fuitable infcriptions.

They marched to the hall of the National Affembly, and required permiffion to walk through it in proceffion. A member

---

* Tyrants, tremble, or be juft,
And refpect the liberty of the people.
† Lewis, the people are weary of fuffering.
‡ Tremble, tyrant, thy laft hour is come.
§ The recall of the minifters, the fanction, or death.

made

made a fpeech againft the granting of this requeft, giving for his reafon, that the petitioners were armed, and in great numbers; but, as this orator's eloquence, while it oppofed the mob's being let in, proved that they could not be kept out, the Affembly gracioufly granted the prayer of the petitioners, and, in confequence, was amufed for three hours with a proceffion of armed men, accompanied by women and children, marching through the hall. Among other ingenious emblems, a pair of old black breeches were carried on a pole, with this comfortable infcription, Libres—et fans-culottes *.

From the National Affembly the armed multitude went to the palace, where there was a confiderable number of troops on duty; but no orders having been given to refift, and many portions of the multitude who formed the proceffion being conducted

* Free—and without breeches.

by

by men dreſſed in municipal ſcarfs, the gardens and courts of the Tuileries were crowded in an inſtant. One body marched with more regularity than the reſt, dragging ſome pieces of cannon with them, and conducted by Santerre, and Legendre the butcher.——The multitude ſoon after ruſhed into every apartment, calling aloud, that they muſt ſee the King ; they had a petition to preſent. M. Acloque, commandant of the ſecond legion of national guards, having placed ſome grenadiers at the door of the apartments neareſt to the King's, told two municipal officers that if they would prevent the mob from proceeding, he would inform the King of their requeſt, and that he was perſuaded his Majeſty would receive twenty of their number, according to the law——He then went to the door of the King's apartment, which he found ſhut—— he knocked, and begged that he might be inſtantly admitted, ſaying, that he came to ſave the King's life——The door of the chamber

ber was opened; he found the King, with
the Queen, the Prince, the Princeſs Royal,
Madam Elizabeth the King's ſiſter, and
the following gentlemen: the Marechal
de Mouchy, Beaulieu, Miniſter of the Fi-
nances, Lajard, Miniſter of War, Terrier de
Monciel, Miniſter of the Home Department,
the Count d'Hervilly, Marechal de Camp
and Commander of the Horſe Guards.

M. Acloque, perceiving that they had their
ſwords drawn, and ſeemed determined to
ſacrifice their lives in defence of the royal
family, entreated them to ſheath their
ſwords, otherwiſe they would increaſe the
danger in which the King was—In a ſhort
time a great noiſe was heard at the door,
the rabble were breaking it open, with
pikes, axes, and the butt end of muſquets.
The King himſelf ordered the doors to be
thrown open:—before this was done, the
ends of ſome of the muſquets and pikes
had been driven through the door—twenty
or thirty of the mob burſt into the room.
M. Acloque

M. Acloque accosted them with a firm voice: " Citizens, respect your King—the law commands it ; and we will all perish rather than suffer his being insulted."—One of the company at the same instant calling out, Vive la nation ! Vive le Roi ! the intruders stopped short.

It was then proposed to the King, that he should stand on a seat in the room commonly called L'Œil de Beuf, to prevent his being pressed upon, and that he might be seen by the people, who were entering in great numbers ; to which he consented.—— The Queen, at the King's desire, with the royal children, went into the adjacent room ; but Madame Elizabeth kept constantly by his side, rejecting every entreaty that was made by the King himself and others to quit him for an instant.

On the sixth of October 1789, when the mob marched from Paris to Versailles and broke into the palace, the Princess Eli-

P zabeth

zabeth attached herfelf to the perfon of the Queen, whofe life fhe knew was at that time more threatened by thofe ruffians than that of her brother; and on the prefent occafion, as he was in greater danger, fhe adhered to him.

Four grenadiers of the national guards appearing at the door, the Princefs, who had betrayed no fymptom of fear on her own account, burft into tears at fight of them, and faid, " *Ah! Meffieurs, defendez le Roi.*"

Thofe four grenadiers, an officer of chaffeurs, a cannonier, with the gentlemen above mentioned, placed themfelves around the King and the Princefs Elizabeth, and with admirable conftancy kept off the preffure of the crowd, and protected the perfon of the King for above three hours; the Marechal de Mouchy, in fpite of his great age, remaining the wholeti me. All the adjacent rooms, mean-while, fwarmed with

with a mixed rabble of men and women, armed with pikes, fabres, fticks with knives fixed at their ends, fufils and piftols; many of them calling, " En bas le veto, au diable le veto!" and fome of them fhewing fo much fury, that thofe around the King's perfon had difficulty in keeping them off.

One fellow, mounted on a chair, fpoke to the King in the moft audacious manner, requiring the recal of the patriot minifters, meaning Roland, Claviere, and Servan, whom the King had a little before difmiffed; he alfo required that the two decrees fhould obtain his approbation.——To which his Majefty anfwered with firmnefs, " Je ferai ce que je croirai devoir faire; mais ce n'eft pas ni le lieu, ni le moment, de me faire une pareille demande *."

A red cap was reached to the King at

---

* I will do what I ought; but this is neither the place nor the time to make a requeft of that nature.

the

the end of a pike, by a man who cried, Vive la nation !—The King faid, " La nation n'a de meillieur ami que moi *." On which the other infolently added, " Eh bien, donnez nous en la preuve en mettant le bonnet rouge, et en criant "Vive la nation !†"

On attempting to put on the red cap, it was found too fmall for the King's head; but a grenadier having ftretched it upon his knee, the King put it on, and wore it as long as the mob remained.

At one time, when the noife and confufion was greater than ufual, a grenadier, addreffing the King, faid, " Sire, n'ayez pas peur." On which he anfwered, " I am not in the leaft afraid, friend." So faying, he preffed the foldier's hand to his breaft, that he might feel that his heart beat calmly.

* The nation has no better friend than I am.
† Prove it then, by putting on the red cap, and by crying " Vive la nation !"

5   Among

Among those armed with various weapons, one ruffian brandished a pike with the heart of a calf stuck on the point, from which hung a label, with this inscription, " Cœur des aristocrates *."

To the noisy requisitions that were made from all corners of " Otez le veto! rappellez le ministres!" the King answered, that he would do what was just.——Legendre the butcher, thinking this expression rather equivocal, took this opportunity of giving the monarch a specimen of his eloquence.—— " *Monsieur*," said Legendre—the King seeming a little surprised at this new style and manner, for this man's manner is as extraordinary as his style——" *Monsieur*," repeated Legendre, " ecoutez nous ; oui *Monsieur*, vous êtes fait pour nous ecouter, vous etes un perfide, vous nous avez toujours trompés, vous nous trompez encore ; mais prenez

* The heart of aristocrates.

garde

garde à vous Monfieur, la mefure eft a fon comble, et le peuple eft las de fe voir votre jouet *."

In a company lately, where the converfation turned on the conduct of Legendre, every body prefent blamed it, except one young Frenchman, who, although of high birth, diftinguifhes himfelf by violent democratic principles : he urged, by way of defending Legendre, that he did not fpeak in his own name, but in that of the nation ; that he reprefented *the majefty of the peuple fouverain.* The company fmiled ; fome of them were deputies, who, however expedient it might be to ufe this language in the tribune, did not expect to hear it in private fociety.——I ventured to repeat a

* Sir, liften to us——yes, Sir, it is your duty to attend to us ; you have always deceived us, you deceive us ftill ; but take care what you are about, Sir, the meafure of our patience is full, and the people are tired of being your dupes.

ftory

ſtory I had heard, of an Engliſh gentleman
celebrated for wit, that, walking in the ſtreets
of London with a democratic acquaintance
of his, who frequently uſed the expreſſion
the majeſty of the people, they met a couple
of chimney-ſweeps; the gentleman took off
his hat, and made them a very formal and
low bow as they paſſed. His acquaintance
aſked what he meant——I was only ſhewing
the reſpect, replied the other, which is due
from every loyal ſubject to two princes of
the blood.

This gentleman, it is probable, judged of
their affinity merely from their external
reſemblance to the Sovereign; but Legendre
could boaſt of an affinity in more eſſential
points, an unyielding firmneſs of heart, a
deciſive promptitude of execution, a diſpoſition which, ſo far from being depreſſed,
finds matter of mirth and pleaſantry in
ſcenes of horror, when they are thought

neceſſary

neceſſary to promote the great cauſe : theſe are features of energy which have diſtinguiſhed the Peuple Souverain ſince the beginning of the Revolution, and in which Legendre bears a ſtriking likeneſs to the monarch he was ſaid to repreſent.

A deputation conſiſting of twelve members of the National Aſſembly, among whom were Iſnard and Vergniaud, at length arrived—Iſnard addreſſing himſelf to the people who filled the room, endeavoured to prevail on them to withdraw, repeating frequently, that he would be anſwerable on his life that they ſhould be ſatisfied.——This had little effect, the noiſe and exclamations of " Rappellez les miniſtres! ôtez le veto!" * recommenced.

Vergniaud alſo ſpoke to the ſame purpoſe, and with as little ſucceſs.

* Recal the miniſters, remove the veto.

The

The noife and confufion continued till paft five in the evening, when Petion arrived, accompanied by Sergent, a municipal officer. Petion approaching the King, faid, " Sire, I was only this moment informed of the fituation in which you are."

That is extraordinary, replied the King, for I have been in this fituation above three hours.

Petion then ftanding on a chair advifed the people to retire, ending his harangue with the following very curious expreffions, which one who was prefent wrote a little after and allowed me to copy : " Citoyens, vous venez de faire entendre vos vœux au reprefentant héréditaire, avec l'énergie et la dignité d'un peuple libre qui connoît fes droits. Le Roi fait maintenant les intentions du *Souverain*, et fans doute il y aura égard. Il convient que vous vous retirez

avec

avec calme et décence, afin qu'on ne puiſſe pas calomnier vos intentions*."

After this, the people at the Mayor's repeated requeſt began to withdraw :—when a ſecond deputation from the National Aſſembly arrived, one of the members of which addreſſed the King in a reſpectful manner, aſſuring him that each member was ready to preſent his body as a ſhield to cover his Majeſty's.

It could not eſcape the King, however, that he might have been cut in pieces three hours before the ſhields arrived.

While theſe things were paſſing in the

---

* Citizens, you have now made your deſires known to the hereditary repreſentative, with that energy and dignity which becomes a free people who underſtand their rights. The King at preſent knows the intentions of the ſovereign, and undoubtedly will pay a proper regard to them. You ought now to withdraw with calmneſs and decency, that your intentions may not be calumniated.

OEil

Œil de Beuf, the Queen entered the council-chamber, attended by the Prince and Princess Royal, by Madame de Lamballe, Mme. Tourzelle, Mme. de Mau, Mme. de Soucy. Her Majesty shewed much uneasiness on account of the situation in which she had left the King, till the Adjutant General of the first legion of Parisian guards, with some soldiers, came and assured her that the King was in safety, and surrounded by faithful servants.

M. de Wittengoff, a general officer, entered the room followed by a number of people of both sexes, among whom was a woman with a red cap in her hand. She presented the cap to Wittengoff, desiring him to give it to the Queen to wear, adding, that she had just left the King, who at that moment had the cap of Liberty on his head.

It would appear that the General did not think it expedient to reject the woman's proposal; which the Queen perceiving, and

2   being

being fhocked at the idea of wearing the cap, faid to Wittengoff, " Vous voyez Monfieur, que ce bonnet ne peut aller fur ma tête :" fhe then put it on the head of the Prince. This fatisfied the woman and her followers.

Santerre entered the council-chamber foon after, followed by a new crowd, who having already feen the King, now demanded a fight of the Queen, which Santerre had undertaken to procure them.—He immediately required that thofe who ftood immediately before her Majefty fhould open to the right and left, that the people who followed him might have a full view of her and the reft of the royal family ; which was done, Santerre *gracioufly* affuring the Queen that fhe had nothing to apprehend from the people, who were *wonderfully good,* and only wifhed to be gratified with a fight of her as they walked out ; and perceiving

that

that the Prince was heated with the cap, he added, " Otez le bonnet à cet enfant *."

Santerre's aſſurances, however, did not prevent ſome of the people, who were not quite ſo good as the reſt, from inſulting the Queen, as they paſſed, with very abominable language.

The crowd having moſtly retired, and the King having left the Œil de Beuf to go to what are called the petits apartemens, the Princeſs Elizabeth was going to wait on the Queen in the council-chamber, when a group of the mob which ſtill lingered in the palace, miſtaking her for the Queen, began to inſult her ; on which one of the Princeſs's attendants was going to undeceive them, but ſhe with nobleneſs of mind prevented this, left the people who were inſulting her, being informed of their miſtake, ſhould have tranſferred their abuſe to the unhappy Queen.

* Take the cap from that child's head.

It

It appeared from the witneſſes examined on this buſineſs, that great pains had been taken with the inhabitants of St. Antoine, for a conſiderable time previous to the 20th of June, to work them up to this criminal meaſure : for it merits that epithet in a high degree, even although what is by no means clear were entirely admitted, namely that no more was intended than to prevail on the King to recall the former miniſters, and to remove the negative he had given to the two decrees ; becauſe, to prevail on the King by ſuch means was open rebellion againſt the government, and ruinous to the Conſtitution, and might have been attended with the immediate maſſacre of the royal family, and other dreadful conſequences, all of which the promoters of this proceſſion were anſwerable for.

The active and apparent promoters of it (for others are ſtrongly ſuſpected who were not ſworn againſt by the witneſſes) were,

Santerre,

Santerre, at that time commander of the battalion of Enfans trouvés, Legendre, Fournier an American, Rotondo an Italian, Buirette a glafs-maker, Rofignol a goldfmith, Gonor who was called the conqueror of the Baftille, Brierre a wine-merchant, and St. Huruge, who rendered himfelf more notorious afterwards in the month of September, and Nicolas, fapeur or miner to the battalion which Santerre commanded. Thefe men had frequent nightly meetings at the houfe of Santerre, where they drew up the motions that were to be made in the groups at the Tuileries, the Palais-royal, the Place de Gréve, and to the multitude which affembled in the Place de la Baftille. They fometimes met alfo in the chamber of the committee of the fection of Enfans trouvés, to compofe placarts to be pofted on the walls; and at thofe meetings Chabot had frequently made harangues, the tendency of which was to encourage the audience to promote

promote the intended proceffion, which he
affured them the National Affembly expected, and would receive with fatisfaction.

From the evidence it alfo appeared,
" that after coming from the National Affembly, the people fhewed no difpofition to force
their way into the palace, till Santerre, accompanied by Saint Huruge, came among
them, and afked why they did not enter the
palace, as it was for that purpofe alone that
they had affembled ; and that it was in confequence of directions from Panis, and another municipal officer, that the gates of
the Tuileries had been broken open."

In confequence of the proof of thefe facts,
the Council of the department of Paris decreed, that the Mayor of Paris, and the Procureur of the Commune, who had been frequently advertifed by the Council of the intended proceffion, had not done what their
duty required to prevent, but had rather
countenanced it, and therefore fhould be fuf-
pended

pended from the exercise of their offices ;
but this decree requiring the sanction of
the King, his Majesty wished to give
no opinion nor decision on the subject,
as he was personally concerned in it. He
therefore referred the whole matter to the
National Assembly ; but his enemies there
being resolved to drive him to the disagreeable alternative of either disapproving of the
decree of the Council, or incurring the
odium of being the immediate cause of sus-
pending the popular Mayor, had sufficient
influence to get the Assembly to refuse giving any opinion on the subject, until the
King should confirm or annul the sentence
of the Council. His Majesty therefore
confirmed the decree ; which he had no
sooner done, than the National Assembly
took the whole matter into their consideration, and reinstated the Mayor and Procureur in their offices.

From this time it was clear that the con-

Q stitution

ftitution was at an end, that a plan was formed for the deftruction of royalty, and that the beft meafure the King could adopt was to attempt at any rifk to remove himfelf and his family out of the reach of the mob of Paris. To this he was often preffed by his friends, who thought, that if he were even removed as far as Fontainebleau, there was fuch indignation in the minds of the moft refpectable citizens all over France at the fcandalous tranfactions on the 20th of June, that they would have united againft the anarchifts of Paris, and given fuch force to the executive power, as, without injuring freedom, would have fuppreffed them, and prevented the dreadful diforders which have fince taken place. But his Majefty, probably deterred by the ill fuccefs of his flight to Varennes, could not be prevailed on to make a fecond attempt of the fame nature.

Difgufted with a feries of crimes which he could neither prevent nor punifh, and

finding

finding that his presence in Paris was neither of use to his country nor to the King, the Duke of Rochefoucauld withdrew from the capital to his villa in Normandy, from whence, on account of his health, he soon after went to the medicinal waters of Forges, where he was during the dreadful period of the massacres in September, and where a commissioner from the general council of the Commune of Paris arrived with an order to arrest and conduct him to the capital. This commissioner was a man, of more humanity than those usually employed by the council on similar occasions; he readily agreed to the proposal of accompanying the Duke in the first place to his own house at Roche-Guyon, with a view that the agitation which existed at Paris might have time to subside before he should arrive, and in the hopes that the Duke's friends might be able to have the order recalled.—In company with Mr. de la Roche-

Q 2

foucauld,

foucauld was the Ducheſſe D'Anville his mother, and the Duchefs his wife. On the road between Forges and Roche-Guyon, they ſtopped at Gifors: during this period, moſt unfortunately a battalion of National Guards arrived, among whom ſome of the Paris aſſaſſins, as is ſuſpected, were mixed.

Theſe villains immediately ſhewed a diſpoſition to murder the Duke, who, being more ſolicitous for the ſafety of his mother and his wife than for his own, and fearing that they might be injured or inſulted if he remained with them, he perſuaded them to go on. The Duke himſelf afterwards walked to his carriage under the protection of the Mayor of Gifors, the Commiſſioner, and ſome of the national guards; but he was, notwithſtanding, followed by the aſſaſſins loading him all the way with abuſive language, till one of them having found means of coming very near the Duke, threw a ſtone with ſuch force that, ſtriking him on

the

the temple, it killed him on the fpot, and fome of the wretches immediately, on feeing him fall, cried, " Vive la Nation !"

The French nation is difgraced by fuch an exclamation on fuch an occafion ; and, were I not convinced that the majority deteft the actions and ficken at the exclamations of fuch wretches, I fhould join in fentiment with thofe who wifh it wafhed from the furface of the globe.

October 24.

In a converfation which I had this day with a member of the Convention, I delivered my fentiments pretty freely upon the fubject of the murder of Mr. de la Rochefoucauld, and fome fimilar events which have taken place of late in France : he expreffed the utmoft horror at them, but added that fcenes of the fame kind had been acted in every country of Europe in times of revolution and diffention, when great interefts

Q 3   were

were at ftake, and when the human paffions were inflamed and agitated in the higheft degree. He mentioned certain barbarous cruelties which had been committed, on both fides, during the conteft between the white rofe and the red in England : he enlarged on the maffacre in Ireland in the reign of Charles the Firft, and on the perfidious affair of Glenco in Scotland in the reign of King William. He added that, every thing confidered, perhaps it belonged lefs to one of my nation than of any other, to complain of the exceffes of revolutions or civil diffenfions ; and with a fmile he quoted from Juvenal :

Quis tulerit Gracchos de feditione querentes ?

I did not choofe to pufh the argument farther, although, with refpect to the reciprocal cruelties which were committed during the conteft between the white rofe and the red, the remark was obvious, that what a nation

a nation had done during an age of barba-
rifm and fuperftition, is not to be compared
with that of another in the days of knowledge and refinement—and perhaps it would
not be difficult to fhew that the barbarities
he enumerated which had been committed
in Great Britain and Ireland, were equalled
by thofe committed in France at the fame
periods ; in which cafe, there has been fuch
an accumulation here of late, that, on comparing accounts, a moft dreadful balance
of horrors would remain with this country.

I find fome people believe, or pretend to
believe, that the murder of the Duke of
Rochfoucauld was the accidental effect of the
fudden frenzy of a few volunteers ; but many
circumftances do not admit of that opinion.
The magiftrates of Gifors, although they
wifhed to protect the Duke, did not feize and
punifh his affaffins, which looks as if they fufpected that the affaffins acted under the direction of fome men whofe enmity the magi-

Q 4   ftrates

strates were afraid of incurring: and when we recollect that the Duke's conduct, immediately before and after the 20th of June, was highly offensive to those who spirited up the shameful insurrection of that day; when we recollect the characters of some of them who were afterwards members of the new formed council of the Commune de Paris, and the orders for arrest which they issued previous to the 2d of September; it will seem much more probable that the death of the Duke of Rochefoucauld proceeded from instructions from some of *them*, than from a sudden impulse of the actual murderers.

If any thing could render this crime more atrocious, it would be, that a man who lies under the highest obligations to the Duke, was the planner of his assassination. This idea has been propagated notwithstanding its enormity, and perhaps is circulated the more on that very account; for the minds of some people are peculiarly attached

tached to the wonderful, and they are fo
fond of repeating what creates the greateft
emotion, of whatever nature that emotion is,
that the very circumftance which renders a
ftory lefs credible, is an inducement for one
fet of people to repeat it, and another to believe it. Much ftronger prefumptive proof
than any I have heard, is neceffary to induce me to think any man capable of fuch
aggravated wickednefs, particularly if the
purfuits of his life have been of a nature to
humanize the heart as well as to enlighten
the underftanding, and if the fact can be
fully accounted for, without fuppofing him
to have had any direct or indirect hand
in it.

October 26.

The party which is formed againft Roland and the Girondifts * manifeft already

as

* Vergniaud, Genfonné, Guadet, and fome others
diftinguifhed for their talents, are deputies from the department

as much enmity to them as the same party did to the court for turning Roland out of office. What renders them very formidable is the influence their leaders have in the Jacobin society, which begins to murmur against Roland and all his friends. To Briffot they shew such peculiar diflike, that he was lately expelled from the society : he

partment of Gironde, and fupport Roland ; many others have joined them, and the whole are called Girondifts or Rolandifts ; and Marat, who has a determined hatred to Briffot, fometimes calls them in his journal Briffotins, and the whole clafs Roland Briffotins. Although Condorcet is of more eminence in the literary world than any I have enumerated as the friends of Roland, I have not mentioned him, becaufe his conduct of late is thought equivocal ; it is not quite clear whether he means to attach himfelf to Roland or Danton.

Barrere, deputy from the department of the High Pyrenées, who was a member of the conftituent affembly without being much diftinguifhed, begins to be thought of more importance in the Convention : he has not hitherto taken a decided part with either party, but, I am told, he is courted by both.

1   probably

probably obtained this diftinction on account
of fome paragraphs which have lately appeared in the daily paper fuppofed to be
conducted by him. Marat is there treated
with a contempt which may be due to his
talents, but which it is not prudent to fhew
for a man who is ftill a favourite of the
rabble, and has fome of the moft defperate
of them under his direction. In the fame
paper Danton is glanced at with feverity,
and Robefpierre is turned into ridicule, in a
manner that would not be readily forgiven
by a man of a lefs implacable difpofition.

Briffot is a little man, of an intelligent
countenance, but of a weakly frame of
body.

While many of the Deputies, even thofe
who are no way obnoxious to the violent
party, carry pocket-piftols, or canes which
contain fwords ; Briffot walks through the
ftreets, at all hours, without fo much as a
fwitch in his hand.

An

An acquaintance of his told me that he had
spoken of this to him as a piece of great imprudence, confidering the number of his enemies, many of whom he thought capable of
affaffination. To this remonftrance Briffot anfwered with a carelefs air, " S'ils font décidés
à m'affaffiner, ils en trouveroient aifément le
moyen de quelque manierre que je fuffe
armé : d'ailleurs je fuis d'une conftitution fi
foible, que ne pouvant faire qu'une trifte dé-
fenfe, je preférerois l'honneur de n'en point
faire du tout."

But timidity is not to be placed among
this man's failings, nor prudence among his
virtues.

If Briffot is too little affected by the rancour of his enemies, Roland fhews too much

---

* If they are determined to affaffinate me, they will
find the means whatever arms I may carry ; befides, I
am of fo feeble a conftitution, that, confcious of being
unable to make a good refiftance, I think it more honourable to make none.

fenfibility

fenfibility to the attacks which are made on him, and this is one reafon perhaps for their being continued with fuch fpirit and perfeverance. Infinuations tending to render him unpopular, not only appear in certain daily journals, but accufations againft him are fometimes pafted on the walls. He alludes to thefe rather too often in his addreffes to the Convention, which are fometimes thought laboured and pompous. While one of this kind was reading in the affembly, I heard one of the deputies fay peevifhly, " Cet homme pretend nous gouverner par des phrafes*." Another, fhrugging up his fhoulders, faid, " Il ne cherche qu'à faire admirer la beauté de fon ftile †." To which the member who fat next him replied,

---

* This man thinks to govern us by fine fentences.

† His only object is to make us admire the beauty of his ftyle.

6

" Auffi

" Auffi y réuffit il quelquefois avec l'aide de
" fa femme*."

The tendency of thefe addreffes and letters generally is, after exculpating himfelf
from the charges above mentioned, to prove
the neceffity of order and fubmiffion to
law.

But if a Minifter takes the trouble of an-
fwering, in the National Affembly, all ano-
nymous accufations made againft him, neither he nor the Affembly will be able to do
any other bufinefs; and if he has no other
means of producing order and fubmiffion
to law than by fpeeches and addreffes, there
is no probability of their being produced
foon.

Some of thefe compofitions however are
very good in themfelves.

Sed nunc non erat his locus.

* In which he fometimes fucceeds, with the affiftance
of his wife.

—Can

—Can it be thought that the men who stormed the King's palace, or those who instigated to the massacres, will be moved from their designs by eloquence or argument?

At the head of the party in opposition to Roland are Danton and Robespierre; after them are Couthon, Bazire, Thuriot, Merlin de Thionville, St. André, Camille Desmoulins, Chabot, Collot d'Herbois, Sergent, Legendre, Fabre d'Eglantine, Panis, Marat.

Robespierre is a man of small size, and a disagreeable countenance, which announces more fire than understanding; in his calmest moments, he conceals with difficulty the hatred and malignity which is said to exist in his heart, and which his features are admirably formed to express. He distinguished himself in the Constituent Assembly by the violence of his speeches, and much more since, in the Jacobin society, by the violence of his measures. His eloquence is employed in invectives against tyrants and aristocrates, and in declamations in praise of Liberty.

Liberty. His speeches are barren in argument, but sometimes fertile in the flowers of fancy.

Robespierre is considered as an enthusiast rather than a hypocrite : some people think him both, which is not without example ; but, to me, he seems to be too much of the first to be a great deal of the second.

He has always refused every office of emolument : his passion is popularity, not avarice ; and he is allowed, even by those who detest many parts of his character, and are his enemies, to be incorruptible by money.

Roland is not supposed to possess all the energy of character that belongs to Danton ; in many other respects they differ. Roland is believed to be a thorough republican : Danton, it is thought, does not lay much stress on the form of government, and would have no objection to monarchy, provided the monarch were a creature of his own ; for I do not find that it is suspected that he aspires to reign in person.

Roland

Roland and Danton were often in opposition with each other when joined in the
fame adminiftration. Roland ftruggled with
all his might againft the ufurpations of
the General Council of the Commune of Paris after the 10th of Auguft: Danton favoured and abetted them. Roland exclaimed againft the maffacres in September,
did every thing he could to put an end to
them, and on that account was himfelf in
imminent danger. Danton, though he was
then minifter of juftice, is accufed of having
been criminally paffive on that very preffing
occafion. Roland ufes his whole influence
to bring the authors of thofe favage fcenes
to juftice: Danton ufes his to ftifle all in-
veftigation of that nature.

In external appearance and manner, thofe
two men differ as in all the reft: Roland is
about fixty years of age, tall, thin, of a mild
countenance and pale complexion. His
drefs, every time I have feen him, has been

the fame, a drab-coloured fuit lined with green filk, his grey hair hanging loofe.

Danton is not fo tall, but much broader than Roland; his form is coarfe, and un-commonly robuft: Roland's manner is un-affuming and modeft——that of Danton fierce and boifterous; he fpeaks with the voice of a Stentor, declaims on the bleffings of free-dom with the arrogance of a tyrant, and invites to union and friendfhip with the frown of an enemy.

He muft be fenfible of the infinite im-portance of internal union, of ftrengthening the executive power, and overawing the factious at the prefent crifis. Thefe might poffibly avert fome of the evils that threaten his country, and tend to the happinefs of twenty-four millions of human creatures. But what muft then become of Danton? he would dwindle in point of importance, and fhare only the proportion of an individual in the general profperity.

In

In the comprehenfive vortex of this extraordinary Revolution, this man, originally placed in the lower ranks of life, has been whirled fo near the fummit as to have the chief direction of government within his hope —He thinks himfelf, no doubt, better qualified for that office than thofe who, according to the prefent fyftem, are likely to retain it; and if his hopes fhould be accomplifhed, he perhaps has it in fpeculation to promote the aggrandifement of his country, and would exert himfelf for that purpofe as long as it went hand in hand with his own. But if the gratification of his own ambition is to be had at no other price than the facrifice of his country's good, he will not refufe the purchafe. This, no doubt, will be thought very profligate; yet in this, perhaps, Danton differs lefs from other ftatefmen than in fome other features of his character.

A perfon who is thought to be well ac-

R 2   quainted

quainted with the characters of the leading
deputies of both parties, and capable of
forming a juſt judgment of their views,
lately hinted to me that there was a probability that Danton and his friends would
overſet their opponents.

" I thought that Roland had the majority
of the members of the Convention with
him ?" ſaid I.

" The majority of the members, if left to
follow the dictates of their conſciences,"
reſumed he, " are certainly inclined to ſupport Roland; but Danton may fall on means
which have been found efficacious in removing ſcruples of conſcience."

" I had no idea of his being ſo very rich.
Where will he find the money ?" ſaid I.

" Money, it muſt be confeſſed, is the
readieſt and moſt effectual," replied he,
ſmiling, " but not the only means—
Danton makes uſe of it the leaſt, he has it
not always at his command; for what he
does

does ufe on preffing occafions belongs to another."

" What other means has he ?"

" Why, eloquence," rejoined he. " Do you count that for nothing in your National Affembly ? I can affure you it has confiderable weight in ours, and Danton may pour it forth with profufion, having at command not only his own noify torrents, but alfo the popular ftream which flows from the lips of Robefpierre."

" Will not the effect of their eloquence," I refumed, " be greatly overbalanced by that of Vergniaud, Buzot, and other friends of Roland ?"

" Perhaps it may," faid he; " but the ally on whom Danton has the greateft reliance has not been yet mentioned,

" Who is he ?"

" Terror ! Terror !" repeated he, " who has acted fo important a part fince the beginning of this Revolution. Do you not

R 3

think

think that his gigantic form ſtalks ſometimes before the eyes of the Deputies? Do you imagine that their ſleep is never diſturbed with the viſions of heads carried on pikes, of murdered priſoners, and the mangled bodies of thoſe victims of cowardly revenge, Briſſac, Montmorin, Deleſſart, and Rochefoucald?"

" I ſhould imagine," ſaid I, " that ſuch viſions would rather diſturb the conſciences of Danton and ſome of his friends."

" They have none," rejoined he; " and Danton ſeems to have nearly as little fear as conſcience."

He then told me, that he was convinced that Danton's plan was to terrify a majority of the Deputies into his meaſures, by means of the rabble of the ſuburbs, which he expects to have at his diſpoſal, through Chabot, Marat, and other emiſſaries and tried conductors; in which view the ſections of Paris were prevailed on to preſent the addreſs

8

already

already mentioned, to the Affembly, which
it is believed was drawn up by Danton
himfelf.

His emiffaries, I have been fince told,
are very active in circulating every report
that they conceive can render Roland and
his friends, particularly the Girondifts, odious
in the eyes of the people. As many of
this party are republicans, and were abufed
by their enemies on that account when fuch
fentiments were not fo popular as they are
at prefent, it was not to be imagined that
they would now be accufed of being royalifts; but as this is the heavieft charge that
can be brought againft any fet of men,
the fame perfons who formerly accufed
them of being republicans, without any regard to confiftency, and trufting to the abfurd credulity of the multitude, now accufe
them of being royalifts—and not entirely
without effect.

The friends of Roland brought to Paris

the

the battalion of Marſeillois, which arrived lately, and unqueſtionably with no other view than to ſerve as a check to the ſans-culottes of the ſuburbs, who are at the command of Danton: their addreſs, which was read in the Convention, is thought to be the compoſition of Barbaroux.

Monſieur Egalité is at preſent ſeldom heard of: he appears however almoſt every day in the Aſſembly; he generally ſtays about half an hour, ſeems to intereſt himſelf little in what is going on, and to intereſt the Aſſembly as little. It has been ſaid that a weak or wrong-headed man of very high rank, or in an eminent ſituation in life, is like a man on the top of a ſteeple, from whence all the world ſeem *little* to him, and where he ſeems *little* in the eyes of all the world——Whether M. Egalité, when in his original elevated ſituation, regarded mankind, or was regarded by them in this light, I will not ſay; but he certainly has been

been at great pains and expence to bring himself low enough to be feen and eftimated at his juft value by all the world.

October 27.

According to a late decree all emigrants who are taken in arms are to be tried by a court-martial, and executed where they are taken. Notwithftanding this decree, thirteen were lately conducted to Paris. They were the fame whom Ruhl had paffed on the road as was mentioned above. When they came near Paris, new fears were ex-preffed in the Convention, of their danger of being maffacred in the ftreets.

If there is really any danger of fuch an event, the inhabitants of Paris muft be the worft of favages ; but the only people I fee of a favage difpofition, are certain members of the Convention, and of the Jacobin Club, and a great majority of thofe who fill the tribunes of both thofe affemblies ; but the fhop-keepers and trades-people (and I take

fome

some pains to be acquainted with their way of thinking) seem to be much the same as I have always known them; and I am persuaded that there is no risk of massacres or assassinations, but from a set of wretches who are neither shop-keepers nor tradesmen, but idle vagabonds, hired and excited for the purpose.——When I hear it asserted from the tribune of the Convention, or of the Jacobin Society, that the people are impatient for the death of the King, or inclined to murder unfortunate men while they are conducted to prison, and yet can perceive no disposition of that nature among the citizens, I cannot help suspecting that those orators themselves are the people who are impatient for those atrocities, and that they spread the notion that this desire is general among the people, on purpose to render it easier to commit them, and to make them more quietly submitted to, after they have been committed.

I remember,

I remember, that for several days before the 2d of September, frequent mention was made of the unaccountable delays of the courts of justice with regard to the trial of the prisoners—Certain members of the National Assembly threw out hints of the people's impatience on that account; and I heard a man at the Jacobins threaten, that if the sword of justice was withheld much longer, the people would exercise it themselves; and yet, at that time, I could perceive no signs of such a disposition among the citizens of Paris.

The dreadful scenes in September began—the citizens were struck with terror—they repeated to each other, " We often heard that the people would be driven to this !" Each of them believed that all the city had risen against the prisoners, except the quarter which he himself inhabited, and from which his anxiety for his family made him afraid to move—They were told that all who spoke

in

in favour of the prisoners were massacred by the people, and that many suspected persons were taken up in the streets. By these means the citizens of Paris remained panic-struck, while a handful of villains, in their name, committed the most shocking enormities.

Reflecting on this, naturally creates a suspicion that something of the same nature is intended by the same means with respect to the King.——It is expected, perhaps, that by dint of repeatedly asserting that the people in general are desirous of his death, they will be driven to some violent measure if his trial is delayed, also that they look upon all who are of contrary sentiments as aristocrates and enemies to the Revolution; and that the citizens will be brought at last to desire, or pretend to desire, what otherwise they would never have thought of.

Whatever there may be in this conjecture, the unhappy emigrants above mentioned were

conducted

conducted to the prifon without any attempt on the part of the people to murder them. They were tried by a court-martial the day before yesterday ; if there really existed in the minds of the people any eagerness for the execution of these unfortunate men, their patience was not put to a long proof: nine of the thirteen prifoners were beheaded this morning, four were officers in the army, one a lieutenant in the navy, one a coun-fellor in the late parliament of Guyenne, the other three belonged formerly to the Garde du corps.

The four who were acquitted were fer-vants, and had not been taken in arms.

What renders it more probable that there are people who wish to renew the fcenes of September is, that a rumour was in-duftrioufly fpread that the Prince of Lam-befc was in the difguife of a footman among the prifoners ; which occafioned a rabble from the fuburbs of St. Antoine,

to

to assemble around the Conciergerie, who exclaimed for the head of Lambesc *; but on the assurances of Commissioners from the municipality that there was no such person in the prison, the mob dispersed.

It is more difficult at present to execute any great atrocity than it was in the beginning of September, because a great number of profligate and idle fellows, who were at that time in Paris, have been sent to recruit the armies, and in the mean time Marat and his gang are kept in check by the arrival of the Marseillois.

* The Prince of Lambesc is peculiarly obnoxious to the mob of Paris, because, in the year 1789, when the insurrection of the Parisians began, and the busts of Necker and of the Duke of Orleans were carried in triumph, this prince was at the head of some dragoons in the square of Lewis XV. Some stones being thrown at them from the gardens of the Tuileries, he charged with his dragoons on the multitude, some of whom were wounded.

October 28.

While I was in the Affembly two days ago, a decree was paffed, which is fevere and unjuft in the higheft degree, and the reafoning in fupport of it was as fophiftical as the decree itfelf is cruel. The queftion regarded the French emigrants; it was firft ftated, that there is an effential difference between thofe who have gone into countries at war with France, to affift with their arms or counfel the enemies of their country, and thofe who have paffed into neutral ftates, fimply with a view to their own fafety—" The former," it was faid, " are traitors, and ought to be punifhed with death; the latter are cowards, who have abandoned their country in the hour of danger, for which they deferve only to be banifhed." Accordingly, by the decree they are banifhed, with this additional penalty, that if they ever return, they fhall be punifhed with death—not for having emigrated (on that

account

account they are only banifhed), but for having broken the law which condemned them to perpetual banifhment."

This is furely a diftinction without a difference; for by this cruel and unjuft decree, the perfon who leaves his native country merely from fear, and takes no part againft it, is in effect fubjected to the fame penalty with thofe who have joined the invading armies, and may be taken in arms——The former is liable to be put to death if he returns to his native country, and the latter cannot fuffer any punifhment till he does the fame.

It is as if two fervants in a family were tried as accomplices with incendiaries who had fet their mafter's houfe on fire: the one is clearly proved to have aided and abetted the incendiaries; nothing appears againft the other, but that he leaped out of the window to fave himfelf from the flames. According to the fpirit of this decree, the judge might

pronounce

pronounce sentence in the suppofed cafe to the following effect : "There is a wide difference between the crimes of thefe two men, and fo there fhall be in their punifhments. The one muft be hanged as an accomplice of the incendiaries ; and as for the other who jumped out of the window, he ought to have been afhamed ever to have fhewn his face ; and if he had ftaid out of the way and never appeared, I acknowledge it would be unjuft to hang him : but fince he is taken, that alters the cafe ; he merits now to be hanged, and I fentence him to that punifhment accordingly ; but obferve, it is not for jumping out of the window, but for the aggravating circumftance of being taken."

By this abfurd and iniquitous decree, many women are punifhed for that timidity which is natural to the fex ; and many men are ruined in their fortunes, and reduced to abfolute want, whofe only view in emigrating was to fave their lives, not from the fword of juftice, but from the poniards of affaffins.

That two parties in a ftate who are contending for the conduct of government fhould diflike each other, is common ; but that rancorous degree to which it is arrived in France is beyond any thing of the fame kind that I ever knew in England, and, I fhould hope, for the credit of mankind, beyond any thing ever known before in any other country. I made this obfervation to a gentleman who pretends to know the French thoroughly.---" The French," faid he, " have been accufed of being very inconftant *lovers :* I know nothing of that ; but I do affure you," continued he, playing on an expreffion recorded of Dr. Johnfon, " that they are very fincere and conftant *haters.*"

In confirmation of this obfervation, I perceive every day the ftrongeft marks of violent

lent hatred between the leaders of the two oppofite parties. They feem to agree in nothing but in a mutual hatred againft the unfortunate emigrants, which however does not in the leaft degree diminifh their reciprocal hatred: and I am told, that the fame hatred prevails among the emigrants themfelves in all the different countries of Europe; that thofe who emigrated at one period of the revolution hate thofe who emigrated at another, as cordially as all of them have very good reafon to hate the men who form this Convention, and are paffing fuch fevere decrees againft them.

October 26.

Marat has carried his calumnies fuch a length, that even the party which he wifhes to fupport feem, to be afhamed of him; and he is fhunned and apparently detefted by every body elfe. When he enters the hall of the Affembly, he is avoided on all fides;

S 2　　　　　　　and

and when he feats himfelf, thofe near him generally rife and change their places. He ftood a confiderable time yefterday near the tribune, watching an opportunity to fpeak. I faw him at one time addrefs himfelf to Louvet; and, in doing fo, he attempted to lay his hand on Louvet's fhoulder, who inftantly ftarted back with looks of averfion, as one would do from the touch of a noxious reptile, exclaiming! " *Ne me touchez pas!*"

Nothing can difconcert Marat; he perfevered in foliciting the privilege of being heard *pour un fait* *. The Affembly fhewed the greateft unwillingnefs to hear him: he exclaimed that it was *un fait qui intéreffoit le falut public* †.

They were at laft under the neceffity of hearing him; he elevated his head as ufual when he fpeaks from the tribune, furveyed

* For a fact.
† A fact regarding the public fafety.

the

the audience with compofure and audacity, and in a hollow voice and with folemnity of cadence faid, " It is not the citizen who now addreffes you, that provokes to murder, or puts public freedom in danger, but thofe in office, men who make ufe of their authority to opprefs the people ; *they* are the tyrants, who, under the pretence of maintaining the tranquillity of Paris, arreft and murder the moft innocent and meritorious citizens." He then accufed Roland of having given orders for arrefting an excellent patriot whom he named.

This turned out to be entirely a mifreprefentation ; but before Marat defcended from the tribune, Barbaroux informed the Affembly that Marat had paid a vifit at the barracks of the battalion of Marfeillois lately arrived ; that, at fight of their accommodations, he had lamented that fo many brave fans-culottes were fo ill lodged, while a regiment of dragoons, compofed of ancient va-

let-

let-de-chambres and coachmen of the nobility, with a mixture of the King's gardes-du-corps, all anti-revolutionists, were superbly quartered in the Ecole Militaire: that he had infinuated many things tending to raife a jealoufy between the Marfeillois and this regiment of dragoons, and had hinted that it was owing to the Convention that the former were fo ungratefully treated : and that he had invited fome of them to breakfaft with him.

It was evident that Marat's defign in this was to have feduced the Marfeillois from thofe who had engaged them to come to Paris, to attach them to his own party, and to engage them, inftead of oppofing the turbulent behaviour of the mob of St. Antoine, to act with them as their townfmen did on the 10th of Auguft.

The Marfeillois however refufed his invitation. But Barbaroux's narrative occafioned a violent outcry in the Affembly againft Marat :

rat : the epithets *scélérat, affaffin,* were often
repeated, and one member faid that Marat
had lately been heard to declare that there
would be no tranquillity in the ftate till two
hundred and fixty-eight heads were cut off.

" I am the perfon," cried another member,
" who heard him fay fo."

I threw my eyes on Marat, to obferve
how he would look on hearing fuch an accufation.

" Very well," faid Marat ; " I did fay fo,
" and it is my opinion."

I fhould have thought I had miftaken or
heard indiftinctly, if he had not refumed—
" I repeat it," faid Marat: " That is my opinion, you will not pretend that men are to
be punifhed for their opinions ; and as for the
filly ftory of Barbaroux," continued he, " it
is a malignant mifconftruction of my patriotic civilities and hofpitality to the Marfeillois. What then does the whole of this
mighty bufinefs amount to ? why, that I

faid,

ſaid, you would not enjoy peace or tranquillity till the oppreſſors of the people loſt their heads, of whom there are two hundred and ſixty-eight at the moſt moderate calculation. I am alſo accuſed of having ſhewn more attention to the battalion juſt arrived from Marſeilles, than any other member of the Convention——If theſe are crimes," added he, ſweeping the edge of his right hand acroſs his throat, " égorgez-moi !"

This new denunciation againſt Marat was tranſmitted to the ſame committee who have the former under their conſideration ; and Marat's accuſation of Roland was conſidered as invidious, and an attempt to obſtruct the courſe of juſtice.

I have never heard of any other of his good qualities——but this man certainly poſſeſſes a great deal of courage both perſonal and political : no danger can terrify him, no detection can diſconcert him ; his heart, as well as his forehead, ſeems to be of braſs.

October

I was prefent when Ruhl of Strafbourg, whom I formerly mentioned, informed the Convention, that being in the commiffion for examining certain letters in the German language, which had been intercepted, he had found one from a corporal in the Pruffian army to his wife in Silefia. In this letter he faid there were many expreffions of conjugal love and parental affection, while in the fame letter the French were painted in the blackeft colours. " This poor corporal," continued Ruhl, " has had the perfeverance and generofity to fave two ducats out of his pay, which he inclofed in the letter to his wife, who, it appears, was then in childbed. I defire to be authorized to tranfmit the money, with what addition I pleafe, to this honeft corporal's wife, with a letter affuring her that the French do not deferve all the ill names which her hufband gives them."

Ruhl

Ruhl is a man about feventy years of age; there is a great appearance of naïveté in his manner. I happened to mention this ftory of the corporal to a Frenchman of my acquaintance:—" Le conte eft beau," faid he, " et ne manque que la vraifemblance pour le rendre intéreffant*."

" He had the letter in his hand," faid I; " how can you doubt it ?"

" If he had twenty letters," replied the Frenchman, " I muft doubt it, becaufe a Pruffian corporal is generous in nothing but in *coups de batons* ; and it is not in the nature of a man who is diftributing thefe from morning to night, to have tender affections of any kind.—Such oppofite and difcordant qualities cannot inhabit the fame breaft."

The incredulity of my French acquaint-

* The tale is agreeable, and only needs probability to make it interefting.

ance I think unreafonable ; and I will here infert an anecdote, although it is much more expofed to his criticifm, becaufe it comes from a quarter which leaves no doubt on my mind of its truth.

Monfieur de Bertrand, chevalier de Malte, and brother to Monfieur de Bertrand de Moleville late Minifter of the Marine, was arrefted and confined in the prifon of the Abbaye, foon after the 10th of Auguft. This gentleman was brought at midnight on the third of September before the dreadful tribu-- nal in that prifon. He is a man of great cool- nefs and firmnefs of mind, which was of in- finite fervice to him in this emergency ; for although the fymptoms of fear ought not on fuch occafions to have been confidered as a prefumption of guilt, yet that conftruction was put on them by the judges, and, with- out any other prefumption, they fometimes proved fatal to the prifoner.

When Mr. Bertrand was queftioned, he
answered

answered with an undisturbed voice and countenance, " that he had not the least idea of what he had been arrested for, that those who arrested him could not inform him, that nobody had informed him since, and that he was convinced he had been taken up by mistake."

Struck with the cool and undaunted manner in which he addressed them, and having no particular accusation nor proof of any kind against him, the judges ordered him to be released.

Two men covered with blood, who had been employed in killing the prisoners, and attended in the expectation of the signal for dispatching Mr. Bertrand, seemed surprised but not displeased at the unusual order. They conducted him through the court of the Abbaye, and on the way asked if he had any relation to whose house he wished to go.

He answered, that he had a sister-in-law to whom he intended to go directly.

6 " How

" How very much furprifed and de-
lighted muft fhe be to fee you !" faid they.

" I am perfuaded fhe will," replied Mr.
Bertrand.

One of the men then afked the other if
he fhould not be glad to be prefent at this
meeting ; to which he eagerly faid he fhould :
and both declared they had a curiofity to be
witneffes to the joyful meeting between Mr.
Bertrand and his fifter-in-law.

The gentleman was aftonifhed and embar-
raffed : he reprefented, that his relation being
a delicate woman, their appearance might
very much alarm her, particularly at fuch an
unfeafonable hour ; that he could not think
of giving them fuch unneceffary trouble :"
and added whatever he thought would divert them from fo unexpected a propofal.

They urged that they would wait in the
parlour till he had advertifed the lady of
their being in the houfe, to prevent her
being alarmed : that fo far from being
a trouble,

would have expected. The firft turn of
mind feems incompatible with the fecond :
I know no theory by which they can be reconciled ; I attempt no explanation : I repeat
the facts as I have them from authority to
which I cannot refufe my belief, and becaufe
they form a new inftance of the aftonifhing
variety, and even oppofition of character to
be found in that wonderful creature, MAN.

October 30.

Part of the equipage of the French Princes
was feized during the retreat of the Duke
of Brunfwick's army, amongft which was
found a pocket-book belonging to *Monfieur*
the King's brother. Several packets of letters, forming a confiderable correfpondence
on various fubjects, between the emigrants
and their friends, were alfo found at Verdun
and Longwy by Kellermann's army. All
thofe papers have been tranfmitted to the
Convention, and by it fubmitted to the examination of a committee.

Moft

Moſt of the letters, I am told, are of a private nature, and no way relative to what concerns the ſtate or the public in general. It would be highly unbecoming therefore in the Convention to order thoſe to be publiſhed, which can have no other effect than to gratify the ſpirit of hatred, envy and ſlander, and create diſcord and jealouſy among families and acquaintance. It is likewiſe ſaid, that important diſcoveries have been made by ſome of theſe letters, and that they form a complete proof of an intelligence between the King and his brothers, for the ruin of the conſtitution*. In ſupport of this aſſertion, a letter was this day read in the Aſſembly, ſaid to have been found in the pocket book above mentioned. The letter is from the Marquis of Toulongeon,

---

* This *complete* proof, I make no doubt, will be of the nature of the proofs already publiſhed, which are alſo called complete, but to every candid mind muſt appear very deficient.

T Lieutenant

Lieutenant General in the French army of the King's brothers : it unfolds certain measures he had taken for arranging the troops in such a manner as to facilitate their desertion to the Austrians ; gives the reason why he had not gone himself to join the Princes at Coblentz ; adds that he is of more use to their cause by retaining a command in the French army ; that the motives of his conduct are known to the Emperor, and approved of by the King, &c.

A decree of accusation immediately passed against Toulongeon, who, fortunately for him, however, has already made his escape : and after the passing of this decree, a member expressed his surprise, that among so many decrees of accusation as had been passed, they had not yet pronounced the most important of all, namely one against the King.

On which Maile, who is of the Committee of Legislation, said, that the process of the

the King required the greateſt ſolemnity, not becauſe there was any difficulty in proving his guilt, nor to demonſtrate it to the French nation, who were already convinced, but to ſatisfy and give a great example to all Europe, and to avoid the errors which the Engliſh had committed in not obſerving all the neceſſary ſolemnities in the trial of Charles the Firſt, for which they were cenſured by many hiſtorians, and juſtified by none.

In anſwer to this, Ruhl obſerved, that the Engliſh nation had been juſtified for the ſentence paſſed on Charles Stuart by a writer of greater genius than all the hiſtorians who ever have written on the ſubject, namely, John Milton, author of Paradiſe Loſt.

Hitherto I had conſidered Ruhl in a favourable light; there is ſomething natural in his manner, and I thought him a man of humanity;

T 2

humanity ; but one of that difpofition would hardly have made fuch an obfervation at this particular time in the Convention.

October 31.

The Trial of Charles the Firft of England, tranflated into French from the State Trials, is to be found of late on all the bookfellers tables around the hall of the Convention. An abridgement of the fame is cried by the hawkers of pamphlets in the Palais Royal and the various entries to the National Affembly : the converfation is now greatly turned to that fubject, and to the expected procefs of Lewis XVI. I never believed, however, that there was a ferious intention in the Convention to bring the King to trial, and ftill lefs did I think it probable that it would be in their contemplation to bring him to the fcaffold ; an idea which I cannot entertain without horror. Befides, however

devoid

devoid of principle fome of them may be, I could not conceive that they would commit fuch an act of cruelty and injuftice, without any of the motives which incite wicked men to deeds of fuch atrocity. Their perfonal intereft evidently dictates the prefervation of the King's life, and it feemed unlikely that any member of the Convention, one only excepted, could be actuated by perfonal enmity: they are almoft all of the middle or inferior ranks of life; none of them have ever had opportunities for that kind of intercourfe with the King, which ufually generates either perfonal friendfhip or hatred: they may like or diflike, refpect or defpife his general conduct and character; but I could fee none of the ufual fources of perfonal hatred either good or bad, efpecially as, with refpect to the exercife of authority, the whole reign of Lewis XVI. has been a reign of moderation. He has always manifefted a defire to meet the wifhes of his fub-

T 3

jects;

jects; and perhaps his averfion to every meafure which had the appearance of being violent, with too great a difpofition to *grant*, have deprived him of the power of *refufing*, and reduced him to the ftate he is in.——I am perfuaded that none of his anceftors had fo juft a claim to the epithets which the public and hiftorians have affixed to their names, as the unfortunate Lewis XVI. has to that of *Louis le trop bon*.

I have excepted one perfon, to whom the preceding reafoning does not fully apply, and who may be fuppofed to be inftigated by hatred or revenge; but allowing this to be the cafe, from all I have obferved or heard fince I have been in this country, there is reafon to think that his influence is infinitely too fmall to engage either party in meafures of which they difapprove.

Thefe confiderations were fufficient hitherto to induce me to believe that there was no ferious intention in the Convention

to

to bring the King to a trial.——But I now begin to fear that a procefs in fome fhape or other will very foon be brought on, and when once begun, there is no knowing what may be the iffue in a town fo much in the power of the populace, and of *fuch* a populace as that which Paris contains at prefent.

I am led to this alteration of opinion from having very lately heard a number of citizens, whom I thought of a different opinion, declare their conviction that the King was betraying the country. The rancorous activity of his enemies has at length perfuaded them, that, inftead of another Henry IV. between whom and Lewis XVI. they formerly found a refemblance, they actually had another Lewis XI. or Charles IX. on the throne.

Befides, whether the King ought or ought not to be judged, is not merely confidered as a matter of juftice or even of expediency,

but

but, moſt unfortunately, it has become a party queſtion, in which paſſion may have more weight than either. Danton's party knows that the Girondiſts wiſh to ſave the King, which is reaſon ſufficient with the former to do every thing in their power to promote his trial and condemnation, and to repreſent the oppoſition of the other party as a proof of their being ariſtocrates and royaliſts in their hearts.

Marat, who is the great agent of Danton and Robeſpierre, declares that it is highly unjuſt, and would be a ſhameful deviation from the flattering tenet of egalité, after having condemned M. de la Porte and other inferior criminals, to paſs over the greateſt criminal of all.

Finally, I have been impreſſed with fears reſpecting the fate of the King from a variety of circumſtances, too minute to be mentioned, which have ſtruck me very lately. It is certainly horrid and diſgraceful to human

man nature, but I am afraid that the populace of this city have heard fo much of a grand example that ought to be exhibited to Europe, and their imaginations have dwelt fo long on the idea of a King being tried for his life, and afterwards led to execution, that they cannot with patience bear the thoughts of being difappointed of fuch an extraordinary fpectacle.

November 1.

When Roland and his friends were attacked by fo active and fo virulent an oppofition, it was not to be expected that they could efcape an accufation fo eafy to make, and fo difficult to refute, as that they were not actuated by the genuine principles of patriotifm, but merely by felfifh motives, and that they had no other object in view than to retain the lucrative offices of the ftate in their own hands.

To ftifle the voice of flander at once, upon this fubject, Genfonné furprifed the Convention lately by a fpeech in which he lamented

lamented that a party-fpirit had manifefted itfelf fo ftrongly among them. He
added that diffidence in each other, the natural effect of the numerous treafons which
had lately been difcovered, alfo prevailed to
an alarming degree; which, joined to the
envy which generates hatred, and produces divifion, might enable defpotifm to
arife again out of anarchy : he added, that
the prefent times required a great example
of felf-denial to dry up one great fource of
party fpirit, filence calumny, and prove to
the world that they had not made war on
royalty on purpofe to divide the regal fpoils
among themfelves, but to obtain freedom to
their country—He therefore moved that it
fhould be decreed that no member of the
Convention fhould be capable of enjoying
any office in the government for ten years
after the decree had paffed.

All the members, as if with one voice,
called out, Yes, yes ; they fprung from their
fcats,

feats, in a fit of enthufiafm, and demanded that the propofal of Genfonnè fhould be inftantly decreed, which was done accordingly.

This practice of paffing decrees the inftant they are propofed, without reflection, may be attended with the worft confequences; as for this decree in particular, it ftrikes fo directly againft the views of the leading men of both parties, and is liable, in other refpects, to fo many weighty objections, that I fufpect it will not be long in force even in France; but if it fhould, it may afford comfort to the minds of Englifhmen at this awful period, when there is a juft dread of the prevalence of French manners and French opinions, to reflect that there is too much folid good fenfe in the Britifh Parliament to adopt fo foolifh a meafure

November 2.

A moft unrelenting fpirit againft the emigrants,

emigrants, appears as often as they are mentioned in the Conventional Affembly— I fpoke of this to one of the deputies this evening, exprefling my furprife that 'no member ever faid any thing in their favour, although I could hardly imagine but that; in fo large an affembly, many of the members had relations or friends among them.

In anfwer to my obfervation the deputy faid, that the greater part of the emigrants were noblefle, of which clafs very few are members of the Convention, fo that there is little or no connection by blood, and as little by friendfhip, between the deputies and emigrants. I take it for granted, added he, that you do not think any meafure too fevere for thofe emigrants who have taken arms againft their country, and as for thofe who do not appear in arms, it is well known that they are doing every thing in their power to excite every nation in Europe, particularly the Englifh, againft France, and

if

if they fucceed, and produce a counter revolution, there is no doubt but thefe emigrants will exercife ftill greater cruelties
againft the patriots.

I replied, that the Affembly had faved
the emigrants the trouble of exciting war,
by declaring it firft ; for that no nation had
declared war with France hitherto till
France declared war with it ; that with
refpect to England, I imagined that whether
fhe fhould enter into a war with France or
not, would depend on the conduct of the
Convention, and not on any thing the emigrants could fay or do ; and, finally, that if
men were to act cruelly towards thofe whofe
perfons or property were in their power,
on a fuppofition that, if the fituations were
reverfed, thofe whom they opprefs would
opprefs them, in that cafe there would be
nothing but oppreffion and cruelty in the
world.

I then mentioned the cafe of one perfon

I

who

who had emigrated in very particular circumftances, and had returned to France foon
after, ftating the cafe in the ftrongeft and
moft favourable light, which I corroborated
with documents that I had in my poffeffion.

Other deputies joined us, to whom I
alfo mentioned this cafe, and one of them
taking me afide, affured me he faw it in the
fame point of view that I did, and that he
would do what he could to ferve the perfon in queftion, which, notwithftanding the
favourable circumftances, muft be attempted
with delicacy, becaufe fuch a hatred prevailed in the Convention againft all emigrants, and fuch a jealoufy of each other, that
whoever feemed active or zealous in their favour, had a greater probability of injuring
himfelf, than of ferving them. You will
readily believe, added he, how difficult it is to
procure any thing like favour to one who is
both a noble and an emigrant, at a period
when thofe nobles who never emigrated,

5   but

but on the contrary have taken an active part in the Revolution, are looked on with diftruftful and jealous eyes.——He then gave me directions how to proceed, and told me to whom, and in what manner to apply—I have followed his advice, and with the beft hopes of fuccefs.

In the gratification of this hatred to the emigrants, as in many other inftances, the Convention overfteps good policy.

General Cuftine has tranfmitted letters to the Convention, which have been addreffed to him from emigrants in foreign fervices, who now wifh to ferve their country, provided they may be allowed to return with fafety.

General Biron has likewife written to the Convention in favour of fome officers who have been in the army of the Prince of Condé, and now implore forgivenefs, and the General's mediation with the Affembly,

that

that they may be permitted to return to France.

In both cafes the Convention paffed to the order of the day—yet as Biron is at prefent a very popular general, and as Cuftine has juft taken poffeffion of Frankfort, and has been always fuccefsful, it might have been expected that more attention would have been paid to their applications.

Befides, at this moment of fuccefs, lenient and conciliatory meafures towards thofe unfortunate people who left their country at a time when, affuredly, there were many reafons for leaving it, would appear generous to all Europe, it would pleafe the numerous relations and friends of the emigrants in every department of France, and go farther to attach the whole nation to the Revolution, than any of the decrees they have lately paffed, or perhaps than even the victories they have lately gained.

But

But there are men in this Convention, and unfortunately leading men too, who are ready to facrifice every confideration to the gratification of their paffions, and whofe ruling paffions feem to be hatred and revenge.

This day the Prefidency of Guadet ended, and Herault de Sechelles was elected to fucceed him.——Herault is a man of about thirty years of age, of an open engaging countenance, and genteel appearance, circumftances which diftinguifh him in this Affembly: it is alfo remarkable, that he is not confidered as fo much devoted to the Girondifts as any of the late Prefidents, which is confidered as a proof that they are rather lofing ground.

November 3.

As the General Council of the Municipality of Paris, which was formed at midnight on the ninth of Auguft, claim the whole glory of the Revolution, they thought

U they

they had the beft right to retain alfo the power of the ftate.

Without confulting the National Affembly, they iffued orders for fearching many hotels, under various pretexts; detachments of national guards, under leaders chofen by the Council, were alfo fent to particular churches and palaces in Paris and the neighbourhood, and confiderable quantities of plate and other valuable effects carried away, under the pretence of being for the public ufe, but of which a large portion has been embezzled.

Some members of the National Affembly began a fhort time after the tenth of Auguft to fpeak on the fubject of thefe embezzlements, and propofed to make an enquiry into that bufinefs: but the National Affembly had then loft all energy; and, according to an expreffion of one of the deputies, it had become a mere engine for manufacturing decrees

decrees at the requifition of the Council of the Commune. As often as any mention was made of eftablifhing a committee to examine into the extent of thefe embezzlements, and by whom they had been committed, the propofal was heard with evident marks of ill humour by all the members of the Affembly who were alfo members of the Commune, and by others intimately connected with them.—They who made fuch propofals, finding themfelves unfupported, dropped them; it was not thought prudent to irritate the men who iffued thofe orders of arreft by which the prifons had been filled, and who, in the opinion of many, had alfo iffued the orders by which they had been emptied.

It was expected that the Convention would be able to effect what the late National Affembly attempted in vain, and to reftrain the power of the Municipality within its proper limits. An account of the ufurpa-

U 2   tions

tions of the General Council had been
written to all the departments of France;
many of the deputies to the Convention
had come to Paris, prepoſſeſſed with the idea
that Paris wiſhed to govern the ſtate independent of all the other departments—that
the General Council governed Paris, and
that Danton and Robeſpierre governed the
General Council.

Having heard that a debate of importance
was expected, I went to the Conventional
Aſſembly two days ago earlier than uſual.

Roland was to preſent a memorial reſpecting the ſtate of Paris. When he appeared,
contrary to cuſtom, they poſtponed the buſineſs then tranſacting, to attend to him.—He
began by ſaying, that if the ſtrength of his
voice was equal to that of his mind, he ſhould
himſelf read the addreſs which he held in his
hand; but as his breaſt was delicate, he begged
that one of the ſecretaries might be allowed

to

to read it for him.——Lanjuinais afcended the tribune, and read.

In this memorial were ftated all the ufurpations and acts of defpotifm which had been committed by the Commune fince the tenth of Auguft, many of which were unknown to the generality of the deputies, and feemed to fill them with equal furprife and indignation.——Roland ftated that he had often required fome account of the money, plate, and effects which had been feized by commiffioners from the Commune at Senlis, Chantilly, l'Hotel de Coigny, and other hotels, without having had any fatisfactory anfwer: that he had alfo addreffed himfelf to them to know how Lewis XVI. and his family were treated in the Temple, but no notice had been taken of his demand. After having demonftrated how both public and private property had been violated, he demanded whether perfonal furety had been better protected. This led him to mention

U 3

the

the horrors of the beginning of September, which he pretty plainly infinuated were committed by the leaders of the Common Council, who, he afferted, were ftill meditating the moft rapacious and bloody defigns in fupport of their avarice and ambition.——With this memorial Roland prefented a letter addreffed to the Minifter of Juftice, in which information is given, "that expreffions of the moft alarming tendency had been ufed by certain perfons of late; that it had been even infinuated that the bufinefs begun in September had not been completed; that the whole cabal of Roland and Briffot fhould be cut off; that there was a fcheme for this purpofe; that Vergniaud, Guadet, Buzot, La Source, and others difpleafed the real patriots; and that *Robefpierre* was the propereft perfon for conducting the government in the prefent emergency.

"Ah the villain!" one of the members

called

called aloud, as foon as this name was pronounced.

There was fuch an uproar in the Affembly for fome time after Roland's memorial had been read, that no perfon in particular could be diftinctly heard : the noife was moftly occafioned by expreffions of rage againft Robefpierre, and partly by a cry that the memorial fhould be printed, and fent to all the departments and all the municipalities in France.

Robefpierre afcended the tribune; the cry againft him was fo violent that his voice could not be diftinguifhed : he at laft was heard to fay, that he wifhed to juftify himfelf from the calumnies of the Minifter. He was interrupted by a new cry to clofe the difcuffion : he then faid he wifhed to fpeak againft the printing of the memorial.

This was alfo refufed by a pretty univerfal exclamation; but on its being obferved, that they could not decree a propofition

U 4   without

without hearing those who wished to speak against it, he was allowed to proceed. He began with a few sentences concerning the printing the paper, and immediately deviated into an eulogium on his own conduct. Guadet, the President, reminded him of the question.

"I have no need of your admonitions," said Robespierre; "I know very well on what I have to speak."

"He thinks himself already Dictator," exclaimed a member.

"Robespierre, speak against the printing," said the President.

Robespierre then resumed, and declaimed on every thing except against the printing.

His voice was again drowned by an outcry against his wanderings. The President strove to procure silence, that Robespierre might be heard; which he no sooner was, than he accused the President of encouraging the clamour against him.

No accusation could be more unjust or more

more injudicious than this, becaufe it was falfe, and becaufe every body prefent was witnefs to its falfehood. The Prefident had done all in his power that Robefpierre might be heard, and had actually broken three bells by ringing to procure him filence.

The Prefident then faid, " Robefpierre, vous voyez les efforts que je fais pour ramener le filence—mais je vous pardonne une calomnie de plus *."

Robefpierre refumed, and continued to fpeak of himfelf a confiderable time in the moft flattering terms.

Many people prefer fpeaking of themfelves to any other topic of difcourfe, as well as Robefpierre ; but in him this propenfity is irrefiftible. Praife acts as a cordial on the fpirits of moft people, but it is the praife they receive from others which has that

* Robefpierre, you are yourfelf witnefs to the efforts I have made to reftore filence ; but I forgive you that additional calumny.

effect :

effect : what is peculiar to Robefpierre is, that he feems as much enlivened by the eulogies he beftows on himfelf, as others are by the applaufe of their fellow-citizens.

The panegyric he pronounced on his own virtues evidently raifed his fpirits, and infpired him with a courage which at laft precipitated him into rafhnefs. " A fyftem of calumny is eftablifhed," faid he with a lofty voice, " and againft whom is it directed? againft a zealous patriot. Yet who is there among you who dares rife and accufe me to my face ?"

" Moi," exclaimed a voice from one end of the hall. There was a profound filence ; in the midft of which, a thin, lank, palefaced man ftalked along the hall like a fpectre; and being come directly oppofite to the tribune, he fixed Robefpierre, and faid, *Oui, Robefpierre, c'eft moi qui t'accufe* *.

It was Jean-Baptifte Louvet.

* Yes, Robefpierre, it is I who accufe you.

Robef-

Robefpierre was confounded : he ftood motionlefs, and turned pale ; he could not have feemed more alarmed had a bleeding head fpoken to him from a charger.

Louvet afcended, and appeared in the front of the tribune, while Robefpierre fhrunk to one fide.

Danton perceiving how very much his friend was difconcerted, called out, " Continue, Robefpierre, there are many good citizens here to hear you."

This feemed to be a hint to the people in the galleries, that they might fhew themfelves in fupport of the patriot——but they remained neuter.

The Affembly was in fuch confufion for fome time, that nothing diftinct could be heard. Robefpierre again attempted to fpeak ——his difcourfe was as confufed as the Affembly——he quitted the tribune.

Danton went into it : his drift was to prevent Louvet from being heard, and to propofe a future day for taking into confideration

fideration Roland's memorial; and as Marat feemed at this time to be rather en mauvaife odeur with the Convention, Danton thought proper to make a declaration which had no connection with the debate, and which nobody thought fincere : " Je déclare à la Republique entière," he exclaimed, " que je n'aime point l'individu Marat. Je déclare avec franchife que j'ai fait l'expérience de fon temperament, et qu'il eft non-feulement volcanique et acariâtre—mais infociable *."

This conveys no favourable idea of Danton's eloquence. After finding the two firft qualities in Marat, it is furprifing that he could fearch for a third. It is as if a man were to give as his reafon for not keeping company with an old acquaintance, that he not only found him quite mad, and always ready to ftab thofe near him with a dagger,

---

* I declare to the whole Republic, that I do not love Marat. I frankly acknowledge that I have fome experience of the man ; and I find not only that he is boifterous and quarrelfome, but alfo unfociable.

but

but that, over and above, he was fometimes a little too referved.

This did not divert Louvet from his purpofe : he perfevered, and the Affembly decreed that he fhould be heard.

November 4.

He began by requefting the Prefident's protection, that he might be heard without interruption, for he was going to mention things that would be mortally offenfive to fome prefent—who, he faid, were already fore, and would be apt to fcream when he came to touch the tender parts.——As he continued a little on fome preliminary topics, Danton exclaimed, " I defire that the accufer would put his finger into the wound."

" I intend it," replied Louvet; " but why does Danton fcream beforehand ?"

Louvet then proceeded to unfold the popular artifices by which Robefpierre acquired his influence in the Jacobin Society : " that he had introduced into it a number of men

.devoted

devoted to him, and, by an insolent exercise of his power, had driven some of the most respectable members out of it; that after the tenth of August he had been chosen of the Council General of the Commune, and acquired equal influence there. Where he was on that memorable day," said Louvet, " nobody can tell; all we know is, that, like Sofia in the play, he did not appear till after the battle. On the eleventh or twelfth he presented himself to the Commune, and under *his* auspices all the orders for arresting the citizens were issued;—that orders had been given for arresting Roland and Briffot, which, by the care of some of their friends, had not been executed;—that a band of men had arrogated to themselves the honour of the Revolution of August, whereas the massacres of September only belonged to them."— Here Talien and some others of Robespierre's faction, who were also of the General Council, began to murmur; on

7   **which**

which a member called out—Silence, les
bleſſés! and Louvet reſumed, with great animation—" Yes, barbarians! to you belong
the horrid maſſacres of September, which
you now impute to the citizens of Paris.
The citizens of Paris were all preſent at the
Tuileries on the tenth of Auguſt, but who
were witneſſes to the murders in September?
Two, or perhaps three hundred ſpectators,
whom an incomprehenſible curioſity had
drawn before the priſons. But it is aſked,
Why then did not the citizens prevent them?
Becauſe they were ſtruck with terror; the
alarm guns had been fired, the tocſin had
ſounded; becauſe their ears were impoſed
on by falſe rumours; becauſe their eyes were
aſtoniſhed at the ſight of municipal officers,
dreſſed in ſcarfs, preſiding at the executions;
becauſe Roland exclaimed in vain; becauſe
Danton, the Miniſter of Juſtice, was ſilent;
and becauſe Santerre, the Commander of the
National Guards, remained inactive. Soon
after

after thefe lamentable fcenes," continued Louvet, " the Legiflative Affembly was frequently calumniated, infulted, and even threatened, by this infolent demagogue."

Here Louvet being interrupted by the exclamations of Robefpierre's adherents, La Croix went up to the tribune, and declared, that one evening, while he was Prefident of the Legiflative Affembly, but not in the chair, Robefpierre, at the head of a deputation of the General Council, came to the bar with a particular petition, which Lacroix oppofed, and the Affembly paffed to the order of the day ; that having retired to the extremity of the hall, Robefpierre faid to him, that if the Legiflative Affembly would not with good will do what he required, he would force them to do it by the found of the tocfin ; on which Lacroix faid, he had taken his feat as Prefident, and related to the Affembly what had paffed.

Other members bore teftimony of Robefpierre's

pierre's having pronounced the threat, and they confirmed the truth of all that Lacroix had related. One added, that Lacroix's friends had entreated him not to return to his own houfe that evening, by the Terrace of the Feuillans, becaufe affaffins were pofted there to murder him.

This interlude excited frefh indignation againft Robefpierre, who made fome efforts to be heard from the tribune. One of the members obferved, that a man accufed of fuch a crime ought not to place himfelf in the tribune, but at the bar.

Robefpierre perfifted ; but the Affembly decided, that he fhould not be heard till Louvet had finifhed.

" The Legiflative Affembly," faid Louvet, refuming the very fentence at which he had been interrupted, " was calumniated, infulted, and menaced by this infolent demagogue, who, with eternal profcriptions in his mouth, accufed fome of the moft de-

X

ferving

serving reprefentatives of the people with having fold the nation to Brunfwick, and accufed them the day before the affaffinations began : in his bloody profcriptions all the new minifters were included except one, and that one always the fame. Will it be in thy power, Danton," continued Louvet, darting his eyes on the late Minifter of Juftice, " to juftify thy character to pofterity for that exception ? Do not expect to blind us now by difavowing Marat, that *enfant perdu de l'affaffinat :* it was through your influence, by your harangues at the Electoral Affemblies, in which you blackened Prieftley, and white-wafhed Marat, that he is now of this Convention. Upon that occafion I demanded leave to fpeak againft fuch a candidate : as I retired, I was furrounded by thofe men, with bludgeons and fabres, with whom the future Dictator was always accompanied : thofe body guards of Robefpierre, during the period of the maffacres, often looked at

me

me with threatening countenances, and one of them said, *It will be your turn soon.*"

Louvet added, that he accused Robespierre of having calumniated some of the most meritorious citizens of the Republic; of having accused them unjustly, at a time when accusation was proscription; of having insulted and menaced the National Assembly; of having domineered over, and by intrigue and terror influenced, the elections of the Electoral Assemblies of Paris; and of having attempted the supreme power. He demanded that a committee might be appointed to examine into his conduct.

He then said that he accused another man who had, to the astonishment of all France, been introduced among them by the former, of whom he was the tool. Several voices called out, Marat! Louvet concluded by saying, that he hoped they would also pronounce a decree against all those monsters who instigate to murder and assassina-

tion,

nation, againſt a faction which from perſonal ambition was tearing the Republic in
pieces ; and that they would alſo decree that
the Executive Power, in caſes of commotion,
might call upon all the military force in the
department of Paris, and order it to act for
the reſtoration of tranquillity in the manner
it judged expedient.

Robeſpierre aſcended the tribune as ſoon
as Louvet had finiſhed.

The Aſſembly feemed unwilling to hear
him : ſome propoſed that the diſcuſſion
ſhould be poſtponed till next day, and that
then Robeſpierre ſhould be heard at the bar.
Louvet moved that he ſhould be heard immediately. Robeſpierre declared that he
did not intend to make his anſwer then, but
deſired that the 5th of November might be
appointed for that purpoſe.——This attack of
Louvet, and the debate which followed,
took place ſeveral days ago. Louvet was
greatly admired for the firmneſs of his be-

3.   haviour

haviour, and the acuteneſs of ſome of his remarks.

Robeſpierre was thrown into ſuch confuſion, that he did not fully recover his ſpirits and recollection afterwards. The effect of eloquence on an aſſembly of Frenchmen is violent and inſtantaneous: the indignation which Louvet's ſpeech raiſed againſt Robeſpierre was prodigious; at ſome particular parts I thought his perſon in danger. I fancy the demand of ſo long an interval before he ſhould make his defence, was ſuggeſted by Danton, or ſome other of his friends; it was a prudent meaſure, had he attempted to anſwer immediately, he muſt have loſt his cauſe: all his eloquence and addreſs could not at that time have effaced the ſtrong impreſſion which Louvet had made.

Although he drew the attack on himſelf by his imprudent boaſting, yet he was taken unprepared: the galleries in particular had been neglected on that day, for the audience

X 3

ſhewed

shewed no partiality—a thing so unusual when he spoke, that it is believed to have helped greatly to disconcert him.

November 5.

Two or three days after the scene above described, Roland wrote to the Convention, that a late address of the Commune of Paris, which had *not* been ordered by the Convention to be printed, or transmitted to the departments, had nevertheless been inclosed in covers directed and franked by the Mayor of Paris, and put into the post-office : that he had ordered them to be stopped, because the Convention had disapproved of the address, and because he believed the name of Petion on the covers to be forged.

Petion immediately rose, and declared that he knew nothing of the intention of transmitting the address to the departments, and had franked none of the covers.

This letter from Roland produced a

8   warm

warm debate, which ſerved only to animate the two parties more violently againſt each other; one accuſing the Commune of a low and factious manœuvre, in endeavouring to circulate an addreſs diſapproved of by the Convention, and which is of a pernicious tendency; the other accuſing the Miniſter of a deſpotic and illegal act in wounding pub- lic confidence, by arreſting the courſe of correſpondence.

Like all debates in a numerous aſſembly, where the paſſions are inflamed, it ſoon de- viated from the object on which it began, and extended to other ſubjects of recrimi- nation; during which Barbaroux of Mar- ſeilles, who had been prevented from ſpeak- ing on the day on which Louvet accuſed Robeſpierre, made a very ſpirited harangue againſt the latter and his partiſans. It was nearly to the ſame purpoſe with that of Lou- vet, but more correct and conciſe: its ob- jects were to remove all jealouſy of the

X 4　　　　　　Marſeillois,

Marfeillois, to urge the neceffity of an armed force to protect the Convention from the brutality of the mob, and to increafe the fufpicions of the ambitious views of Robefpierre.

He began by afking " if the reprefentatives of twenty-five millions of men were to bend their heads to thirty factious perfons,"

" The inhabitants of the South are accufed of having projected a federal republic," continued Barbaroux ; " yet we, their reprefentatives, declare, that they have inftructed us to oppofe every project of that nature. I call on Marat to rife and prove that ever there was fuch a project, or to own himfelf to be a calumniator."

" The friends of Roland are accufed of wifhing to domineer by means of the armed force which is requifite to maintain the independence of the Convention ; I undertake to prove, when that queftion comes regularly before us, that this is rendered impoffible by the very manner in in which that force is proposed to be established. It is not to be formed of Swifs guards, but of French citizens from the eighty-three departments.

" Those agitators," continued Barbaroux, " who for villanous purposes wish to spread anarchy over the nation, have the audacity to say *they* brought on the revolution of Auguft, and by that falsehood try to make us forget their project of a Dictator, their numerous robberies and their horrid murders in September : but they never can be forgotten ; nor shall I ceafe to act against that faction, till the murderers are punished, the effects restored, and the dictators thrown from the rock.

" What," continued Barbaroux, " can more plainly demonstrate the ambitious projects of those men, than that which has already been mentioned in the Convention ; namely, that immediately before the 10th of Auguft, Robefpierre invited Rebecqui and

and me to his houfe ? He fpoke to us of the
neceffity of our rallying all our force under
fome man who enjoyed great popularity ;
and Panis, as we took our leave, named
Robefpierre as the propereft man for being
Dictator. And Robefpierre himfelf propofed in the committee of twenty-one,
that the Council General of the Commune
fhould be authorifed to form itfelf at
once into a jury of accufation, a jury of
judgment, and a tribunal for applying the
law. Let it be remembered that he himfelf
had the chief influence in the General Council. And finally," faid Barbaroux, " this very
man, on another occafion, eager to obtain
a decree, came to the bar of the National
Affembly, and threatened the reprefentatives
of the nation to make the tocfin be founded,
if they did not form one as he thought
proper to dictate."

This difcourfe, while it increafed the indignation already kindled againft Robefpierre, muft alfo tend to make his adherents
more

more zealous to defend him :—it is their own caufe :—when the murderers of the prifoners, and the embezzlers of goods are threatened, many members of the Convention, and more of the General Council, muft be in a ftate of fevere alarm. And feverely will this alarm be avenged if thefe men fhould ever obtain the afcendency in the Convention. On the 2d of September, they fhewed what is to be expected from them when in power.

November 6.

Great inconveniency was found in the Convention, from the petitions which formerly were allowed to be prefented at all times. By a late decree, all petitions are ordered to be referved for Sunday, when, unlefs fomething of great importance intervenes, the fole bufinefs is to attend to them.

This renders it the leaft interefting day for attending the Convention. I went laft Sunday, in company with an Englifh gentleman, to St. Cloud. This was the fummer refidence

refidence of the Orleans family from the time that *Monfieur*, brother to Lewis XIV. built the chateau, till lately.

From the houfe itfelf, as well as from many parts of the delicious park, there is an extenfive view comprehending Paris, all the villas around it, a rich landfcape of hills, woods and meadows, through which the Seine flows in many graceful windings. The cafcade is greatly admired, and the park has been confidered as the happieft effort of the genius of Le Noftre, who has made a delightful ufe of all the variety of furface it contains, as well as of the Seine which flows by it.—St. Cloud, in the opinion of many, was preferable to any of the royal villas before it became one of them : it was purchafed by the Queen from the Duke of Orleans about five or fix years ago, fince which time, the apartments within the chateau have been altered at a great expence, and much improved. Nothing can

be

be conceived more commodious. Notwith-standing the richnefs and magnificence of fome of the apartments, this palace, with all its fplendid furniture, has remained hitherto undefpoiled and unfullied.

The contraft between the magnificence we were beholding, and the wretched apart-ment in which the perfon for whom that magnificence was prepared is confined, natu-rally prefented itfelf to our minds. This idea, with that of the various aggravating circum-ftances which attend her confinement, made us contemplate the fplendour of St. Cloud through a very gloomy medium. The whole manner of the man who conducted us through the apartments, fufficiently evinced that his thoughts fprang from the fame fource, and flowed in the fame channel with ours.

Thofe who have had the curiofity to vifit the houfes of princes and villas of nobility, may have remarked with what oftentation

and

and pride the houfe-keeper and fervants conduct ftrangers through magnificent apartments : they enjoy the admiration of the vifitors, and fwell with felf-importance in proportion to the richnefs of the furniture. They are not, however, more grofsly miftaken than thofe proprietors, who, deriving all their importance from the fame quarter, think it amounts to a great deal.

Nothing of this kind, but all that is oppofite, appeared in the demeanour of the man who attended us through the palace of St. Cloud : his mind evidently borrowed no pride from the magnificence he had under his care, but feemed rather to be engroffed with the fad fate of the owners, and the folicitudes

———— —— laqueata circum tecta volantes.

The annals of the unfortunate do not record any fituation more dreadful than that of the unhappy Queen of France.

Any

Any woman in her situation would be exceedingly miserable; but we cannot help thinking that she must be more miserable than any other woman in the same situation.

The distance at which her rank seemed to have placed her from the reach of the misery which now surrounds and threatens to overwhelm her, renders her sufferings more acute. This circumstance, independent of any absurd prejudice in favour of rank, must increase the sympathy of every feeling heart. Although she is the daughter of an Empress, the sister of Emperors, and the wife of a King who was lately considered the most powerful in Europe, she seems now more pre-eminent in wretchedness than ever she was in rank and splendor.

She was not only a queen, but is a beautiful woman ; not only accustomed to the interested and ostentatious submission that attends power, but to that more pleasing atten-

tion

tion and obedience which are paid to beauty.
Fortune accompanied her friendſhip, and
happineſs her ſmiles. She found her wiſhes
anticipated, and ſaw her very looks obeyed.—
How painful muſt now be the dreadful reverſe! Shut up in a priſon, ſurrounded with
barbarians, wretches who rejoice in her calamity and inſult her ſorrow, with what
affecting propriety might this unfortunate
Queen adopt the pathetic complaint of Job!
" He hath fenced up my way that I cannot
paſs, and he hath ſet darkneſs in my paths.

" He hath ſtripped me of my glory, and
taken the crown from my head.

" He hath deſtroyed me on every ſide,
and I am gone : and mine hope hath he removed like a tree.

" He hath put my brethren far from me.

" My kinsfolk have failed, and my friends
have forgotten me."

What has this moſt unfortunate of women already ſuffered? what is yet reſerved
for

for her to endure ? She has been shocked by the cruel murder of many of her servants and friends, some of them for no other reason than their fidelity to her. She now suffers all the agonies of suspense—her heart throbbing from recent wounds, and her mind terrified, not for her own fate only, but for those of her sister, her husband, and her children.——No ; the annals of the unfortunate do not record, nor has the imagination of the tragic poet invented, any thing more dreadfully affecting than the misfortunes and sufferings of Marie Antoinette queen of France ; and for ages to come, her name will never be pronounced unaccompanied with execrations against the unmanly and unrelenting wretches who have treated her, and suffered her to be treated, in the manner she has been.

November 7.

From St. Cloud we wished to drive to

Mont Calvaire, but found part of the road impaffable for a carriage, and were obliged to return and go directly to Paris.——It feems very ftrange, that a road between a royal palace and a neighbouring hill to which there is fo great a refort from other places fhould be in this ftate. The day was one of the fineft I ever faw. On coming to the barrier, immediately before we entered Paris, a waggon ftood acrofs the road, which ftopped our carriage : the coachman had fome words with the waggoner, who was drinking with fome fans-culottes. He feemed in no hurry to move his waggon out of the way, notwithftanding the repeated requefts of our coachman, who, after a little altercation, loft his temper fo far as to make ufe of the term *canaille*, which has fuch an ariftocratic found, that it alarmed me. I inftantly and very loudly rebuked the coachman; which pleafed the audience fo much, that they

they removed the waggon, and we paſſed unmoleſted to Paris.

I was the more alarmed at this expreſſion, on account of a ſcene which I had been witneſs to in the gallery of the National Aſſembly. A man dreſſed like a gentleman had a diſpute with two perſons of a poor appearance: he called them *canaille*, which drew the ſevereſt of all repartees from one of them, namely, that he was an ariſtocrate. The people around took part againſt the accuſed perſon, who tried in vain to refute the charge; they would not liſten, but obliged him to leave the gallery.

A gentleman who had entered with him was very near being reduced to the ſame neceſſity. One addreſſed him in an angry tone, ſaying, " The people are not to be treated in the inſolent manner your friend did, Sir."

To which the other anſwered with mildneſs, " Il n'eſt pas probable, Monſieur, que

Y 2　　　　　　　j'aie

j'aie la moindre intention d'infulter le peuple, puifque j'ai l'honneur d'en faire partie*."

November 8.

On the day on which Robefpierre made his defence, the galleries of the Conventional Affembly were crowded at an early hour; but having an order from the Prefident for the box of the Logographe, I was admitted at the ufual time.

There was not fo great a crowd of the populace at the entry to the Affembly, as I have fometimes feen; but thofe who were there expreffed their partiality for him, and diflike to his accufers. On the terrace of the Feuillans, the groups were moftly formed of his partifans: one fellow accompanied by two or three others carried tripe on a pole, which they fwore they would force thofe to eat, who fhould vote againft fo diftinguifhed a patriot.

* It is not probable that I fhould have any intention to infult the people, fince I have the honour to be one of them.

Imme-

Immediately before Robefpierre afcended the tribune, a deputy complained that the galleries were unfairly filled ; that certain privileged perfons, chiefly women, had been introduced for the purpofe of applauding, while all the impartial citizens were kept out : " Des citoyennes," he exclaimed, " font à la porte des tribunes, tandis que d'autres porteufes de cartes privilégiées font facilement entrées*."

This obfervation occafioned an univerfal laugh, and every body turned their eyes to the galleries, which were almoft entirely filled with women. Robefpierre's eloquence is faid to be peculiarly admired by the fex ; and it has been remarked, that on the nights when he was expected to fpeak at the Jacobins the proportion of females in the galleries was always greater than ufual.

* Some female citizens are kept at the door, while other females with privileged tickets are feated in the tribunes.

When

When Robefpierre appeared in the tribune, it was evident that he had entirely recovered his fpirits, and he certainly made a much better figure than he did when he was laft there.

"I am accufed," faid he, "of having aimed at the fupreme power. If fuch a fcheme is criminal, it muft be allowed to be ftill more bold. To fucceed, I muft have been able not only to overthrow the throne, but alfo to annihilate the legiflature, and above all, to prevent its being replaced by a National Convention. But, in reality, I myfelf was the firft who, in my public difcourfes and writings, propofed a National Convention as the only means of faving the country. To arrive at the dictatorfhip, to render myfelf mafter of Paris, was not fufficient; I muft alfo have been able to fubdue the other eighty-two departments. Where were my treafures? where were my armies? what ftrongly fortified places had I fecured? All the

the riches and power of the ftate were in the hands of my enemies. In fuch circum-ftances, to make it credible that I had fuch a fcheme, my accufers muft demonftrate that I am a complete madman."

" Ce n'eft pas la l'embarras*," faid one of the deputies near me to thofe around him.

" And when they have made that point clear," continued Robefpierre, " I cannot conceive what they will gain by it, for then it will remain for them to prove that a mad-man can be dangerous in a ftate."

" Bah!" faid the deputy who had already fpoken, " ils font les plus redoutables†."

Robefpierre denied having ever had much connection with Marat, and he explained by what means he had been induced to have the little which he avowed; and he afferted, that Marat had not been chofen to the Con-vention from *his* recommendation, nor per-

---

* That would not be difficult.
† They are the moft dangerous.

haps

haps from any high opinion which the electors had of that Deputy, but from their hatred to the ariſtocrates, whoſe mortal enemy they knew Marat to be.

"I am accuſed," continued Robeſpierre, of having exerciſed the deſpotiſm of opinion in the Jacobin Society. That kind of deſpotiſm over the minds of a ſociety of freemen could only be acquired and obtained by reaſoning. I find nothing therefore to bluſh for in this accuſation. Nothing can be more flattering to me than the good opinion of the Jacobins, eſpecially as Lewis XVI. and Monſ. de la Fayette have both found that the opinion of the Jacobins is the opinion of all France. But now, that ſociety, as Louvet pretends, is not what it was, it has degenerated ; and perhaps, after having accuſed me, his next ſtep will be to demand the proſcription of the Jacobins. We ſhall then ſee whether he will be more perſuaſive and more ſucceſsful than Leopold and La Fayette.

"Louvet

" Louvet next tries to vilify the General Council of the Commune ; thofe men who, chofen by the fections, affembled in the Town Houfe on that awful night when the confpiracy of the Court was ready to burft forth ; thofe men who directed the movements of that infurrection which faved the ftate ; who difconcerted the meafures of the traitors in the Tuileries, by arrefting the Commander of the National Guards, who had given orders to the leaders of battalions to allow the people to pafs towards the Caroufel, and then attack them in the rear : thofe patriots are of too much energy of character to be efteemed by the flaves of monarchy ; but it is not in the power of calumny and impofture to preclude the heroic fervice they were of to the Republic from the records of hiftory.

" They are accufed," continued he, " of arrefting men contrary to the forms of law. Was it expected, then, that we were to ac-
complifh

complifh a revolution in the government
with the code of the laws in our hands? Was
it not becaufe the laws were impotent, that
the Revolution was abfolutely neceffary?
—Why are we not accufed alfo of having
difarmed fufpected citizens, and of exclud-
ing from the affemblies which deliberate on
the public fafety, all known enemies of the
Revolution? Why do you not bring accufations againft the Electoral Affemblies
and the Primary Affemblies? they have all
done acts, during this crifis, which are *illegal,*
as illegal as the overthrowing of the Baftille,
as illegal as Liberty itfelf.

" When the Roman conful had fuppreffed
the confpiracy of Catiline, Clodius accufed
him of having violated the laws. The
Conful's defence was, that he had faved the
Republic.

" We are accufed of fending Commiffioners to various departments.—What! is it imagined that the Revolution was to be com-

pleted

pleted by a simple coup de main, and seizing the Castle of the Tuileries? Was it not necessary to communicate to all France that salutary commotion which had electrified Paris?

" What species of persecution is this, which converts into crimes the very efforts by which we broke our chains? At this rate, what people will ever be able to shake off the yoke of despotism? The people of a large country cannot act together; the Tyrant can only be struck by those who are near him. How is it to be expected that they will venture to attack him, if those citizens who come from the distant parts of the nation shall, after the victory, make them responsible by law for the means they used to save their country? The friends of freedom, who assembled at Paris in the month of August, did their best for general liberty. You must approve or disavow their whole conduct taken together, and cannot, in candour, ex-

amine

amine into partial diforders, which have ever been infeparable from great revolutions. The people of France, who have chofen you as their delegates, have ratified all that happened in bringing about the Revolution. Your being now affembled here is a proof of this: you are not fent to this Convention as Juftices of the Peace, but as Legiflators: you are not delegated to look with inquifitorial eyes into every circumftance of that infurrection which has given liberty to France, but to cement by wife laws that fabric of freedom which France has obtained —Pofterity will pay attention to nothing in thofe events but their facred caufe, and their fublime effect."

Robefpierre denied however having any connection with the flaughter of the prifoners, which, he afferted, was entirely owing to the indignation of the public for M. Montmorin's being acquitted by the Criminal Tribunal, the efcape of the Prince de Poix and

and other people of importance, joined to the emotion occasioned by the taking of Longwy. In this part of his defence he feems to have copied from a pamphlet written by Tallien, entitled, *La Verité fur les Evénemens du 2 Septembre* *, in which is hardly a word of truth.

Robefpierre then added (and it required a moft determined firmnefs of front to add this), " I am told that *one innocent* perfon perifhed among the prifoners, fome fay more ; but one is without doubt too much. Citizens, it is very natural to fhed tears on fuch an accident. I have wept bitterly my-felf for this fatal miftake. I am even forry that the other prifoners, though they all deferved death by the law, fhould have fallen facrifices to the irregular *juftice* of the people. But do not let us exhauft our tears on them; let us keep a few for ten thoufand patriots

* The real Truth refpecting the Events of the 2d of September.

5

facrificed

facrificed by the tyrants around us ; weep for your fellow-citizens, expiring under their roofs, beat down by the cannon of thofe tyrants : let us referve a few tears for the children of our friends maffacred before their eyes, and their infants ftabbed in the arms of their mothers, by the mercenary barbarians who invade our country.——I acknowledge that I greatly fufpect that kind of fenfibility which is only fhewn in lamenting the death of the enemies of freedom. On hearing thofe pathetic lamentations for Lamballe and Montmorin, I think I hear the manifefto of Brunfwick. Ceafe to unfold the bloody robe of the tyrant before the eyes of the people, otherwife I fhall believe you wifh to throw Rome back again into flavery. Admirable humanity ! which tends to enflave the nation, and manifefts a barbarous defire of fhedding the blood of the beft patriots !"

Robefpierre, having finifhed his fpeech, came

came down from the tribune, amidft the applaufe of the galleries, and of part of the Convention.

Louvet took his place, and declared, that he was ready to refute every argument, or fhadow of argument, that had been urged in his defence. The uproar prevented his proceeding: fome called for the printing of Robefpierre's fpeech — others declaimed againft it——there was a great confufion for fome time——the queftion was at laft put, and the printing decreed.

Merlin of Thionville faid, that Roland had difperfed 15,000 copies of Louvet's accufation: he therefore moved, that the fame number of the defence fhould be printed.

When a great debate is expected, thofe members who intend to fpeak give their names to the Secretaries, and the Prefident calls them in the order in which the names have been given. Thirteen members gave their names on this occafion: three declared

they

they intended to fpeak in defence of Robef-pierre, five againft him, and five on the fubject in general. This formidable num-ber of fpeakers, and the known tedioufnefs of fome of them, appeared fo awful, that the Affembly became difpofed to preclude the difcuffion. Barrere propofed to clofe it im-mediately. Barbaroux was fo eager to be heard, that, when refufed as a member, he prefented himfelf at the bar as an accufer. Couthon and other friends of Robefpierre exclaimed againft this, and infifted on the bufinefs being ftifled, by paffing to the order of the day.

Barbaroux retired from the bar, and Louvet attempted to fpeak—he could not be heard.

One member remarked that, if Robefpierre felt himfelf innocent, he would defire that his adverfaries fhould be heard.

Barrere at laft afcended the tribune, and immediately there appeared a difpofition in the

the Affembly to hear him, he was confidered
as an impartial man, who belonged to neither party. His fpeech feemed to have been
prepared : the tendency of it was to fhew
that accufations and recriminations only
ferved to irritate individuals, and injure the
intereft of the public; that the time of the
Convention was due to the nation, and
ought not to be engroffed by deliberations
on the crimes or virtues of one or two
perfons. " It is time," faid he, " to efti-
mate thofe little undertakers of revolutions
at their juft value; it is time to give over
thinking of them and their manœuvres :
for my part, I can fee neither Syllas nor
Cromwells in men of fuch moderate capaci-
ties; and inftead of beftowing any more time
on them and their intrigues, we ought to
turn our attention to the great queftions
which intereft the Republic."

He then moved to pafs to the order of
the day; which, after fome further debate,

was agreed to ; feveral members who had fhewn great eagernefs to proceed with feverity againft Robefpierre immediately after Louvet's accufation, having, during the interval, either been gained by his friends, or influenced by their own reflections, that it was beft to give up a meafure, which, however proper in itfelf, feemed inexpedient in the prefent ftate of men's minds. Some of them think that, if Robefpierre were ordered to be arrefted, it would occafion an infurrection, and that an attempt to punifh the authors of the maffacres would occafion their renewal.

Thus this bufinefs ended in a kind of drawn baitle, which is perhaps the worft end it could have for the intereft of the Republic ; for the parties remain too nearly equal in force, and likely to ruin the common intereft by their mutual animofity.

November 9.

An account of Louvet's fpeech againft

I   Robef-

Robefpierre was given the fame night at the Jacobin Society; it excited great indignation. What is fuppofed to have provoked fome of the members moft, was the propofal to examine into the fource of the maffacres, and to punifh the authors. This, however, could not be avowed; they affected therefore to feel only for the attack on Robefpierre, which was denominated by various fpeakers a confpiracy againft patriotifm itfelf, by a fet of men of ariftocratic principles, who were in the pay of Roland.

The names of Louvet, Rebecqui, and Barbaroux, were ftill on their lifts as members of this Society : it was propofed to expel them, and the vote was carried.

Robefpierre himfelf was not in the Society, but his brother was. He made a fpeech on the occafion, in which he declared, that he had been often afraid, during Louvet's fpeech, that fome members of the Convention would have ftabbed his brother; that

Z 2

he

he had heard one of them fwear that he was determined on it. There was an outcry immediately that he fhould name the horrid wretch ; but the brother of Robefpierre acknowledged that *he did not* know his name.

The Convention's having paffed to the order of the day after hearing Robefpierre's defence, is confidered by his friends as a victory : their triumph on that account is as great as their rage was at his accufation, and they leave no means untried to infpire the citizens with hatred to his enemies. Legendre and Tallien afferted lately in the Convention, that a party of the Marfeillois, with fome dragoons of the Republic, had appeared with drawn fwords in the ftreets, crying, " Off with the head of Marat!" A bas la tête de Marat ! and finging a fong, the burden of which is,

> Robefpierre, Marat, Danton, et tous ceux
> Qui s'en mêleront, à la guillotine, ô gué, &c.

Tallien

Tallien added, that thefe fame *fédérés* had curfed thefe Deputies in a coffee-houfe on the Boulevards, and had cried, " Vive Roland ! point de procès au Roi !"

It is true that fome *fédérés* and dragoons, being in liquor, fung the words above mentioned in the ftreets : but the other article is without foundation, and added on purpofe to throw odium on the Minifter ; for the moft dangerous afperfion that can be thrown out againft any perfon at prefent, is, that he wifhes to prevent the condemnation of the King.——In the mean time, Marat thinks proper to keep himfelf concealed; and an uncommon number of patrols have been remarked in the ftreets, particularly near the dwellings of Robefpierre and Danton, ever fince Louvet's accufation. Some people affert, that Santerre has given orders for this, merely to convey the notion that the lives of thofe great patriots are in danger from the Marfeillois. Whether this is the cafe or not, I

Z 3

cannot

cannot tell; but I do obferve, that thofe who fay they are in danger with them to live, and thofe who infift upon it that they are quite fafe would be very happy to hear of their death.

As for Santerre, whatever his motive may be for ordering thofe patrols, it was well obferved in one of the late journals, that if he had paid half the attention to protect the poor prifoners, that he now fhews to guard Robefpierre, there would have been no maffacres in September.

November 10.

The Girondifts affect to turn the triumph of Robefpierre's friends into ridicule: they infift upon it, that paffing to the order of the day on an accufation of the nature of that brought by Louvet againft Robefpierre, would be the moft fevere and humiliating of all mortifications to a man of good character and common feeling. Whatever truth there may be in that, it is evident that his party

party are in higher spirits, and have gained strength since he made his defence. The friends of Roland certainly expected that Louvet's accusation would have thrown such an odium on Robespierre and all his adherents, as would have gone far to annihilate their influence in the Convention; instead of which, those members who spoke with horror of his conduct before, mention it with caution and moderation now.—— Barrere, by alluding to him with contempt as a dictator, has removed part of the indignation that prevailed against him; and in moving the order of the day he rendered a very important service to Robespierre, and did what was highly agreeable to Danton, who had done every thing he could, from the beginning, to prevent any scrutiny from being made relative either to the conduct of Robespierre, or the murder of the prisoners. I am persuaded, therefore, that Barrere thinks Roland's party, notwith-

Z 4   standing

standing the majority which on some questions they may still have in the Convention,
is on the whole the weaker of the two, and
that he means to attach himself to that of
Danton.

Condorcet, however, judges otherwise;
for his conduct, which some time since was
thought doubtful, now plainly indicates a
decided preference of the Girondists.

M. Condorcet very seldom speaks in the
Conventional Assembly: in a public paper
under his direction he delivers his political
sentiments with more effect than he could
by speaking: in this he has of late directed
such strokes of ridicule against Robespierre,
as no man would do who wished to keep
on good terms with him.

In the Chronique de Paris of yesterday
is the following curious article, which I shall
insert, because it shews M. Condorcet's idea
of a man who has made so much noise in
this country, particularly of late.

" II

" Il y a, dans la Révolution Françaife, des hommes et des événemens qui n'y font un•certain bruit paffager, que parceque la turbulence nationale groffit et gonfle tout, et qu'il y a peu d' obfervateurs tranquilles. Ces petits hommes et ces petits faits ne tiendront que quatre lignes dans l'hiftoire.

" Une de ces circonftances de huit jours, c'eft l'accufation intentée contre Robefpierre, par un homme de beaucoup d'efprit et de talent, mais qui a beaucoup plus d'imagination encore. L'accufateur et l'accufé ont été tous les deux entendus, et tous les deux ont prouvé qu'il étoit impoffible de faire de Robefpierre un Dictateur.

" Tout le monde a remarqué que l'on avoit amené beaucoup de femmes à la féance : les tribunes en contenoient fept ou huit cents, et deux cents hommes tout au plus, et les paffages étoient obftrués de femmes.

" On demande quelquefois pourquoi tant de femmes à la fuite de Robefpierre, chez lui,

à la

à la tribune des Jacobins, aux Cordeliers, à la Convention ? C'eſt que la Révolution Françaiſe eſt une religion, et que Robeſpierre y fait une ſecte : c'eſt un prêtre qui a des dévôtes ; mais il eſt évident que toute ſa puiſſance eſt en quenouille. Robeſpierre prêche, Robeſpierre cenſure ; il eſt furieux, grave, mélancholique, exalté à froid, ſuivi dans ſes penſées et dans ſa conduite ; il tonne contre les riches et les grands ; il vit de peu, et ne connoît pas les beſoins phyſiques ; il n'a qu'une ſeule miſſion, c'eſt de parler, et il parle preſque toujours.——Il refuſe les places où il pourroit ſervir le peuple, et choiſit les poſtes où il croit pouvoir le gouverner ; il paroit quand il peut faire ſenſation, il diſparoit quand la ſcéne eſt remplie par d'autres ; il a tous les caracteres, non pas d'un chef de religion, mais d'un chef de ſecte ; il ſe fait une réputation d'auſtérité qui viſe à la ſainteté ; il monte ſur des bancs ; il parle de Dieu et de la Providence ;

il

il fe dit l'ami des pauvres et des foibles ; il fe fait fuivre par les femmes ; il reçoit gravement leurs adorations et leurs hommages ; il difparoit avant le danger, et l'on ne voit que lui quand le danger eft paffé. Robefpierre eft un prêtre, et ne fera jamais que cela*."

Bazire,

---

* In the French Revolution certain men and certain events have made a temporary noife, only becaufe national turbulence fwells and enlarges every thing, and becaufe there are but few cool obfervers. Thofe little men, and thofe unimportant events will not employ four lines of hiftory.

One of thofe incidents of a week is the accufation of Robefpierre, by a man of great underftanding and talents, but whofe imagination is more extenfive than either. The accufer and the accufed have both been heard, and both have proved that it is impoffible to make a Dictator of Robefpierre.

Every body remarked that a great many women had been brought to the galleries of the National Affembly when Robefpierre made his defence ; among feven or eight hundred which the galleries contain, there were at the moft two hundred men, and all the paffages were filled with women.

November 11.

Bazire, one of the deputies for the department of the Côte d'Or, and ſtrongly attached
to the party of Robeſpierre, made a rep* report
lately

It is ſometimes aſked, how it happens that ſuch numbers of women are continually attending Robeſpierre
wherever he is, at his own houſe, at the galleries of
the Jacobins, of the Cordeliers, and of the Convention?

It is becauſe the French Revolution is conſidered as
a religion, of which Robeſpierre is the leader of a ſect.
He is a prieſt who has devotees, but it is evident that
all his power is *en quenouille**. Robeſpierre preaches,
Robeſpierre cenſures; he is furious, grave, melancholic,
affectedly exalted, followed in his opinions, and in his
conduct; he thunders againſt the rich and the great;
he lives on little, is moderate in his natural appetites;
his chief miſſion is to ſpeak, and he ſpeaks continually.
He refuſes thoſe offices in which he might be of ſervice
to the people, and chooſes thoſe in which he expects
to govern them; he appears where he can make a
figure, and diſappears when the ſcene is occupied by

* This expreſſion is uſed in the ancient French chronicles relative to the
ſucceſſion of the crown, to declare that women are excluded, *la couronne en
France ne tombe jamais en quenouille*. It is now applied in other caſes, and
here implies that Robeſpierre's power is chiefly over women.

others;

lately from the Committee of General Safety on the prefent ftate of the city of Paris.

In this he reprefented Paris as in great tranquillity—with a view, no doubt, to prove that the armed force which has been fo often required for the fecurity of the Convention is not neceffary.

He endeavoured to juftify in a great meafure the maffacres of the prifoners in September, and afterwards made one of the moft improbable affertions that ever was imagined, namely, that fome fervants of a lady of the court (it was imagined he meant Madame

others; he has all the characteriftics, not of the leader of a religion, but of the leader of a fect; he attempts to eftablifh a reputation of aufterity which points to fanctity; he mounts on forms, and talks of God and of Providence; he calls himfelf the friend of the poor and of the weak; he makes himfelf be followed by women, and gravely accepts of their homage and admiration; he retires before danger, and nobody is fo confpicuous as he when the danger is over. Robefpierre is a prieft, and never can be any thing more.

de

de Lamballe) began the affaffinations, with a view to fave their miftrefs. His words are:

" Je dois dire cependant, qu'il eft prouvé que les domeftiques d'une femme célébre à la cour fe déguifèrent en fans-culottes, s'armèrent de piques et de tranchans, fe portèrent aux prifons, et les premiers égorgèrent des prifonniers avec des marques de fureur affez atroces, et des propos affez violens, pour acquérir quelque crédit dans la foule, et fauver par ce moyen leur maitreffe.

" Voilà quels furent les premiers auteurs de ces maffacres !

" Celui des prifonniers d'Orléans s'eft fait particulièrement par des gens attachés au fervice de la Reine, reconnus à la tête de l'attroupement de Verfailles *."

And he added, that as he was in the Committee of Surveillance during thefe fcenes,

---

* I muft declare, however, that it has been proved that

scenes, he knew some important facts relating to them, which it would be improper to reveal at present, but which he would publish perhaps at some futur eperiod†.

Bazire terminated his discourse by blaming

that the servants of a lady of the court disguised themselves like sans-culottes, and, being armed with pikes and other deadly weapons, went to the prisons, and joined in the massacres of the prisoners with such fury as they imagined would gain credit with the populace, and enable them to save their mistress.

Those men were the first authors of the massacres.

As for the massacre of the Orleans prisoners, that was chiefly executed by men in the service of the Queen, who are known to have put themselves at the head of the band of assassins at Versailles.

† When I heard Bazire pronounce this, I considered it as entirely false ; but I have been since assured, from good authority, that some servants of Madame de Lamballe and of the Princesse de Tarente, particularly the valet-de-chambre of the latter, actually joined the mob that surrounded the prison of La Force, and, by adopting the furious language of the mob, endeavoured to gain so much credit as would enable them to save their mistresses. But these servants in no other way joined with the assassins ; and the plan, which certainly was

ing the conduct of thofe who were continually mentioning thefe fcenes in September, which, he infinuated, had been of more
fervice to the confolidating of the Revolution
than at firft fight might appear; and he advifed all parties to forget their former diffe-
rences, wave all idea of accufations on the
account of the fcenes in September, and unite
in mutual confidence and friendfhip for the
public welfare.

While Bazire was in this manner preaching peace and tranquillity, the Affembly was
in an uproar, and the actions and exclamations of the members indicated fury and
deadly hatred.

Some called out for printing and difperfing the report, others oppofed it.

At laft St. André, formerly a calvinift

was formed on the moft generous motives, did fucceed
with regard to Madame de Tarente.
The affertion refpecting the Queen's fervants at Verfailles is without any foundation.

minifter,

minifter, now a deputy for the department
du Lot, one of the moft violent partifans of
Robefpierre, made a fpeech, the tendency of
which was to prove the utility of printing
and difperfing the report; which would fhew
the good people how unanimous the Convention was ; that all former feeds of diffen-
fion were now blafted; that there was no appearance of diftruft or accufation ; and would
remove the error in which the departments
were, in believing there was any need of a
guard for the Convention, where mutual
confidence, freedom of opinion, and tranquillity reigned.

The falfehood of thefe reprefentations,
which were delivered in a canting hypocritical tone, were fo well known to the Affembly, that they produced a laugh ; after which
Buzot faid, " I fhould be glad to fee real union
founded on mutual efteem eftablifhed among
us ; but there can be neither efteem nor
union between the heroes of the 10th of Au-

guft and the affaffins of September; there
can be no union between virtue and vice."

At this phrafe, murmurs were heard.

" I defpife thefe murmurs," refumed Buzot; " I am as little enriched by the maffacres as by the civil lift. I confider Bazire's
report as an apology for the maffacres, and
entirely falfe, and I oppofe its being printed."

Buzot's fpeech prevented Bazire's report
from being printed; but the debate on this
occafion augmented that hatred and animofity which before was too violent between
the two parties. The Girondifts in general
have expreffed fuch a determination of profecuting the authors of the maffacres, and
have fhewn fuch contempt for the underftanding of their opponents, as feems to have
kindled mortal hatred, and an implacable
thirft of revenge in the breafts of the latter.

November 12.

An event has taken place which has raifed
the

the spirits of the Convention, before too lofty, to the highest pitch of exaltation.

I was in the Assembly when letters were received from Dumourier with an account of a victory obtained by him at Jemmappe, which was followed by the surrender of Mons. to the French troops. An aid-de-camp of the General stood at the bar. After the letters had been read, he addressed the Convention to this effect :

" Citizens Representatives,

" I am a soldier, and no orator; but I will inform you of one memorable thing of which I was witness on that day. Baptiste, valet-de-chambre to General Dumourier, rallied some squadrons in the midst of the battle, put himself at their head, led them again to the enemy, and seized, sword in hand, a post of importance."

One of the secretaries then read a passage from a letter of the General to the War Mi-nister, in which he recommends Baptiste,

A a 2

confirms

confirms the account which the aid-de-camp had given of his gallant behaviour in the action, with this additional circumftance—that when Dumourier offered a pecuniary recompenfe to Baptifte, the latter declared that he defired no other reward than that of being permitted to wear the national uniform.

Baptifte was brought to the bar, and in the midft of loud and repeated applaufe it was decreed, " That the citizen Baptifte, who had rallied a regiment of dragoons, and four battalions of volunteers, at the battle near Mons, fhould receive the fraternal kifs of the Prefident of the Convention ; that he fhould be clothed and armed at the expence of the Republic ; and that the Minifter at War fhould authorife General Dumourier to give him a commiffion in his army."

A variety of letters were then read relative to Dumourier's operations before the battle, and until his making himfelf mafter of Mons ; in which the officers who had
most

moſt diſtinguiſhed themſelves were mentioned, many of whom were ſeverely wounded : one officer in particular of the Gendarmerie Nationale, received one-and-forty wounds with ſabres, after having killed ſeven of the enemy with his own hand. Dumourier alſo highly praiſes young General Egalité for his intrepid and ſkilful conduct, and Lieutenant-colonel Larue his aid-de-camp, with whom he ſends the diſpatches.

Monſieur Egalité himſelf, who had never before ventured to ſpeak in the Aſſembly, thought this a favourable moment for him to appear in the tribune : he ſaid that he wiſhed to communicate to the Convention what General Dumourier's modeſty had prevented him from mentioning ; namely, that he had perſonally led on the troops who had taken ſeveral redoubts ſword in hand.

Cambon ſaid, " As many citizens may be

near

near death in the various provinces of France, I require, that extraordinary couriers may be immediately fent to all the departments, that our dying countrymen may enjoy the comfort of being acquainted with the triumph of the Republic before they expire."

Jean Debry propofed that the fixth of November, on which the victory of Jemmappe was gained, fhould be appointed as a day of annual rejoicing.

Lafource oppofed this. " Let us wait," faid he, " until the triumph of Liberty is complete, by the defeat of all the tyrants at war with us ; let us not by partial diftinctions create jealoufy in the other armies of the Republic : remember the fuccefs of Cuftine, and the 20th of September, which does fo much honour to Kellermann."

" Let us decree no national rejoicing," faid Barrere, " when fo many men have perifhed. The ancients, after their victories,
appointed

appointed funeral ceremonies only. Tyrants order rejoicings, although their subjects have perished. Shall republicans imitate the unfeeling joy of tyrants? You ordained with propriety a public rejoicing for the conquest of Savoy, because it cost no blood. Here 4000 men have perished; the Austrians are men; 300* French have likewise perished, and yet you talk of rejoicing!"

But Vergniaud, with a discernment superior to such unnatural and affected sentiments, said, " Undoubtedly men have perished, but the cause of freedom is triumphant. Let us beware of metaphysical abstractions: the love of glory, of our country and of liberty are natural to man; and we, as legislators, ought to cherish those generous sentiments in the hearts of our countrymen.

* It cannot be believed that this account of the killed and wounded is just. Private letters from the army state a much greater number of the French among the slain.

Wretched

Wretched is the philofophy which damps them! If fuch fentiments had not glowed in the breafts of Frenchmen, where fhould we now have been? where our armies? where our victories? One way to keep this facred fire alive, is public rejoicings on fuch occafions as the prefent. Let a national feaft, therefore, be decreed for the fuccefs of all our armies. To a funeral oration's being pronounced on the fame occafion I give my confent; but that a national feaft be decreed, I demand.''

The feaft was decreed.

Baptifte, who had withdrawn immediately after the decree had paffed in his favour, now appeared again at the bar, dreffed in the uniform of the National Guards: he is a handfome and genteel young man. The aid-de-camp, who had remained at the bar while the other was withdrawn, threw his arms around his neck and embraced him
the

the inftant he appeared. The hall refounded with reiterated applaufe.

" Brave citizen," faid the Prefident, " enter within the fanctuary of law; the legiflators are impatient to have one who deferves fo well of his country, feated among them; they are impatient till you receive the recompenfe due to your intrepidity."

Baptifte and Lieutenant-colonel Larue entered into the Affembly; the former was led up to the tribune, where the Prefident faluted him, and prefented him with a fword as the gift of his country. How exquifite muft have been the fenfations of this young man at that moment! the mere idea of them was delightfully affecting. When a gentleman diftinguifhes himfelf by any noble action, he attracts praife and admiration, although we prefume that he has had honourable fentiments inculcated into his mind from his infancy; but when one born in the loweft rank, who has not received the advantage of education, and whofe chief concern

cern

cern for a confiderable part of his life, probably, was to ward off the mifery of want,
and fecure daily bread, difplays a mind fuperior to every fordid confideration, and
capable of the moft generous effort—fuch a
man affuredly is an object of ftill greater admiration.

November 13.

The battalion of Marfeillois and fome
fédérés from other departments, now at Paris, give uneafinefs to the party of Danton
and Robefpierre, in fpite of their influence
in the General Council and in the fuburbs:
they find that Roland is fupported by a majority in the Convention: they fear that this
will continue to be the cafe as long as the
Marfeillois and fédérés remain in the capital.
Their prefence damps the energy of the patriots of St. Antoine, and prevents Danton
from reaping the full benefit of their attachment. Great pains have been taken to render the Marfeillois odious, and excite a jealoufy

loufy of them in the minds of the fuburb
fans-culottes. It was expected that, confid-
ing in their numbers, the latter would have
driven the ftrangers out of Paris; but the very
name of Marfeillois keeps the fuburb patriots
in check; and although the courage of the former has not been put to the proof fince their
arrival at Paris, that of their townfmen, to
which the fans-culottes were witneffes on the
10th of Auguft, impreffes their minds with
an awful refpect for the fmall band from the
fame town, now at the capital.

As it was found difficult to drive them
out of Paris by force, a plan was formed to
get rid of them by policy.

Pache has been War Minifter ever fince
Servan was appointed to the command of
the army on the frontiers next to Spain. He
owed his fituation entirely to the recommendation of Roland; but Danton and Robefpierre have had the addrefs to convince him
that he will have the beft chance of retaining

ing it, by attaching himself to them, and Pache like many others, being more influenced by the favours he expects than by those he has already received, is supposed to have entered into their views.

Custine lately made a requisition of reinforcements for his army : Pache informed the Military Committee of this, and at the same time hinted that it would be proper to send all the fédérés now at Paris, as part of the reinforcement. This plan had the better chance of succeeding, as the first suggestion came from Pache, a man supposed to be the friend of Roland, and as none of the principal members of Danton's party seemed to interest themselves in it.

It was no sooner mentioned in the Convention, however, than Buzot saw through the whole scheme, and unfolded it at full length, as an intrigue to expose the Convention to the most mortifying of all situations, and subject them to the insolence of a

faction

faction which had the direction of the inhabitants of two of the suburbs.

Barbaroux also represented it as an abominable conspiracy, which, if carried into execution, might expose the lives of many of the Deputies, and end in the pillage of Paris : he insisted that the *fédérés* could not be of so much service to their country any where as at the capital, where they were ever ready to join with the most respectable citizens in defence of the legislative body, and for the protection of property.

Cambon being struck with the observations made by Buzot and Barbaroux, and with the recollection of some scenes that had been acted immediately after the tenth of August, ascended the tribune with a precipitation, and raised his voice to a pitch that surprised the Assembly, and commanded their attention. He put them in mind of the tyrannical manner in which the last

Assembly

Aſſembly had been treated by thoſe men
who had the direc ion of the Fauxbourgs,
and by that General Council who on the
tenth of Auguſt had ſeized the government,
and inſulted the Repreſentatives of the Nation. He aſked if they had forgotten that
thoſe uſurpers had ordered the barriers to
be ſhut, the tocſin to be ſounded; that they
had threatened the members; and that when
the Swiſs who had reſigned their arms were
placed within the walls of the Aſſembly,
and under the ſafeguard of the public faith,
a gang of blood-thirſty ruffians had come
to the doors of the Aſſembly-hall, and demanded that they ſhould be delivered up
to their ſavage rage; that thoſe furious
men were on the point of burſting into
the Aſſembly, and dragging them out to
be ſlaughtered; and that they were not
turned from their purpoſe till Lacroix and
ſome other deputies begged of them *upon*
their

7

their knees not to proceed to so horrid an outrage * !

" Would you be again subjected to the same tyranny?" continued Cambon. " If so, order the *fédérés* to leave Paris before an armed force is decreed and established for the protection of the Convention; put yourselves again in the power of those whose despotism you have experienced—the very tyrants who enslaved the Legislative Assembly; and soon, in the midst of anarchy and civil war, the French Cromwell will appear, and tell you that he will be your Protector, and give you peace ; that you stand in need of his popularity and despotism to render you happy. But no ; we will have no Protector, no King, no Triumvirs, no Tribunes, we will be free ; for which purpose, let us secure the independency of the National

* Although I was in the National Assembly when this happened, I was ignorant of it at that time, and therefore it is not inserted in the Journal ; but Lacroix, on the present occasion, confirmed the truth of Cambon's assertion.

Assembly,

Affembly, and on no pretext allow the *fédérés* to be removed from Paris till an organized force is formed from all the departments of the Republic, which can prevent the Reprefentatives from being under the influence of one department only."

Cambon pronounced this with great fire and energy, which feemed to proceed entirely from the ftrong conviction he felt of the importance of his fubject; and which had the greater effect, as his ufual ftyle of fpeaking is uncommonly cold and uninterefting. His manner is awkward, and his countenance dull. He is of a methodical, calculating turn of mind, and confidered as their beft financier. I have frequently heard him fpeak before; and generally when he began, I heard it obferved—" Now we fhall have fomething worth hearing; this is a man of admirable good fenfe;" but I always found his good fenfe fo exceffively tirefome, that I never could

liften

liften to it long. But on this occasion
he commanded all my attention, and
his difcourfe made a ftrong impreffion
on the Affembly; it is believed to have
contributed more than all that had been
previoufly faid, to the failure of the plan
which had been very artfully arranged for
fending away the *fédérés*.

The importance put on fuch a queftion as
this, fhews how very loofe and unfettled the
affairs of this country are; and that in whofe
hands the government is to remain, depends
more on the fans-culottes of two or three of
the fuburbs of Paris, and a handful of determined fellows from Marfeilles, than on
the unbiaffed will of the Conventional Affembly.

Roland and the Girondifts feem to be in
fomething of the fame fituation that the
Court was in a little before the tenth of
Auguft. The party of Danton and Robefpierre are as earneft for the deftruction of

the firft, as ever they were for that of the fecond; and they feem preparing to attempt it by the fame means.

The Court a little before that epoch had the majority of the National Affembly with them—Roland's party have the majority of the Convention with them at prefent.

The Court had a battalion of Swifs and a band of gentlemen to protect them. The Girondifts have a battalion of men from Marfeilles and fome *fédérés* from other departments for their guards : whether thefe laft will prove more fuccefsful than the Swifs is yet to be tried. In the mean time it is evident that each party is more afraid of the other, than either is of all their external enemies.

November 14.

Some days ago I faw the following article in the Chronique de Paris :

" Lorfque Louis a été conduit aù Temple,

il

il n'avoit pas le fols ; le citoyen Pétion lui a prêté deux mille livres. Voici fon billet :

"Le Roi reconnoit avoir reçu de M. Pétion la fomme de 2526 liv. y compris 526 liv. que MM. les Commiffaires de la Munici-palité fe font chargés de remettre à M. Hue, qui les avoit avancés pour le fervice du Roi.

Paris, ce 3 Septembre

1792.   (Signé)   Louis *."

I had the curiofity to fhew this to a per-fon whom I knew to be of Petion's acquaint-ance, afking him, at the fame time, if he believed it.

* When Lewis was conducted to the Temple, he had not a penny; Citizen Petion lent him two thoufand livres—here follows his receipt :

The King acknowledges having received from M. Petion the fum of 2526 livres, 526 livres of which the Commiffioners of the Municipality are to pay to M. Hue, who had advanced them for the fervice of the King.

Paris, this 3d of Sept. 1792.   (Signed)   Louis.

B b 2   He

He faid he could not tell whether it was true or not, but that he would inform me of fomething to the fame purpofe, which I might depend upon was true. He then told me, that, having fome bufinefs with the Mayor, he had waited on him on the 31ft of Auguft; that while he was with him a letter was delivered to the Mayor, which having read he threw carelefsly on the table, and faid to the fervant, *Very well.* He then turned to my acquaintance, and converfed with him on the bufinefs which had brought him there ; and afterwards, as he happened to have his eyes fixed on the letter, which lay open on the table, the Mayor faid, You may read it, if you pleafe. —It was from the King, and what follows is a literal tranflation :

" The King would be glad that Mr. Petion gave an anfwer to the letter written to him five days ago--this is the laft day of the month, and he has received no money to defray his ex- pences :

pences : the King will be obliged to Mr. Petion, if he will let him know what he is to
receive, and fend him an anfwer to-day.

(Signed)   Louis."

Counterfigned by two other names.

The patience with which the King has
endured every hardfhip which preffed on
himfelf alone, gives reafon to believe that
he has been prevailed on to write on this
fubject from a confideration for others ; it
is probable that the firft letter was written
by fome attendant, and that this not having
been anfwered, the King has been under
the neceffity of writing the fecond himfelf.

That either was neceffary is abominable,
and betrays real meannefs of fpirit in thofe
who are affecting grandeur of mind and a
manner of thinking fuperior to vulgar prejudices.

November 15.

It is difficult to be informed of the treatment which the Royal Family are subjected to in the Temple. Many circumstances of a public nature, however, indicate, that it is indelicate and harsh in the highest degree.

A Committee appointed by the General Council of the Commune of Paris sit there constantly, and, accordingto directions given, regulate every thing respecting the Royal Family.

As they have been more closely confined of late, and not seen by the Guards which do duty at the Temple, a report was spread that the King had escaped, although the same number of men as usual continued to mount guard: it was said, that this was done merely to deceive the people, till some excuse could be thought of to avert the public indignation from the Committee for their negligence or treachery. Full of this idea, a body of men from the Sections of Paris, who were on guard at the Temple, insisted upon seeing the King and Royal Family,

that

that they might be fatisfied themfelves, and enabled to fatisfy their fellow citizens, that the King actually was in the Temple, and that they were not guarding empty apartments, as was ftrongly fufpected.

The Municipal Officers refufed to comply with this demand; the guard infifted, and threatened to force their way into the apartments. Santerre was fent for: he expoftulated with thofe mutineers, and affured them, that all the family were fafe in the prifon. This at length fatisfied the volunteers from the Sections; but the cannoniers perfifted in their demand, and Santerre was under the neceffity of appealing to the multitude affembled at the gates of the Temple, who in character of Peuple Souverain decided againft the cannoniers, and they were obliged to give up the point.

The Municipal Committee, to whofe care the Royal Family are peculiarly entrufted, have made frequent reports to the General

B b 4 Council,

Council, in which they pretend, that there feems to be a plan of delivering them from the Temple—and the fmalleft accidental circumftances which occur are confidered as fignals from without, which are fully underftood by the prifoners within.——Mention has been made in thofe returns to the General Council, of a man's being heard playing on a flute at midnight, of the fongs that are fung in the ftreet, the expreffions ufed by the common criers that pafs; and it is infinuated that by all thefe, more is meant than meets the ear. Some time fince, the Committee reprefented, that when the family walked in the garden, or appeared on the balcony, a number of perfons came to the windows of the adjacent houfes, and made fignals, which feemed to be underftood by the prifoners.——One Member of the Council propofed, that, to prevent this laft, the King and Royal Family fhould never be permitted to come into the open air, till it

was

was fo dark that they could not to be feen; another propofed to raife the walls in the garden, and make fuch alterations in the Temple as would effectually prevent the prifoners from being feen by any perfon without.

Both thefe ingenious propofals were rendered unneceffary by an order from the Council, that all the family fhould be prevented from walking in the garden, or even appearing at the windows of their apartments; and when they affemble at the hour of dinner, which is always in the prefence of one or two Municipal Officers, every look, word, or gefture of the unhappy prifoners is obferved, interpreted, and frequently reported to the Council General as having a myfterious meaning.

Among other circumftances equally unimportant, it was mentioned in one of the memorials of the Committee, made a confiderable time ago, that the King continued to wear his ftar and ribbons, which raifed the

petulance

petulance of the author of a daily journal,
who, on the subject of this memorial, expref-
fes himfelf in the following indecent terms :
" Si Louis avoit le fens commun, il auroit
quitté lui-même toutes ces chamarrures féo-
dales : il feroit aujourd'hui Republicain, c'eft
à-dire, plus qu'un Roi; car un Roi n'eft que
le premier efclave de fon empire*."——He then
adds, that, fo far from ftripping him of them,
it would be better, provided the nation allows
him to live, to condemn him to wear thofe
fhameful emblems for life ; and propofes
that all who fhould be convicted of certain
crimes fhould be fentenced to the fame punifhment——and concludes : " Qu'on les ex-
pofât aux regards du peuple bardés de cor-
dons, et l'habit garni d'aigles, de pigeons,
d'éléphans, de moutons: les Romains ne

---

* If Lewis had common fenfe, he would of his own
accord have thrown afide all thofe feudal trappings ;
he would by this time have become a Republican,
which is being greater than a King ; for a King is only
the higheft flave in his own dominions.

dépouilloient

dépouilloient pas les rois vaincus des attributs de la royauté; ils les en revêtoient au contraire avec grand foin, et cela pour cracher deſſus*."

The Council General however ſaw this in a different point of view. Eager to diſplay a contempt for ariſtocracy, and conſtantly aſſerting that the people in general deteſt monarchy, they cannot help often betraying a dread of the firſt, and a ſuſpicion that the nation ſtill retains its old affection for the ſecond——they ſeem afraid of every thing that puts them in mind of either. Manuel was ordered to go to the Temple, and announce to the King, that as royalty was aboliſhed, there was no propriety in his wearing his former ornaments any longer. The dialogue which paſſed between the

* Let them be expoſed to the view of the people covered with ribbons, and their clothes trimmed with pigeons, elephants, eagles and ſheep ; the Romans did not ſtrip the vanquiſhéd Kings of the emblems of royalty. On the contrary, they carefully dreſſed them in them for the purpoſe of ſpitting on them.

King

King and Manuel on this occafion, has been publifhed in fome of the Journals, probably by Manuel himfelf : even from this account it appears, that the King received this meffage with that manly indifference, and undif-turbed refignation, which he has fhewn fince the beginning of his misfortunes. I have always heard that Lewis XVI. never was much affected by the magnificence of royalty, even when he poffeffed it in its higheft fplendour ; he feems now to be as little affected by the lofs of it ; and the malice of his enemies, difplayed in thefe paltry inftances, inftead of throwing difgrace on the Monarch, renders his good qualities more confpicuous.

November 16.

In a work publifhed fome years ago*, I endeavoured to give an idea of that enthu-fiaftic attachment and affection, which the

* View of Society and Manners in France, &c.

French

French of thofe days had, or pretended to have, for their Monarchs.

They fpoke of loyalty as a quality of the mind, like generofity or courage : they feemed proud to think that they poffeffed this quality, if not exclufively, at leaft in a higher degree than any other people ; and every Frenchman wifhed to be thought loyal, as every man wifhes to be thought generous or brave. They feemed even to confider it as a virtue, which ought to be cherifhed in the breaft of the fubject, independent of the good qualities, and in fpite of the bad qualities, of the Sovereign; and they were vain to point out to ftrangers how far their countrymen furpaffed all others in the exercife of it.

An Englifh officer, after having paffed fome days at Verfailles during the reign of Lewis XV. fupped in company with feveral French Gentlemen on the evening that he returned to Paris. The converfation turned

on

on the great attachment and affection of the
French nation to their monarchs ; and one of
the company underftanding that the court
had been greatly crowded, and that many
people of diftinction from Paris had been at
Verfailles during the officer's refidence there,
afked him if he had not been furprifed at
feeing fuch marks of loyalty.

"No," replied the officer, "I fhould have
been furprifed if I had not feen them."

"To be fure," refumed the Frenchman,
"the King is the moft amiable man in the
world, and it is quite natural that all the
world fhould love him."

"That is indifputable," faid the officer ;
"but I was thinking of other reafons which
thofe I faw fo affiduoufly paying their court
to the King might have, and which are fufficient to account for all the zeal and attachment they difplayed."

The other affected not to underftand
him,

him, and asked with great politeness what other reasons they could have.

" Why," replied the officer, " has not the King governments, and regiments, and bishopricks, and many other very beneficial things to bestow ? I should imagine that this consideration might render the King an object of great attention, and produce many marks of zealous attachment to his person, even although he were not quite the most amiable man in the world, as all the world allow him to be."

" Be assured, Sir," rejoined the Frenchman, " that there is no people on earth who have such a veneration for their Kings, and so much disinterested loyalty as the French."

" Forgive me," said the officer, " I know a people who can dispute those qualifications with them, and whose courtiers give stronger proofs of veneration and loyalty to their Prince than even those of Versailles."

" What people ?"

" The

" The fubjects of the Emperor of Mo-
rocco," replied the officer : " there is a monarch for you, gentlemen, who hardly ever
fpeaks to his fubjects *qu'à coup de fabre*, and
yet they venerate him in the moft aftonifhing manner. When I was in garrifon at
Gibraltar, I paffed over to his dominions,
and had the honour of fpending fome time
at his court at Fez :—one of this beloved monarch's morning amufements, is fhooting ar-
rows at his fubjects ; when he chances to
mifs, which feldom happens, for by frequent
practice he is an excellent markfman, the
perfon at whom it is directed takes up the
arrow, and with all the zeal of the moft devoted courtier prefents it on his knee to
the Emperor.

" On fome occafions, he does his fubjects
the honour of cutting off their heads with
his own hands, and is much praifed by the
courtiers around for his dexterity ; in fhort,
they difplay every mark of attachment to his
perfon

perſon, and may be ſaid with truth to love their ſovereign to diſtraction.——This is, gentlemen, what I call diſintereſted loyalty." But now the French, at leaſt all of them who remain in France, are as ſolicitous to declare that they never poſſeſſed this enthuſiaſtic loyalty, as formerly they were anxious to have it thought they did ; and as they began to diſavow this principle during the reign of the moſt mild and moſt equitable monarch they ever had, as ſoon as his power began to be abridged, and continued to profeſs the moſt ardent loyalty towards the moſt oppreſſive and tyrannical of his predeceſſors while they retained their power, it is pretty clear on what that boaſted loyalty was founded.

But as the men ſhew an abject and ſlaviſh diſpoſition, who affect attachment and veneration for a fooliſh or wicked prince, ſo thoſe on the other hand betray a malevolent and odious character, who are deficient in reſpect and gratitude to a mild and equitable

VOL. II.   C c   monarch,

monarch, who through the whole of his reign has manifefted a love of juftice, and an equal regard for the rights of his fubjects and for his own prerogative.

The loyalty of a man of fenfe and fpirit arifes from a due refpect for the firft magif-trate in the ftate, whofe lawful authority he is ready to fupport for the good of the com-munity, independent of every other confide-ration. To this fentiment of loyalty to the monarch as firft magiftrate, efteem for per-fonal good qualities, if they exift, and gra-titude for favours received, will be added in every well formed mind. But thefe fenti-ments do not exclufively belong to loyalty, but are felt for every perfon of our ac-quaintance who poffeffes great or amiable qualities, and from whom we have received favours. But the oftentatious indications of loyalty which are fometimes exhibited, in the vulgar, generally proceed from a mere love of noife; in fome of fuperior rank, from

the

the desire of being looked on as the particular friends of the royal family, uncon-
nected with any idea of their good qualities;
and in many it is founded on a lucrative office in possession or in expectation.

November 17.

At the beginning of the revolution, when
a veneration for the christian religion was
still pretty general in the minds of the people, a democratic abbé, with a view to inspire
his audience with a detestation for aristocrates, assured them in his sermon that Jesus
Christ was crucified by the aristocrates of Je-
rusalem.

Some people imagine that the same assertion made in a sermon now, would not produce the same horror in the minds of a
French audience that it did three years ago,
being of opinion that religious impressions
are much weaker now than they were then.

One distinguishing doctrine of christia-

nity,

nity, namely, the forgiveneſs of injuries, ſeems to be greatly exploded, and conſidered rather as the effect of weakneſs than magnanimity: revenge, on the contrary, is applauded as a virtue, and proclaimed as a duty, and the people are ſtimulated to vengeance, on every real or ſuppoſed injury.

Thoſe who excite the populace againſt the King, tell them, that his execution is neceſſary, to *avenge* the murder of their brethren in the Carouſel on the 10th of Auguſt; and that the affairs of the nation cannot proſper, until their ſlaughter is amply *revenged.*

It was mentioned in the National Aſſembly, that ſome of thoſe patriots, while they lay expiring on the ground, had had the conſolation of ſeeing the Swiſs cut in pieces, before their eyes were entirely cloſed.

The new levies are aſſured by way of encouragement, that in caſe they ſhould be killed in battle, they may make themſelves

perfectly

perfectly eafy, for that their deaths fhall be
fully revenged.

A poor woman was weeping bitterly for
the death of her fon, killed at the battle of
Valmy: the foldier who had brought her
the news endeavoured to comfort her, faying, " Confolez-vous, Marguerite, je vous
reponds qu'il a été bien vengé *."

At the civic feaft, which took place on
account of the conqueft of Savoy, a new
ftanza was added to the hymn of the Marfeillois, and was fung by a company of
young boys on that occafion:

> Nous entrerons dans la carrière,
> Quand nos aînés n'y feront plus:
> Nous y trouverons leur pouffière
> Et la trace de leurs vertus.
> Bien moins jaloux de leur furvivre,
> Que de partager leur cercueil,
> Nous aurons le fublime orgueil
> De les *venger* ou de les fuivre.
> Aux armes, Citoyens!—Formez vos bataillons!
> Marchez!—Qu'un fang impur abreuve nos fillons.

* Comfort yourfelf, Margaret, for I can affure you
that he was well avenged.

I was

I was at the Convention lately, when a young officer belonging to the regiment of Beaurepaire appeared at the bar.

He had been at Verdun when the Colonel ſhot himſelf : he ſpoke highly of that offi-cer, by whom, he ſaid, the garriſon had been animated to ſuch a pitch of enthuſiaſm, that they had reſolved to be buried in the ruins of the town, rather than ſurrender : he gave an affecting account of the indignation and grief of the ſoldiers, when they found that the Magiſtrates had capitulated, and were told of the cataſtrophe of their Colonel : he ſaid, he was deputed from his regiment, to demand vengeance on the traitors who had betrayed Verdun to the enemy, and driven their Commander to deſpair. He read the names of thoſe he accuſed, conſiſting of the Magiſtrates of Verdun, and ſome of the Field Officers of the National Guards.

This young officer was handſome, and of a genteel figure : he ſpoke with fluency and grace;

grace; and what interefted the audience greatly in his favour, was, that a letter from Dumourier was read, which informed the Convention, that the regiment to which he belonged had behaved remarkably well againft the Pruffians; and that the officer who brought the accufation had diftinguifhed himfelf in a very gallant manner.

Some of the Members began to talk of avenging the death of Beaurepaire on the heads of the perfons accufed by the officer; and the Affembly feemed fo much enraged againft them, that I was afraid of their decreeing fomething very violent inftantly—but one Deputy, who had preferved coolnefs in the midft of all this emotion, fhewed the impropriety of coming to any refolution againft the accufed citizens, in the prefent ftate of their minds, and begged that the accufation might be referred to the confideration of a Committee.

This meafure was at laft adopted.

November

November 18,

There are eight or ten theatres for dramatic entertainments of one kind or other at prefent in Paris: moft of them are open four times a week. The pieces reprefented are generally new, and adapted to the fpirit of the times, and to fortify the minds of the audience in fentiments favourable to the Revolution. Kings and Princes are reprefented as rapacious, voluptuous, and tyrannical; Nobility as frivolous and unfeeling, fawning to the fovereign, and infolent to their fellow fubjects; Priefts as hypocritical, artful, and wicked. To infpire a hatred to monarchical government, and a love of republicanifm, is one great object of almoft every new piece —even in thofe comic pieces whofe plots turn on an amorous intrigue, or fome object equally remote from politics or forms of government, fentiments of the fame tendency occur, and however awkwardly introduced

duced they are fure of being received with applaufe. A ftrict adherence to the unities of time and place, and other critical rules, for which the French theatre was formerly diftinguifhed, is now little attended to.

The dramatic writers hate fetters, as much as the Sans Culottes, and fometimes defpife decorum as much.

I was lately at the Theatre de la Variété; the piece was entitled *La Mort de Beaurepaire.*

The hero, on hearing that the Magiftrates of Verdun have delivered a gate of the town to the Pruffians, fhoots himfelf on the ftage. The Duke of Brunfwick, furrounded by his guards, enters, and finds a French foldier lamenting over the body of his commander: while the Duke is queftioning him, another French foldier is brought in, who has juft fhot a Pruffian officer in the ftreet. The Duke afks, who bribed him to commit this affaffination? The foldier replies,

3   " That

" That he needed no bribe to determine him to deftroy the enemies of his country; that he had no part in the infamous capitulation, by which the Pruffians were permitted to enter Verdun; that he had miftaken the officer he had killed, for the Duke himfelf, and highly regrets the miftake."—— The foldier in his turn demands of the Duke, " who had bribed *him* to invade a country which had renounced conqueft, and to make war on a people, who wifhed only to be governed by laws of their own making, under a form agreeable to their own tafte ?" The Duke makes fome reply to this, and the difpute becomes warm : but although the foldier is reprefented as having by much the beft of the argument, he is ordered to immediate execution. It appears foon after, that on his way he has leaped over a bridge, and by that means efcaped a more painful death. The firft foldier concludes the piece, by affuring the Duke, that he will make nothing

of

of his prefent enterprife, which he had beft relinquifh in time; for *the fhorteft follies are the fooneft remedied.*

Many little dramas are daily exhibited on the Boulevards, to the fame tendency, and ballads are fung in the ftreets and public walks: one is entitled, Comparaifon du Régime Ancien avec le Nouveau; the laft ftanza is as follows:

> Jadis, quand pour l'armée un fils partoit,
> Sa bonne mere tout auffi-tot pleuroit,
> Et le retirer elle ne pouvoit;
>   C'étoit régime defpote.
>
> Aujourd'hui, l'on voit toutes les mamans
> Faire le paquet, armer leurs enfans,
> Et les envoyer fervir dans les camps;
>   Vive un régime patriote.

The two following ftanzas are from another, which is much relifhed by the people:

> Savez-vous la belle hiftoire
> De ces fameux Pruffiens?
> Ils marchoient à la victoire
> Avec les Autrichiens;
> Au lieu de palme de gloire
> Ils ont cueilli des—raifins.

Le Grand Fredéric s'échappe,
Prenant le plus court chemin;
Mais Dumourier le ratrappe,
Et lui chante ce refrain :
N'allez plus mordre à la grappe
Dans la vigne du voisin.

A writer in one of the Journals observes, that small springs are capable of moving great machines; and that popular ballads have had considerable influence in the revolutions of nations;—he adds, " La chanson des Marseillois éclaire, inspire, et réjouit à la fois. Je conclus à ce que l'on attache quatre chanteurs à chacune de nos armées. Faire notre Révolution en chantant, est un moyen presque sûr de l'empêcher de finir par de chansons *."

What truth is in this observation, is not worth examining; but, if the termina-

* The Song of the Marseillois at once enlightens, inspires, and rejoices. I therefore move, that four good Singers shall be appointed to each of our armies. To accomplish our Revolution with gaiety and good humour, is one sure way to prevent its ending in a song.

tion

tion of the French Revolution depends on the good humour and humanity with which it has of late been carried on, it will have a difmal ending.

Marat has kept himfelf concealed for fome time, but his Journal is continued as ufual. He dates it from a fubterraneous habitation (d'un Souterrain); in which, he fays, he is obliged to bury himfelf alive, that he may be fafe from the daggers of affaffins. And why am I obliged to hide myfelf? he afks of the people, to whom his Journal is addreffed—" O peuple, que je chéris, que je porte dans mon cœur, pour avoir pris votre défence, pour avoir été votre ami, &c. &c.*"

It feems extraordinary, to addrefs the mob of Paris in the ftyle of a lover to his miftrefs; but it is ftill more extraordinary, that a mob, who have given fuch proofs of fe-

* O people, whom I love, who are always neareft my heart, for having always been your friend and advocate.

rocity,

rocity, fhould be deluded by the language which feduces a fond girl.

The general turn of his Journal, however, is not in the fame tender ftrain, even fince he dated from below ground. The manner in which he vindicates himfelf from the accufation of being fanguinary, will be thought curious.

" Le grand cheval de bataille de mes détracteurs eft de me peindre comme un homme fanguinaire, qui eft fans ceffe à prêcher le meurtre et l'affaffinat. Mais je les défie de faire voir autre chofe dans mes écrits, fi ce n'eft pas que j'ai demontré la néceffité d'abatre quelques centaines de têtes criminelles pour conferver trois cent mille têtes innocentes*."

In his Journal of this day, is the following paragraph: " Je ne croirai pas à la Re-

---

* The great aim of my detractors is to paint me as a fanguinary man, who is always preaching murder and affaffination. But I defy them to point out any thing in my writings, unlefs that I have demonftrated the neceffity of cutting off a few hundred criminal heads to preferve three hundred thoufand innocent ones.

publique, que lorſque la tête de Louis Capet ne fera plus ſur ſes épaules, et que les ſoldats de la liberté ne feront plus menés à la boucherie par des géneraux courtiſans *."

In the midſt of all the ſucceſs of Dumourier, this man exclaims againſt him for having permitted the Pruſſians to eſcape out of France ; and he writes in the ſame ſtyle of the other Generals, whom he deſcribes as men of ariſtocratic principles, and enemies of the people ; and adds whatever he thinks moſt likely to excite the populace againſt Louvet, Barbaroux, Genſonnet, Guadet, Buzot, Vergniaud, Kerſaint, and all the faction Rol-Briſſotine, as he denominates them. But what may lead to more extenſive miſchief than all the reſt is the drift of the motto of his Journal: " Ut redeat miſeris, abeat fortuna ſuperbis:" that is to ſay, " Take the money from the rich,

* I ſhall never think the Republic eſtabliſhed, until the head of Lewis Capet is no longer on his ſhoulders, and until the ſoldiers of Liberty ſhall be no longer led to ſlaughter by generals who are courtiers.

that

that it may be reſtored to the poor." This plainly prompts to univerſal pillage : and perhaps the wickedneſs of faction never was puſhed farther than in the protection given to ſuch an incendiary as this Marat; for, notwithſtanding all the public diſavowals that have been made, that he is powerfully protected ſeems to me evident. ——He dates from a cellar, but every body believes he is now living at his eaſe in very good quarters, above ground ; and nobody can doubt, but that it would be a very eaſy matter to diſcover them, if it were thought ſafe and prudent to ſeize the man. But they cannot even ſuppreſs his Journal ; it is cried every night in the Palais Royal: a little boy came bawling after me with it, as I returned home a few nights ago, " Journal par Marat, l'Ami du Peuple !——combien voulez-vous, Citoyen Anglais? Journal par l'Ami du Peuple!——Ah, c'eſt bien intéreſſant aujourd'hui——vous prendrez deux ou trois, n'eſt-il pas vrai, mon cher Milor ?"

November

November 20.

It is moſt unpleaſant to obſerve how little ſenſation the cruel ſtate in which the Royal Family is occaſions in Paris, and how ſmall a part of general converſation it occupies: as for the loweſt mob, they never mention them but with ſome foul epithet of abuſe: this does not ſurpriſe me, becauſe they are either hired for the purpoſe, or, like all mobs, join in the cry that is ſuggeſted, and preſs blindly on, according to the impulſe given by others; I ſpeak not therefore of them, but of the other ranks of ſociety.

Whatever people's ſentiments are with regard to the Revolution, whether they are what is here called Ariſtocrates, or Democrates, one ſhould think that ſo ſevere a reverſe of fortune, and one ſo unexampled in the political ſtate in which Europe has ſo long been, would occaſion more general ſympathy. That this ſympathy ſhould not be difplayed in public, is eafily accounted for: but even in private and confidential converfations, where no referve is ufed on topics equally dangerous, the misfortunes of the Royal Family feem to be felt in a very flight manner, by fome who might have been expected to feel them moft feverely.

What an affecting contraft does this indifference and neglect make with the obfequious attention, almoft to adoration, which was paid to this family by the whole French nation ; with the emulation and unwearied affiduity of all ranks to captivate their notice and gratify their wifhes ; with the proteftations of efteem, refpect, and affection they have been accuftomed to hear from their childhood !

All thofe external marks of veneration were accompanied, no doubt, with the ftrongeft affurances of their being the offspring of genuine fentimental preference, beftowed on perfonal

4

fonal virtues, uninfluenced by any expectation from their power, and purified from
all felfifh confiderations.

The cannon of St. Antoine, and the fabres of the Marfeillois, exterminated the
virtues of the King on the 10th of Auguft;
and every day of his imprifonment in the
Temple feems to have added fome new article to a lift of vices of which he is now
accufed, and which were never heard of before.——I never fee a man in the Conventional Affembly, or elfewhere, eager to diftinguifh himfelf by violent fallies againft
the King and his unfortunate family, but
I imagine I behold a wretch who would be
the moft abject of his courtiers, if, by an
unexpected turn of affairs, the Monarch
were re-eftablifhed on the throne. Nor
did I ever know any men, who were diftinguifhed for adopting the prejudices,
abetting the caprices, and affecting wonderful attachment to the perfons of Princes in

the

the fulnefs of power, without fufpecting that they would be the moft turbulent demagogues, and the bittereft enemies of thofe very Princes, if by any accident they fhould ever be in the fame fituation with the Royal Family of France.

November 21.

When a man, who, from his fituation in life, or from the commiffion he enjoys, is guarded from retaliation, treats another, who is in his power, with infolence or cruelty, it naturally excites feelings of indignation and contempt. When an inferior behaves with infolence to his fuperior, a blackguard, for example, to a gentleman in the ftreets of London, it raifes difguft, but not contempt as in the former inftance, becaufe the blackguard *may* run fome rifk—he is not abfolutely fure of impunity.

It was natural to fuppofe, that the imprudent introduction of the term *égalité* would produce

produce an univerfal infolence among the lower claffes of people in France towards their fuperiors: and I am ftill convinced it will in procefs of time be the cafe; but I confefs I have not hitherto remarked any difagreeable inftance of this nature. No perfon, indeed, of whatever rank, is allowed to drefs his footmen in livery, but every one is allowed to have as many footmen as he pleafes; and when L. L's carriage was driving, a day or two fince, in at the gate of the Louvre, it was ftopped by the fentinel, who had obferved that the hammercloth had fringes of a different colour; and informed his Lordfhip, that fuch a kind of diftinction was no longer permitted in France, being contrary to that égalité which every Frenchman had fworn to. The coachman had been ordered never to ufe any but a plain cloth; but, having a fringed one in his poffeffion of which he was very vain, he had ventured to

adorn

adorn his coach-box with it on this unfortunate day. As the poor fellow was taking it off with a very mortified air, the valet de place reproached him for having put it on; which the sentinel overhearing, said angrily to the coachman, "Il sied bien à un gueux comme toi d'être aristocrate *."

A few days since I saw a man dressed in the uniform of a General Officer come up to a poor fellow, who, with a pike in his hand, stood sentinel at a gate, and, addressing him by the name of "*Citoyen Soldat*," asked him the way to a particular street.

The pike-men were formerly considered as of a rank inferior to the National Guards, who are armed with muskets: but of late they are put on a footing, and do duty together; but still it might have been expected, that this gentleman's rank in the army would have commanded the strongest marks of respect from a common soldier,

* It well becomes a beggar like you to give yourself the airs of an aristocrate.

if

if his laced coat failed to produce them in a poor fellow almoſt in rags.

" Tenez, mon camarade," ſaid the pike-man: " you will firſt turn to the right, and then walk ſtraight on until, &c."

The Officer having heard the directions returned thanks to the Citoyen Soldat, and, moving his hat, walked away.

November 22.

Some time ſince I was walking with a man, who has the rank of Lieutenant Colo-nel in the National Guards :—ſeven or eight men belonging to his battalion came up to him with a complaint ; they pretended that injuſtice had been done to their company, in the arrangements reſpecting the duty ; and they alſo complained of ſome other grievances :—the perſon they had choſen to ſpeak for them ſeemed to be of rather a fiery temper ; and he ſtated the grievances with more heat and leſs ceremony than I had been accuſtomed to ſee ſoldiers uſe when

D d 4

addreſſing

addreffing their officers.——The Lieutenant
Colonel on his part heard the complaints
with attention and coolnefs; only faying,
from time to time, as the orator proceeded,
" Tu as raifon, tu as raifon, mon ami"——and
gave no other interruption or anfwer, till
he had quite finifhed. The officer then began with the phrafe he had already ufed fo
frequently, " Tu as raifon, mon ami, cela eft
clair; but there is one point in which you
are a little miftaken."

This one point turned out to be the
whole affair in queftion. The officer proceeded to put the bufinefs in a very different
light; fometimes addreffing himfelf to the
orator, and fometimes to others of the circle; and in a fhort time convinced the
whole, that what they afked was unreafonable, and difmiffed them fatisfied, and repeating " *Le Colonel a raifon.*"

When they were gone, he faid to me fmiling, " This is my conftant method, when

they

they come with an unreasonable request :. I hear them with patience; and after I have acknowledged two or three times that they are in the right, they allow me quietly to convince them that they are in the wrong: —whereas, were I to tell them at once they were in the wrong, they would think me unjust; but not that they themselves were unreasonable.

"When their complaint is well found-ed," continued the officer, "and in my power to remedy, there is no need of rea-foning; I get the grievance redressed as soon as possible, and am happy it is in my power."

"All this," said I, "will do very well in civil life; but I should hardly think it would answer in the military, where sub-ordination and implicit obedience are so necessary."

To this the officer answered, "That men who clothe themselves and serve without

pay,

pay, cannot be treated with the same severity as soldiers who are paid and clothed
by the public: it is rather to be wondered
at, that so many poor tradesmen and day-
labourers all over France submit to lose the
profit of their work for one day, and sometimes two, in a week, bear so much fatigue,
and perform the military duty required of
them, so cheerfully as they do. When
those men are ordered to the frontiers, and
obliged to perform the duty of soldiers
every day, they then receive pay, and are
subjected to a severer discipline."

" I cannot help thinking," resumed I,
" that a General, who commands soldiers
who are taught to obey without thinking,
has a great advantage over one whose army
must be reasoned with. The Duke of Brunswick has only to issue his orders, and he is
as sure of being obeyed, as I am certain this
watch will strike when I press the spring,"
continued I, making the watch, which I
held

held in my hand, repeat the hour; " whereas I underſtand, that Dumourier is often
obliged to convince his ſoldiers *qu'il a
raiſon,* before they will execute his orders."

" The temper and national character of
the ſoldiers muſt be conſidered by the General who commands them," reſumed the
officer: " Frenchmen would be diſpirited,
rendered good for nothing, or would deſert,
if they were treated with as much ſeverity
as German and Ruſſian ſoldiers. I am of
opinion, that the introduction of the puniſhment of the cane (coups des batons)
was one reaſon of the defection of the army
at the beginning of the revolution. I know
that many regiments were quite diſguſted
with that practice. The French and Germans are as different animals as greyhounds
and fox-hounds ; they accompliſh the de-
ſtruction of their enemy by different en-
dowments, and require a very different
treatment."

" I do

" I do not wish to depreciate the merit of Dumourier," continued the officer; " but I must observe, that the disadvantage you mention might be compensated by that enthusiasm, which in the present emergency acts on the minds of French soldiers with an energy beyond the force of any mechanical spring. Besides, you must recollect, that it has always been the custom in France, to enlist soldiers for three or four years only; for which reason, great numbers of young tradesmen and labourers choose to go and serve during that time in the army; after which, they return to their trades and villages, where their adventures in the army are a source of conversation to themselves, and of admiration to their wives and children for the rest of their lives: and when the whole country is called forth as on the present occasion, there are among the recruits of every department a considerable number of old soldiers, who not only instruct the

the new men in the essential parts of the exercise, but also give them an example of regularity and obedience; so that the hasty levies with which Dumourier was reinforced at St. Menehould were not entirely raw recruits.

November 23.

In keeping this journal, my object was not to confine myself to the public events which take place in this country at this critical period, but to give also some idea of the effect which these events have on the manners and sentiments of the people, which I imagine is better done by relating facts and incidents, than by general description. With this view, I mention the following which occurred to an English gentleman and lady of my acquaintance: Hearing there was to be a debate on an important subject in the Convention, the gentleman hired two persons to go early and keep places for them in the front of the gal-

lery

lery oppofite to the Prefident. The gentleman and lady went themfelves an hour after. A fentinel who was placed within the
gallery, told them there was no room. They
faid that two perfons in the front would
yield them their places, and the two perfons
rofe accordingly and offered to withdraw ;
but the people in the gallery objected to the
new comers taking their places, which, they
faid, naturally belonged to thofe who fat
neareft. The Englifhman appealed to the
fentinel : " Ma foi, citoyen," faid the fentinel, " l'affaire eft un peu épineufe ; you muft
let it be judged by the company."

This is the ufual way on all difputes in
the galleries ; a jury is immediately formed
of the people neareft, who decide by the
plurality of votes, and their verdict is always
obeyed.

The Englifhman then afked of the company, whether the two perfons whom he
had fent to the gallery had not a right to
keep

keep their places. It was unanimoufly agreed that they had ; but that, if they retired, the two who fat neareft them had a right to the places they left ; and fo every couple might advance in fucceffion, but thofe who came laft muft be content with the worft places, till new vacancies occurred. "But," refumed the Englifhman, " I have paid thofe two men for keeping places for this lady and me, and that we fhould have them is founded on juftice."——" Mais non pas fur l'*égalité*," faid one of the jury ; to which opinion all the reft adhered.

" You fee, citizen," refumed the fentinel, " that the caufe is given againft you, and there is no more to be faid."

It is not furprifing that this idea of equality is very favourably received by the loweft order of fociety, particularly according to the fenfe in which many of them underftand it; and I make no manner of doubt but that there are men of acknowledged dulnefs, and women decidedly ugly, who

who would rejoice in a decree for an equality of genius and beauty, and who, to that variety in which nature delights, would prefer an infipid monotony of talents and looks all over the world.——But until Nature shall issue such a decree, the decrees of all the National Conventions on earth to establish égalité will be vain. Were equality decreed by the univerfal confent of mankind this year, there would be inequality of riches and importance all over the earth the next.

November 24.

As I walked to-day on the terrace of the Feuillans, which is contiguous to the hall of the National Affembly, I obferved a young man ftanding on a chair: at his fide, there was a pike thruft into the ground, on the upper end of which a fmall board was fixed with this infcription : *L'Apôtre de la Liberté.* A crowd furrounded him, to whom he harangued in praife of the glorious revolution of the 10th of Auguft, and of the patriots to

whom

whom France owed its liberty, which he asserted to be those determined men who were on the preceding night appointed to be of the General Council of the Commune, and not the Briſſots, Vergniauds, Guadets, Buzots, and ſtill leſs Louvet the calumniator of Robeſpierre. He ſaid that all theſe men, with Roland at their head, were doing every thing they could to ſave the life of Louis Capet, the various inſtances of whoſe perjury he attempted to prove, as well as his ingratitude to the Nation, which had behaved ſo generouſly to him. " But," he added, " Lewis the traitor has now filled up the meaſure of his treachery ſo high, that even his friends in the aſſembly could not deny his guilt, though they were ſtriving with all their cunning to ſave his life."

This fellow was evidently hired to animate the populace againſt Roland and his friends, and make them conſider every attempt to poſtpone or evade the condemna-

tion of the King as a proof of their aristo-
cracy and treachery. No sovereign that
ever reigned has had more pains taken to
mislead and impose upon his judgment,
than the Peuple Souverain who at present
governs France; and being naturally of a
thoughtless and giddy character, it is no
wonder he falls into the snares which are so
artfully laid for him.

November 25.

That spirit of hatred and accusation which
prevails in the Convention, has extended to
the Generals of the armies, and seems to aug-
ment daily in this place.

Some weeks ago, Custine, in a letter which
was read in the assembly, accused Kellermann
of negligence, or something worse, in having permitted the Prussians and Hessians to
escape out of France, and reach Coblentz.

He asserted, that if Kellermann had passed
the Mozelle and the Sarre, he would have
made

made himfelf mafter of Treves and Coblentz with little difficulty ; and he referred to ftate-ments which he fent at the fame time, to prove the truth of his accufation.

The Commiffioners who had been in Kel-lermann's army, and had feen the correfpon-dence between him and Cuftine, declared that it would have been highly imprudent in the former, to have joined Cuftine with his caval-ry at Treves at the time it was demanded.

When Cuftine fent this letter to the Con-vention, he wrote at the fame time to Kel-lermann informing him of it. Kellermann alfo wrote to the Convention, and has this expreffion in his letter : *Les inculpations de Cuftine n'ont pu être écrites que dans le vin* *.

On this occafion, it happens fortunately that thofe Generals are particularly attached to neither party. If they were, their mili-tary fkill, as well as their patriotifm, would be eftimated, as is the cafe in other coun-

* The accufations of Cuftine muft have been made in his cups.

E e 2

tries,

tries, according to the political party to which they belonged ; and he, who was efteemed a good General by one fet of men becaufe he was of their party, would have been called a bad one by another for that very reafon.

But as in this inftance the fpirit of party has not interfered, both are fpoken of as good officers and faithful fervants to the public, and their mifunderftanding is univerfally regretted.

A member in the Convention having fpoken highly of the recent fucceffes of Cuftine, another immediately obferved, that if the fucceffes of Cuftine, which were immediately before their eyes, had enlarged their external dominions, Kellermann's victory on the 20th of September had faved the interior parts of France.——This was equally applauded by both parties.

In confequence of Cuftine's accufation, Kellermann was called from his army, and

has

has been for some time in Paris. He is by birth a German, and served for many years in the German armies. I have been several times in company with him. Once, when several Deputies were present, he could not abstain from speaking with indignation of the accusation of Custine, which gave him no otherwise uneasiness, he said, than as it obliged him to remain inactive at Paris, while the brave army he had commanded were in the field. Kellermann is a man of plain manners conveying the idea of sincerity, and whose talents are calculated to render him much more brilliant at the head of an army than in conversation. There is no doubt of his being soon restored to his command.

November 26.

In a company of bourgeois, a person was lamenting yesterday the fatal effects which might happen from discord; but added, he

understood

underftood that the two political parties were on the point of uniting.

On which a chemift who was prefent, fhaking his head, faid, he queftioned it very much: " becaufe," continued he, " fince fear did not comprefs them together when the Pruffian and Auftrian armies were advancing into the heart of the country, there is little probability that fuch heterogeneous fubftances will unite by elective attraction."

However pedantic the chemift's language may be thought, his argument feems juft.— Every day, I am more and more confirmed in the opinion, that the animofity between the two parties will never end but in the deftruction of one of them ; and fome people think that Roland and his party would have been overfet before now, had it not been for the fédérés, particularly thofe from Marfeilles, who are now at Paris.

The effect which their name has on the minds of the fuburb fans-culottes is wonderful

derful—this greatly vexes Marat. In one of his Journals, he infinuates that Dumourier expofed the Parifian battalions at the battle of Jemmappe, more than the reft of the army, on purpofe to have them deftroyed ; and that this was done in compliance with the directions he received from Roland, Briffot, and that party. His words are : " Pour affurer le fuccès de leurs projets ambitieux, ces tyrans ont enlevés notre bouillante jeuneffe, toujours la premiere à marcher contre les fuppôts du defpotifme, et à former une barriere autour des défenfeurs du peuple." He afterwards mentions what this bouillante jeuneffe confifted of : " nos forts-de-la-halle, continues he, " nos charbonniers, nos cochers de place." .

Thofe who have feen Marat, and are acquainted with the manners and fentiments of Chabot, Legendre, Merlin de Thionville, and fome other of his coadjutors, will not be furprifed at their having fome partiality to

E e 4

hackney

hackney coachmen, colliers, and whatever is rough and vulgar.

A writer of great ingenuity and eminence regrets, that " we fhall never more behold that generous loyalty to rank and fex, that proud fubmiffion, that dignified obedience, that fubordination of the heart, which kept alive, even in fervitude itfelf, the fpirit of an exalted freedom ;" and adds, that with thefe are alfo fled " that fenfibility of principle, that chaftity of honour, which felt a ftain like a wound, which infpired courage while it mitigated ferocity, which ennobled whatever it touched, and under which *vice itfelf loft half its evil, by lofing all its groffnefs.*"

Notwithftanding the fplendid elegance and force of this paffage, the concluding fentiment has been cenfured. No man however can with lefs reafon than the honourable gentleman above alluded to, be fuppofed to mean this as a palliative for vice of any kind; and it is moft certain, that in in general fociety, politenefs is a convenient fubftitute for benevolence, and that when rude and polifhed men are equally vicious, the latter are always lefs difgufting and fometimes lefs mifchievous than the former. A favage, when he hates a man, or has violent defire for a woman, will murder the one and ravifh the other; in polifhed fociety, a man with the fame paffions will do neither. It is equally true, that a great deal of the groffnefs of vice may be removed, without a grain of its intrinfic wickednefs being removed with it. The courtier, who, in elegant terms, profeffes friendfhip to the man he is endeavouring to fupplant, and politely careffes thofe he means to betray, exhibits as much genuine vice as the moft vulgar footpad that ever knocked a man down, or informed againft his accomplice.

All the refinement of Courts cannot alter the nature of falfehood, ingratitude, or treachery; nor can all the perfumes of the

Eaft

Eaſt ſweeten the corruption of vice. On the whole, though poliſh in ſome caſes renders vice leſs miſchievous than it would otherwiſe be, in other caſes it may make it more dangerous by being more attractive; like furbiſhing the knife of a child, which does leaſt harm when ruſty, and is moſt dangerous when brilliant.

The Deputies above mentioned, and others of the Convention, cannot have this laid to their charge; their nauſeous manners and debaſing ſentiments exhibit vice in its native deformity.

November 27.

Aſſertions frequently and boldly repeated ſeldom fail to make an impreſſion on the minds of the populace, and at length to gain belief, in ſpite of the moſt clear and rational evidence of their falſehood.

Marat has been exciting the people to mutual rancour, to pillaging, and cutting
each

each other's throats, fince the beginning of the Revolution; but he affures them in all his fpeeches, and he tells them every morning in his Journal, that he is l'Ami du Peuple!—and the populace believe them.

It is univerfally known, that the Girondifts exculpate the citizens of Paris from the horrid crimes of September; whereas Robefpierre, St. André, Tallien, Chabot, Bazire, and all that party, affert, that the maffacres were committed by the people. But as, at the fame time, St. André always calls them " le bon peuple," Marat fays " he carries them in his heart," and Robefpierre declares " he would willingly facrifice his life for them," the populace confider this faction as their friends, and look on Roland and the Girondifts as their calumniators.

It is alfo notorious, that Roland, Claviere, Genfonnet, Guadet, and the other leaders of that party are republicans; that they

they made open attempts to eftablifh that form of government, at the time the King was brought back from Varennes; that Robefpierre, Danton, and many of their friends oppofed it, and declaimed in the Jacobin Society againft it, and in favour of monarchy. Yet, as the favouring of monarchy is now confidered as the greateft of all crimes, thofe very perfons accufe the Girondifts of that crime, and of being determined enemies to the Republic; which affertions, by dint of repetition, begin to be believed ; and Roland, Briffot, Guadet, and the whole of that party, are of courfe becoming daily lefs popular.

In a fmall company, a few days fince, a perfon remarked, " That the great fondnefs which Robefpierre, Danton, and fome others, fhewed for a republican form of government, was of a very late date ; and that although they difplayed fuch deadly rancour againft Lewis XVI, by whom they thought

thought they never could be forgiven, yet they had no hatred to monarchy, provided they could have a King of their own choofing."

Another of the company obferved, " That he could not believe that fo fierce and infolent a fpirit as Danton would bear to fee any King eftablifhed in France."

" I am convinced, however," faid a third, " that he would like well enough to fee M. Egalité on the throne."

" Remember," refumed the firft fpeaker, " what Benferade faid, when he was told that a certain lady was fond of the Duc de la Vantadour, who was the uglieft man in France: " Parbleu, fi elle aime celui-la, elle en aimera bien un autre*."

November 28.

It is not furprifing, that a people of great

* If fhe can love him, fhe will foon love another.

fenfibility,

fenfibility, and naturally verfatile, fhould fly from one extreme to another,; yet one would hardly have expected that Republican manners would have been much to the tafte of the French nation.

There is however in Paris at prefent, a great affectation of that plainnefs in drefs, and fimplicity of expreffion, which are fuppofed to belong to Republicans. I have fometimes been in company, fince I came laft to Paris, with a young man, of one of the firft families in France, who, contrary to the wifhes and example of his relations, is a violent democrate. He came into the box where I was laft night at the playhoufe; he was in boots, his hair cropt, and his whole drefs flovenly: on this being taken notice of, he faid, " That he was accuftoming himfelf to appear like a Republican." It reminded me of a lady, who being reproached with having a very ugly man for her lover,

lover, faid, *C'eft pour m'accoutumer à la laideur de mon mari**.

They begin to *tutoyer* each other, that is, to ufe in converfation the fingular pronoun *tu*, inftead of the plural *vous*, as the Romans did, and the Quakers do. They have fubftituted the name Citoyen, for Monfieur, when talking to or of any perfon; but more frequently, particularly in the National Affembly, they pronounce the name fimply, as Buzot, Guadet, Vergniaud. It has even been propofed in fome of the Journals, that the cuftom of taking off the hat and bowing the head fhould be abolifhed, as remains of the ancient, flavery, and unbecoming the independent fpirit of free men; inftead of which they are defired, on meeting their acquaintance in the ftreet, to place their right hand to their heart as a fign of cordiality.

* It is to accuftom myfelf to the uglinefs of my hufband.

All

All this appears a little premature. If the Republic is permanent, new manners will gradually be introduced, and a new national character will of courfe be formed ; but fo very fudden a change of decoration is too much in the ftyle of a harlequin entertainment to be durable. The example of the Greeks and Romans is, in my opinion, too often held out ; and when I hear the names of Lycurgus and Brutus and Cato repeated in the Convention, it raifes recollections which are not favourable to thofe legiflators and patriots to whofe debates I am liftening. One of the beft obfervations I have feen in any of Marat's Journals, is the following: After fneering at fome of the Deputies, on account of their high pretenfions to patriotifm, he adds, " Thefe are the men, who are on every flight occafion telling us, ' Souvenez-vous que nous fommes Républicains, que tout ce qui n'eft pas grand et fublime n'eft pas digne de nous.'——

5 Meffieurs,

Meffieurs, foyez d'abord honnêtes gens: après cela, vous ferez des Camille, des Regulus, des Catons, fi vous le pouvez*."

David, the celebrated painter, who is a Member of the Convention and a zealous Republican, has fketched fome defigns for a republican drefs, which he feems eager to have introduced; it refembles the old Spanifh drefs, confifting of a jacket with tight trowfers, a coat without fleeves above the jacket, a fhort cloak, which may either hang loofe from the left fhoulder or be drawn over both: a belt to which two piftols and a fword may be attached, a round hat and feather, are alfo part of this drefs, according to the fketches of David; in which full as much attention is paid to picturefque effect as to conveniency. This artift is ufing all

* Remember that we are Republicans, that nothing but what is great and fublime is worthy of us.——Pray, gentlemen, try in the firft place to be honeft men: after that, each of you may become a Camillus, a Regulus, or a Cato, if he can.

his influence, I underſtand, to engage his friends to adopt it, and is in hopes that the Municipality of Paris will appear in it at a public feaſt, or rejoicing, which is expected ſoon. I ſaid to the perſon who gave me this account, "that I was ſurpriſed that David, who was ſo great a patriot, ſhould be ſo anxious about an object of this kind."

He anſwered, "that David had] been a painter before he was a patriot."

Part of this dreſs is already adopted by many; but I have only ſeen one perſon in public completely equipped with the whole; and as he had managed it, his appearance was rather fantaſtical. His jacket and trowſers were blue; his coat, through which the blue ſleeves appeared, was white with a ſcarlet cape; his round hat was amply ſupplied with plumage; he had two piſtols ſtuck in his belt, and a very formidable ſabre at his ſide: he is a tall man, and of a very warlike figure; I took him for a Major of Dragoons

8   at

at leaft : on enquiry I find he is a miniature painter.

November 29.

General Kellermann is reftored to his command, and is to fet out for the army in a few days: having heard that he was to be at the Jacobin Society laft night, I went there.

The General made a fhort fpeech, importing that he had come to take his leave of the friends of the people previous to his leaving Paris. The General is no orator, nor did he attempt eloquence ; what he faid, however, was applauded. One of his friends rofe, and demanded that he might be received as a member into the Society : this propofal occafioned a murmur, which furprifed me after the applaufe with which the General himfelf had been heard.

I foon underftood from thofe around me, that this manner of propofing a member was contrary to the rules of the Society ;

that

that if he wished to be admitted, he ought to have made the proposal himself, since he was present, and not by deputation. One of the Members whispered the General, who immediately rose, and asked the favour of being received as a member of the Society.

Still there was a demur and whispering through the hall. I heard some who were near me say, that the usual formalities ought not to be dispensed with, it was a bad precedent; others might expect to be admitted in the same manner: it was unworthy of Republicans to pay any regard to his rank in the army, &c. &c.

The General rose again, and declared, that he had not been acquainted with the particular forms of the Jacobin Society of Paris, otherwise he would have strictly observed them in the application he made; that perhaps it was too late, as he should be obliged so soon to set out for the army; that he

2 had

had imagined they might be the lefs neceſſary in his cafe, as he was already a member
of the Jacobin Society of Straſbourg, and
had been ſometimes honoured with the
name of the Jacobin General. Cicero could
have ſaid nothing more perſuaſive than this.
Kellermann was declared a member amidſt
the applauſe of all preſent.

The Preſident gave him the kiſs of frater-
nity, and made him a ſhort addreſs, the tendency of which was to wiſh him victory, and
that he might ſpread the ſentiments of liberty
and equality among the ſuperſtitious ſlaves of
Italy, and inſpire the ſubjects of the Pope
with the ſentiments of the Roman Republic:
he finiſhed by exhorting the General not to
allow his mind to be elated by the victories which he had already obtained, or thoſe
which the army of the Republic might
hereafter obtain under his command; but
remember, that after them all, he muſt return
to the condition of a private citizen, and be

reſpected,

respected, not according to the rank he was raised to in the army, but according to his virtues, and the service he had rendered to his country.

Kellermann heard this admonition with the grave and respectful air of a timid student receiving instructions from a Professor.

After this, a member of the Society, whose face I had never seen, and whose name I do not remember, ascended the tribune, and made a tedious and disgusting harangue, to prove the right the Nation has to try and condemn the King; representing all the arguments in favour of his inviolability as sophistical, and hinting that those who used them were traitors to their country: the orator added every thing that malice could suggest, to inflame the audience against the unfortunate Monarch. Among other assertions, unsupported by probability or proof, he said, " that the King had gone from the Tuileries to the Assembly Hall

partly

partly from fear of being wounded or killed during the attack which he had ordered to be made on the people, and partly with a view to point out the members he wiſhed to be murdered by the Swiſs, and by the Chevaliers du Poignard, whom he expected every moment to ſee enter the hall, reeking from the ſlaughter of the citizens. He repreſented the Queen in the ſame light ; and concluded, that both merited an immediate and ignominious death :" at which ſome woman in the galleries, who had ſhewn much ſatisfaction during the diſcourſe, exclaimed, " *Oui, oui.*"

November 30.

When I returned from the Jacobins laſt night, I expreſſed to the perſon who had procured me admiſſion, my ſurpriſe at the heſitation in receiving Kellermann as a member. " I ſhould have thought," ſaid I, " that they would have been eager to admit a victorious General."

F f 4 " In

" In my opinion they were in the right to hefitate," he replied: " no fet of men are fo apt to over-value themfelves as thofe who are at the head of armies :——they talk of their victories as if they had been gained, like that of Samfon, by the ftrength of one arm ; whereas nothing is more certain, than that victories are often obtained by the valour of the troops, in fpite of the blunders of their Generals. Kellermann," continued he, " did his duty at Valmy ; fo did every foldier of his army, in which it cannot be doubted there are at leaft an hundred who are as fit to command as he, and fome of them, in all probability, more fo :——and are thofe gentry to expect to be admitted into a focie-ty like that of the Jacobins, without obferv-ing the fame forms with others ? No, no, fuch diftinctions are dangerous to liberty, particularly when beftowed on the General of an army. Who was it," continued he, " that overturned the Roman Republic ?

Julius

Julius Cæsar, the General of an army. Who dismissed the Parliament of England, and established military despotism ? Oliver Cromwell, the General of an army. Who restored royalty in the same country ? Monk, the General of an army."

" Do you imagine," said I, " that little mortifications of this kind will prevent similar events from happening in France? All those who are at the head of your armies may not have the moderation of Washington."

" We do not rely on the moderation of our Generals," answered he, " but on the spirit of freedom which pervades the French armies, and will prove a check to the ambitious or treacherous views of their leaders. This spirit did not exist in any of the armies above mentioned. The army of Cæsar looked up to him, and to him only ; at his order they marched with as little reluctance

luctance againſt the Senate, as againſt the Gauls : the armies of Cromwell and Monk were ſo deceived and modelled, as to become the blind inſtruments of the will of their Generals : the armies of France are more enlightened, and are organiſed in a different manner ; they will follow their leaders againſt the foreign enemy, but not againſt their country. No General was ever more popular than La Fayette ; yet he would have been arreſted in the midſt of his own army, if he had not fled ; and if the Convention thought proper, they could arreſt Dumourier to-morrow in the middle of his, notwithſtanding all his victories. But civil honours and diſtinctions would render the Generals of armies more dangerous ; and therefore, in civil ſociety, they ſhould be made to feel themſelves on a level with their fellow citizens, and obliged to ſubmit to the ſame regulations in public ſocieties with the other members. Every kind of
particular

particular diftinction fhewn to profeffional rank, or to birth, is unworthy of the independent fpirit of Republicans; " and you might obferve," continued he, " that when citoyen Egalité entered and feated himfelf by you, his appearance produced no fenfation :—no notice was taken of him."

" Forgive me," anfwered I, " his entrance did produce a fenfation; and if I had not before been acquainted with his perfon, I fhould have gueffed it to be him, by an affectation which I remarked in thofe around, not to take notice of him."

December 1.

Few things fhock a ftranger more on his firft arrival in this country, than the unrelenting and indelicate ftyle in which the Queen is fpoken of; and nothing feems more contrary to what was formerly confidered as characteriftic of the French nation. They have been often accufed of
paying

paying fo great an attention to politeneſs, that they neglected morality ; they are now in danger of neglecting the firſt, without paying more attention to the fecond, and of loſing every attribute of courtiers, except that of abandoning the unfortunate.

The report in the name of the Committee of Legiſlation, on the mode of conducting the King's trial, was read lately in the Convention by Mailhe:—after which, he faid, " We have faid nothing of Marie Antoinette; what right has ſhe to have her cafe confounded with that of Lewis XVI? The lives of thoſe women who have had the titles of Queen of France were never confidered as more inviolable or more ſacred than thoſe of other rebels or conſpirators; therefore, in cafe you think proper to bring a decree of accuſation againſt her, ſhe will of courfe be tried by ſome of the ordinary criminal courts."

As the mode of trying the King was the

fole object fubmitted to the confideration of
the Committee, I was reflecting what could
be this man's motive for departing from the
fubject of the report, on purpofe to make
this brutal attack on the Queen; but when
he had finifhed, and I heard the galleries refound with applaufe, I was no longer at a
lofs.   As foon as the noife was over, I heard
one of the Deputies fay to his neighbour,
" I fhould not be furprifed, that fhe were
condemned to occupy Madame de la Motte's
vacant place at the Bicêtre *."

But what furprifed me more than any
thing I have had occafion to obferve on
this fubject, was a converfation I had at a
coffee-houfe, in the Palais Royal, with a
perfon I have fometimes accidentally met
there: he is a man of a grave and refpect-

---

* The perfon's name who made this harfh and indecent fpeech, is in my original Journal; I omit it
here, becaufe I afterwards knew of a very effential fervice which he rendered to an unfortunate Emigrant.

able

able appearance, of about forty-five or fifty years of age, well dreſſed, but rather in the ſtyle that was faſhionable before, than ſince the Revolution. He is not a member of the Convention, but I had ſeen him there often, and had ſometimes converſed with him : I took him for a man of moderation and humanity, he now convinced me how much I had been miſtaken.——I aſked him a queſtion concerning the intended trial of the King——there was nothing remarkable in his anſwer. I then ſaid ſomething expreſſive of ſympathy for the deplorable ſituation of the Queen : his eyes kindled, and his countenance altered at the name; the mention of the Queen affected him as that of chivalry did Don Quixote ; his diſcourſe, from that of a man of ſenſe, became the ravings of a madman ; he poured out the moſt illiberal torrent of rancorous abuſe againſt her that I ever heard; and concluded the whole with this horrid ſentiment, which I tranſlate literally:

terally : " I hope *that* woman will be obliged to drink the full draught of mifery
which is poured out for her, to the very
dregs."

The rancour which in this country is
manifefted againft the Queen, is more violent and more unaccountable than even that
which appeared in Scotland againft Mary
Queen of Scots, though many circumftances concurred to create a jealoufy in the
minds of the people of Scotland, againft
their Sovereign, which do not exift in the
other inftance. Endowed with unrivalled
beauty, and adorned with every elegant ac-
complifhment, Mary had been accuftomed
to the fplendor of a licentious Court, over
which prefided an unprincipled woman,
of whofe politics, gallantry was a principal
engine. She returned to her native country
at a time when it was fo overfhadowed with
fanatical gloom, that the inhabitants confidered

fidered gaiety as finful, and pleafure as a profanation.

Mary was of a religion which the Scottifh nation held in abhorrence: how could a people endure the varied ornamented robes of Popery, in whofe eyes the decent furplice of the Church of England was detefted, as a rag of the ftrumpet of Babylon, whofe worfhip they fufpected their young Queen wifhed to introduce into her native country?

The manners of the Court of Vienna were very different from thofe of the Louvre; and the character of Maria Therefa was the reverfe of that of Catherine of Medicis. ——That their Queen was beautiful, and elegant, and gay; that fhe loved fplendor, and was a Roman Catholic, were circumftances of a nature to gain, and not to alienate a people like the French.

Befides, the crimes imputed to Mary, whether

ther true or falfe, were of a much deeper dye than any which calumny has ever laid to the charge of the Queen of France. And although the fate of the former was moft affecting and deplorable, yet the caufes which brought it on are not uncommon. Mary fell the victim of hypocrify, female jealoufy, and political fear; whereas the fufferings of the Queen of France are as contrary to policy as to humanity, and proceed from a people, who, before they could behave to her in the barbarous manner they did, muft have renounced every amiable quality imputed to them by their friends, and adopted the difpofition of which they are accufed by their bittereft enemies.

December 2.

The moft deplorable circumftance which diftinguifhes this Revolution from others, is, that when its original object was in a great meafure obtained, order, tranquillity,

VOL. II.   G g   and

and fubmiffion to law did not return. One
revolution has been grafted on another;
new alterations have been imagined, and
executed by men more violent, and means
more bloody, than the former; the populace, ftimulated by unprincipled leaders, have
committed all the exceffes of revolted ne-
groes, or of flaves who have burft from the
galleys. At this moment, four years after
the firft infurrection, inftead of the bleffings
of freedom, the unhappy people of France
are, under the name of a Republic, fuffering
more intolerable oppreffion than they ever
did under the moft defpotic of their monarchs; and are at the fame time expofed to
the attacks of external enemies, whofe number is daily increafing by the imprudent
conduct of their new governors.

Of all the evils which have attended this
extraordinary Revolution, the moft important to mankind in general, perhaps, is, that
it weakens the indignation which every
liberal

liberal mind naturally feels for defpotifm, and inclines them to fubmit to the awful tranquillity of methodifed oppreffion, rather than rifk fuch fcenes of anarchy and carnage as have been of late exhibited in this country.

Yet it ought to be remembered, that, defpotifm, though lefs favage, is more hopelefs than anarchy, which contains within itfelf the feeds of its own deftruction; whereas, the pillars of defpotifm, being artfully arranged for the fupport of each other, as well as of that of the general fabric, may ftand for ages. Were it not for this circumftance, and if there were no choice but to live under arbitrary government, or to be expofed to the unreftrained ravages and cruelties of a frantic populace, perhaps the former would be preferred as the leffer evil. —For, in fpite of the vitiating tendency of unlimited power on the human heart, hiftory affords inftances of perhaps one in a

dozen

dozen of Princes whofe power was unlimited, and who yet preferved the virtues
of humanity; whereas a mob is always furious, brutal, and cruel.

But Heaven has not confined mankind
to this miferable alternative; nor is every
nation poffeffed of the impetuofity of the
French, which, at the firft fenfation of freedom, has hurried them headlong into exceffes without any rational object—like the
lunatic, who having fpoken the language of
moderation, and announced a peaceable difpofition, makes ufe of his liberty in attacking every body around, and fighting furi-
oufly, till, his ftrength being exhaufted, he
is again brought back to his fetters.

The emigration of the Nobleffe was moft
unfortunate; I fpeak of that which took
place at the beginning of the Revolution,
when it was ftill fafe for them to remain in
their country; and not of thofe which have
happened fince, and were abfolutely neceffary

fary for, felf-prefervation : but it is more than probable that the neceffity for thefe laft emigrations arofe from the unneceffary one which took place at firft. Had all the Nobleffe remained, it cannot be imagined but that a body of men of the moft extenfive property muft, in fpite of the torrent of the times, have retained great influence, and prevented many of the diforders which have diftracted this unhappy country. Numbers of the Nobleffe would have been elected into the Affemblies, and thus have precluded fome Deputies who perhaps have been the caufe of great mifchief: by accommodating themfelves in fome degree to the prevailing opinions, they would have gradually rendered them more mild and conciliatory, and prevented that degree of acrimonious prejudice which at prefent prevails againft the whole body of Nobility. The earlieft emigrants being confidered as the inftigators of a combination of foreign

powers

powers againſt France, as determined to re-eſtabliſh the ancient government, and as filled with the moſt implacable deſire of vengeance; the odium againſt them became ſtronger every day, and was by the populace, ever incapable of diſcrimination, extended to the whole claſs. The Nobleſſe who remained in the country were daily provoked by new injuries from their countrymen within, and piqued by letters from thoſe without, accuſing them of meanneſs in ſubmitting to the new order of things, and of cowardice for not joining the armies of the Princes. It is not to be wondered at, therefore, that many of them left their country. After the tenth of Auguſt, it became dangerous for any of them who had ſhewn themſelves the friends of limited Monarchy, and eager to ſupport the Conſtitution, to remain in France.

As for that party which is known by the name

name of Girondifte, and to which Roland, Briffot, Buzot, Condorcet, and many other deputies who do not come from the Gironde, belong, they are certainly free from the dreadful guilt of the maffacre of the prifoners; I am perfuaded also, that they not only wifhed to fave the life of the King, but that fome of them have rifked their own lives in the various meafures they have ufed for that purpofe: yet being acquitted of thefe, other charges of a highly criminal nature remain againft them.

After the Conftitution was accepted by the King, and after they themfelves had fworn to maintain it, they continued their efforts to overthrow it.

Judging of the King from what they thought muft be his fecret wifh, and what, it is probable, they were confcious would have been their own conduct in his fituation, they could never believe that he would remain faithful to the Conftitu-

G g 4   tion;

tion; they were convinced that in his heart
he abhorred it, and would feize the firft opportunity to overturn it, to punifh all who
had any hand in eftablifhing it, and to reftore the ancient fyftem with renewed force
and augmented terror. They were convinced that the freedom of France could have
no fure foundation but in a Republic; and
on this conviction, they fcrupled not to ufe
the moft perfidious means to introduce that
form of government.

They endeavoured to vilify the character
of the King, with a view to render royalty
odious and contemptible; they gave circu-
lation to innumerable ftories, to the prejudice of others of the Royal family, which
they either knew to be falfe, or had no
proof of their being true.

On mere conjecture, they accufed the
King and Queen of undermining the Conftitution to reftore defpotifm, while they were
confcious of undermining it themfelves, on
purpofe

purpofe to rear a Republic. They invol-ved their country in a war with the Em-peror, on pretexts which they knew to be groundlefs, and folely in the expectation that it would increafe that jealoufy of the King which already exifted, and give rife to incidents and circumftances on which plaufible accufations againft him and his Minifters might be founded.

By thofe means, they rendered a bene-volent Prince, who was anxious for the welfare of his fubjects, unpopular; by thofe means they produced the infurrection of the 20th of June, and prepared the minds of the populace for that of the 10th of Au-guft; and by making it be believed, that a Prince of fuch a quiet, unambitious charac-ter as Lewis XVI. could not remain fatis-fied with the power granted by the Confti-tution, but was fecretly confpiring to reftore defpotifm, conveying the idea, that every one who could be placed on the throne would

would do the same, the French nation were tricked into a republican form of government, when there is great reason to believe that a vaſt majority would have preferred a limited monarchy.

December 3.

That fickleneſs of diſpoſition which has been conſidered as the general characteriſtic of the populace of every nation, certainly belongs in a ſtronger degree, and more peculiarly to the French than to any other, and has appeared more perſpicuouſly ſince the preſent Revolution than it perhaps ever did before.

Nothing could ſurpaſs the popularity of Necker at one period. Although a ſtranger and a proteſtant, the whole nation, fixing their eyes on him, ſeemed to exclaim, *Tu maximus ille es*——and to conſider him as the only perſon who could ſave the country from ruin, and reſtore their affairs. A ſhort
time

time after he had been recalled by the united voice of the people, he began to be neglected, and is now almoſt forgotten.

La Fayette, who was adored, is now de-
teſted.

The popularity of Petion, which was in
its meridian when we arrived in France, begins already to decline.

Orleans and others have had their moments of popularity, which, as a genuine
poet beautifully obſerves of pleaſures, has
had the fate

Of ſnow that falls upon the river,
A moment white—then melts for ever ;
Or like the borealis race,
That flit ere you can point their place ;
Or like the rainbow's lovely form
Evaniſhing amid the ſtorm *.

The ſame ſickleneſs which the French
have diſplayed in a manner ſo ſtriking, with
reſpect to their favourites, at various pe-

* Burns's Poems.

riods

riods of the Revolution, is also conspicuous
with regard to their taste in government.
When the attempt was made to introduce
a republican form, after the King's return
from Varennes, it was rejected.

In the month of July last, a member of
the National Assembly declared, that he was
as much against a Republic being established
in France, as a despotic Monarchy; and he
invited all who were of the same opinion,
to avow it by standing up.

All the members instantly stood up.

This happened in the month of July, and
the National Convention decreed the abolition of monarchy on the 21st of September.

I stated this to a Member of the Convention yesterday, as a proof that his countrymen were free from that stubbornness of
which some people are accused.

He answered, " that although he did not
believe the change of opinion to be so uni-

versal

verfal as fome wifhed to have it thought, yet he *did* believe, that there was a confiderable change fince the 10th of Auguft, which he imagined was in a great meafure owing to two caufes: Firft, the idea that prevailed, that the papers found in the King's cabinet on that day, and thofe lately difcovered in the iron cheft, in the wall of the palace, formed a convincing proof of the King's having confpired with the foreign enemy to betray the country. " This," he faid, " had raifed a general indignation, and had reconciled many minds to the idea of a Republic, who formerly thought that form of government very unfuitable to France.

" A fecond caufe which contributed to the fame effect," he faid, " was the prodigious fuccefs of their arms; which was in a great meafure imputed to the energy which the idea of being republicans and freemen impreffed on the minds of the French."

I ob-

I obferved, " that if this laft confideration had any weight, it muft entirely proceed from the infpiriting fentiment of freedom, and the French might have been free without being Republicans."

The perfon with whom I was converfing, being himfelf a Republican, fhook his head at this obfervation ;—on which I added, " It is equally certain, that they may be Republicans without being free *."

Accounts of towns taken, battles gained, and fuccèfs of every kind, are announced in the Convention almoft daily. Four ftandards taken from the Piedmontefe were prefented to them yefterday, by an aid-decamp of General Anfelme, fent from his army for that purpofe; the colours were unrolled and difplayed in the middle of the hall; the applaufe and fhouting were of

---

* This perfon, who was attached to the party of Roland and Briffot, has had fevere experience of the truth of this remark.

3

courfe

courfe loud and perfevering.——In his addrefs to the Affembly, the officer made ufe of fome expreffions which indicate pretty juftly to what a height national vanity is mounted in this country: I tranflate them literally.

" Legiflators, our enemies had the audacity to appear: Anfelme fhewed himfelf, and they fled as ufual. Our army ardently defires to enter into the heart of Italy. Naples infults you, Rome excommunicates you, the King of Sardinia does not acknowledge you his conquerors: only give us the order, and all the crowns of the South fhall be brought to your bar. Our foldiers declare, that each of them has a heart to blefs your decrees, and two hands to execute them. The Romans in their degeneracy called out for bread, and public fpectacles; the French, being regenerated, demand bread and the profperity of the Republic."

The Imperial Eagle, which formerly ftood on the top of the fteeple of Namur, has been removed

removed to Paris: it was placed on an open carriage, and drawn in the moft oftentatious manner from the gate of the city to the door of the Affembly hall, efcorted by a party of dragoons, one of whom rode immediately before the carrriage, holding a chain, the other end of which was around the Eagle's neck.

I was at the Convention when the commander of the party came to the bar, and addreffing the Affembly faid: " Legiflateurs, Monfeignieur l'Aigle Imperiale attend vos ordres."

One Deputy moved, that it fhould be placed, with the claws and beak cut off, on the top of the obelifk now erecting in the Place de Victoire. Merlin of Thionville propofed that it fhould rather be hung by the legs from the fame monument. Another defired that the Eagle fhould be permitted to ftand in his ufual pofture, but with the cap of Liberty on his head.

These

Thefe witticifms, fuch as they are, afforded great entertainment.

The prodigious torrent of fuccefs which
has flowed on the Republic of late, might
have intoxicated a nation of foberer brains
than the French. Had this produced no
other effects than huzzas. and proceffions in
the ftreets, allufions to their victories, and
felf-praife in fongs and declamations at the
theatres, or the rhodomontades of a few
orators in the Convention, there would have
been no great harm ; but moft unfortunately the intoxication has affected the judgment of a majority of the deputies, as evidently appears by the decifion of the Executive Council of the 16th of November,
fent to the French Generals commanding
the expedition to Brabant, to ufe every meafure in their power to open the navigation
of the Scheldt ; and by the inconfiderate and
rafh decree of the 19th of November, by
which the Convention declares, " au nom

de la Nation Françoise, qu'elle accordera fraternité et fecours à tous les peuples qui voudront recouvrir leur liberté * ;" and likewife by charging the Executive Power to give the commanders of the French armies orders to protect the citizens of every country who may be difturbed or vexed for the caufe of liberty.

Which is in effect telling the inhabitants of every country, that whenever they choofe to rife in infurrection againft their government, they will be affifted by the French.

So far from adhering to their former profeffions of a love of peace with all their neighbours, it is proclaiming a challenge to all Europe, and laying the foundation of everlafting war; for what country exifts, or ever did exift, in which part of the inhabitants did not think that they laboured un-

* In the name of the French nation, that they will affift the people of every country who wifh to recover their liberty.

der

der inconveniences, which they might call vexations or infringements of their liberty? This decree therefore announces to all the people of Europe, that as often as any part of them chooses to rebel againft their government, it will be fupported by France. By a decree of the 27th of November, Savoy is declared an eighty-fourth department, under the name of the department of Mont Blanc; which, contrary to their former declarations, renouncing every idea of conqueft, is to all intents and purpofes making a conqueft, and evincing as great an ambition for extent of dominion as Lewis XIV, or any French monarch ever difplayed; and of courfe the Republic will roufe the jealoufy of Europe as much as he did.

December 4.

A Committee had been appointed to examine certain papers, lately difcovered in an iron cheft, concealed in a cavity of the wall of the palace.

H h 2

As

As a report was this day to be made to the Convention concerning thofe papers, we went to the Affembly to hear it, although we had previoufly determined to leave Paris early in the morning.

Some very important difcoveries were expected from thofe papers. When Rhul, of Strafburgh, who was Prefident of the Committee, afcended the tribune to make the report, a moft profound and awful filence took place; it was underftood, that there were a number of letters to the King, and his Minifters, among thofe papers. Every Member of the Convention muft therefore have been in a ftate of anxiety, either on his own account or on account of fome of his friends: an imprudent expreffion in a letter to a Minifter might, in the prefent ftate of men's minds, expofe the writer to great danger. The papers however proved to be of very little importance. Barrere, who at prefent is Prefident of the Convention,

tion, is mentioned in fome of thefe papers ; fo are Dumourier, Claviere, Kerfaint, all as having had fome connection or intercourfe with the Court, but not in a way that can be confidered as criminal.——But, although no fufpicion of treafon could be inferred from them, one particular letter does afford one of the ftrongeft proofs of felf-fufficiency and prefumption that has been recorded in hiftory or fable fince the days of Phaeton.   It is from Rouyer, a member of the Convention, who had alfo been of the former Affembly.

The man had frequently drawn my attention before : he is remarkably noify and buftling; but as his importance feemed to be founded on his own fingle opinion, and what he faid, although pronounced with great force, had little weight, I had never inquired his name.

The letter is dated in March, and is addreffed to the King himfelf.

The following are extracts from it :

H h 3   " Pro-

" Profondement occupé des maux qui dechirent ma patrie, j'ai dû compter auſſi ſes innombrables reſſources ; j'ai ſondé ſes bleſſures et calculé ſes forces ; j'ai tout comparé, tout aprofondi, tout prévu *." He then declares, that he has a ſecret which will within two months reſtore the health of the empire, " cicatriſer ſes plaies, diſſiper ſes alarmes, annihiler ſes périls, rendre à la France le repos qui la fuit, la dignité qui lui convient, et au trône l'amour qui l'affermit avec l'éclat qui le décore †." He at laſt reveals his ſecret, which is, only that the King would place the whole power of the State in his hands; and he continues, " Sire,

---

* —Deeply concerned for the misfortunes of my country, I have alſo reflected on her innumerable reſources ; I have founded her wounds and calculated her force ; I have compared them, I have fathomed them, I have foreſeen every thing——

† That will heal her wounds, diſſipate her alarms, annihilate her dangers, and reſtore to France the tranquillity which has fled from her, and the dignity which becomes her; and to the Crown the public love which renders it ſecure, and the ſplendor which adorns it——

je le repète encore à votre Majesté, je m'engage à rétablir dans deux mois la paix au dedans, la confideration au dehors, la félicité publique et l'autorité royale ——— J'irai vous révéler ce que vos Miniftres vous cachent, ou vous apprendre ce qu'ils ignorent———Pour moi, Sire, je connois fi bien nos forces et nos moyens, qu'en jetant les yeux fur les ennemis qui nous menacent, j'ai peine à me defendre d'un fentiment de pitié.——J'ai porté mes regards fur toutes les Cours de l'Europe, et je fuis bien fûr de les forcer à la paix.———Je jouirai, dans le filence, du fruit de mes confeils—Heureux du bonheur de tous, je dirigerai vers vous feul la reconnoiffance publique *."

This

* Sire, I again repeat to your Majefty, that I engage to re-eftablifh, within the fpace of two months, peace within, importance from without, general felicity, and the royal authority ——

I will reveal to you what your Minifters conceal, and I will inftruct you in what they are ignorant.——As for my own part, Sire, I am fo intimately acquainted

with

This letter had, it is probable, been kept as a curiofity of its kind, and thrown into the cheft with the other papers found there.

Barrere's name having been mentioned in one of them, namely, in a letter from M. de la Porte to the King, he thought proper to demand leave to be heard before any other perfon ; as the Prefident of the National Convention ought not to remain a moment under fufpicion.——He defired Guadet to occupy his place as Prefident, while he himfelf went to the tribune, to explain how he came to be mentioned in De la Porte's letter.

Before he began, Charlier fuddenly ftood up, and faid, that the fame delicacy which had prompted Barrere to quit his place as

with our force, that on contemplating the enemies who threaten us, I can fcarcely fupprefs a fentiment of pity. I have thrown my eyes on all the Courts of Europe, and I am certain of being able to force them into peace.———I fhall enjoy in filence the fruit of my counfel.—Satisfied with the general profperity, I fhall direct the public gratitude to your Majefty.

Prefident,

Prefident, ought to have prevented Guadet from taking it.

Many voices exclaimed, that Guadet was not mentioned in any of the papers.

Charlier infifted, that although his name had not been read to the Convention, yet he was pofitively included in the defcription given by the Member who had made the report.

The way in which he attempted to make out this, is fingular enough : "For," continued Charlier, "in one of the papers addreffed to the King, it is faid, that thirteen or fourteen of the moft eloquent Members of the Convention were *dans les bonnes difpofitions* ; and although none of them are named, yet it is evident that Guadet muft be one of them ; for every body knows, that there are not thirteen members of the Convention more eloquent than he."

Rhul, who was the organ of the Committee in making the report, was fo much offended at hearing this, that he declared

8   with

with great heat, that if his expreffions were to be twifted into accufations, he would refign his place as a Member of the Committee.

Charlier's conftruction was condemned; Rhul was appeafed; Guadet was allowed to perform the function of Prefident, until Barrere made his defence, which was eafily done; after which he refumed his office.

Guadet then quitting the Prefident's chair, afcended the tribune, and, in reply to Charlier's infinuation, declared, that he had never been connected with the Court—" But if I had, and if I were confcious of guilt, I know how I could obtain my pardon : I know," continued he with animation, and looking to that part of the hall which the party of the Mountain occupied, " I know under whofe ftandard *thofe place themfelves, who have need of forgivenefs for the moft horrid crimes.*" This apoftrophe threw the Mountain into convulfions, in the midft of which I left the Convention, and foon after we fet out from Paris.

7   Lille,

Lille, December 7.

As it was late in the afternoon before we left Paris, we got no farther than the fmall town of Louvre that night, to which, a little after our arrival, a party of National Guards brought about fixty prifoners. The guards fung the hymn of the Marfeillois as they marched through the town; the prifoners had their hair entirely cut from their head; they were tied two and two together, the right arm of one being bound to the left of another. Thofe men had behaved ill at Jemappe, and Dumourier had ordered them to be carried in this difgraceful manner to Paris, to be difpofed of as the Convention fhould ordain. The National Guards of each town through which they paffed, guarded them to the next. They were to be marched to St. Denis the following morning by a party from Louvre, and the National Guards of St. Denis would the day after conduct them to Paris.

The

The punifhment feems well imagined, and muft make a ftrong impreffion on the troops on the whole route from Mons to Paris.

At Pont St. Maxence, a Courier from the Cabinet, with difpatches for Dumourier, overtook us; he travelled in a cabriolet a- dorned with the Cap of Liberty and other infignia of the Republic. This man, un- derftanding that our road and his was the fame as far as Cambray, made a propofal to take one of the fervants into his carriage on certain conditions, informing us at the fame time, that it would be ádvantageous to have him with us, becaufe he being a meffenger from the Cabinet, the gates of all the towns through which we were to pafs, would be opened to us at whatever hour of the night we might arrive.

We agreed to his propofal, and proceeded to Peronne, where we arrived an hour after it was dark: there we fhould have remained
that

that night, but as the gates were to be opened at any hour for the Courier, we were perfuaded by him to go on, for he affured us, "that we were within three pofts of one of the beft inns in France, which was protected by General Dumourier, and where he always lodged when he travelled on that road, for the landlord and landlady were the moft hofpitable and obliging people in the world." The Courier gave fuch an inviting defcription of this inn, that in fpite of the exceffive rain and darknefs of the night we left Peronne, travelled three pofts farther, and arrived at the gate of this famous inn about midnight. After a great deal of knocking, a fervant looked out of a window, and having in a very angry tone faid, "*On ne loge pas ici,*" fhut the window with a great deal more force than was requifite: this was rather difagreeable news to people who had been travelling fince five in the morning, and flattering their imagi-

nation

nation during the laft four hours, with the hopes of refreshment and reft.

Our Courier was a good deal confufed at this ; but on farther inquiry, he was inform-ed that the landlord and landlady were both ill of a malignant fever, which had proved fatal to one of the principal fervants, and many other perfons in the neighbourhood.

It is fortunate for men, when the beft meafure they could adopt is the only one which is left in their power. Our not paf-fing the night at this inn, in fpite of the malignant fever, did not depend entirely on our prudence. We were under the necef-fity of proceeding in the midft of the rain to Cambray ; the Courier renewing his affurances, that as he was un Courrier du Cabinet, the gates would be opened as foon as he fhould be announced.

At about two or three in the morning, we ftopped at a moft miferable hovel, immediately without the gates of Cambray.

Had

Had we been ever fo much difpofed to complain of hardfhip or fatigue, every expreffion of that kind would have been fuppreffed by the behaviour of a young dragoon,
who jumped from behind our carriage as
foon as it ftopped. His arm was in a fcarf:
he informed us, " that his thumb and two
of his fingers had been fhot off at the action near Menehould; that he had been at
Paris to folicit a fmall penfion, to prevent
him from ftarving, becaufe," added he,
holding up his wounded hand, " avec cette
b— de main, I can neither fire a mufket,
nor work:—the Secretary of the Minifter
told me, that I could not obtain a penfion
without a recommendation from my Colonel; I faw very well, qu'il fe ——— de moi *,
for he knew that my Colonel was with the
army. I immediately determined to fet
out for it myfelf, being fure of getting

* That he made a jeft of me.

a re-

children : fhe is a very induftrious woman, and ufed to get three livres ten fols for making a fhirt, when fhe made for people of quality; but at prefent, when there are no people of quality, fhe receives only forty fols for each fhirt. Je ne me plains pas, parce que je fuis bon Patriote moi—mais il y a une grande difference entre 40 f. et trois livres dix. Malgré cela j'ai toujours eu du bonheur."

" Eh votre main," faid the Courier.

" Ma main—ma main," anfwered the dragoon ;—" ça pouvoit être mon bras : un de mes camarades à deux pas de moi a eu la cuiffe emportée—eft-ce que le General Kellermann n'a pas eu auffi un cheval tué fous lui?—c'eft une plus grande perte que mes f— doigts pour le General. Ainfi vous voyez, Citoyen, combien j'ai toujours été heureux *."

We

* I do not complain—becaufe I am a good Patriot
—but

We were indebted to the high fpirits and gaiety of this young fellow, for keeping us in tolerable good humour during two hours that we remained in this wretched place; the horfes being all the time expofed to the rain, for there was no ftable.

Our Courier of the Cabinet mean while was bluftering and fwearing at the fentinel on the rampart, who could not immediately find any body to fend to the Magiftrates for an order to open the gates—for there was no regular garrifon at this time in Cambray; and when the order was obtained, a good deal of time was loft before the man who kept the keys could be roufed.

—but there is a great difference between 40 fols and three livres ten. In fpite of that, however, I have always been fortunate.

What fay you to the wound in your hand?

My hand—why, I fay, it might have been my whole arm: one of my comrades, within two fteps of me, had his thigh carried off; and had not General Kellermann a horfe killed under him? and that was a greater lofs to the General than my fhabby fingers.—So you perceive that I have always been fortunate.

Three

Three men armed with muskets, but without uniforms, came at last, and informed us, that the gates were open. The Courier recommenced his blustering, and threatened the whole Municipality of Cambray with the vengeance of Dumourier. He also expressed a fear that the General would blame him for the delay.

The dragoon, who was of the happy disposition to view every thing in the most favourable light, endeavoured to console him, saying, " Non ; Dumourier ne vous blamera pas : il est trop bon soldat pour ne pas savoir, que quand on ne peut pas prendre une ville d'assaut, il faut attendre qu'elle se rende *."

On entering Cambray, the Courier went directly to the town-house, and got a formal attestation of the time he had been de-

---

* Dumourier will not blame you : he is too good a soldier not to know, that when a town cannot be taken by assault, it is necessary to wait till it surrenders.

tained

tained at the gate, to fhew to Dumourier, as an excufe for his delay—and immediately proceeded on his journey, accompanied by the dragoon.

As no gate was allowed to be opened except that at which they went out, we were detained two or three hours longer, till the ufual time of throwing open all the gates.

We paffed through Douay, and arrived the fame evening at this town.

We have vifited the quarter where the Auftrians formed their entrenchments and batteries, from which the town was bombarded: a large village, near which the entrenchments were formed, was, before the main body of the Auftrian army advanced, unexpectedly furrounded by their light troops ; and, as we are told, the wretched inhabitants, with many more peafants driven there by the body of the army, were forced to work in the trenches, fo that the fire from the ramparts deftroyed a much greater num-

ber

ber of the country people than of the foldiers.

The anfwer returned by the municipality
to the fummons of Prince Albert of Sax-
ony, was firm and laconic.

"Nous venons de renouveller notre fer-
ment, d'être fideles à la nation, de maintenir
la liberté et l'égalité, ou de mourir à notre
pofte. Nous ne fommes point des per-
jures*.

"Fait à la Maifon Commune, le 29 Septembre 1792, l'an 1. de la République
Francaife.

"Le Confeil permanent de la Commune
de Lille.

(Signé) ANDRE, Maire.

ROHART, Secretaire-Greffier."

* We have juft renewed our oath of fidelity to the
nation, that we are determined to maintain liberty and
equality, or to die at our poft.
We are refolved not to be perjured.

The

The bombs and red hot bullets were particularly directed againſt that part of the town where the poorer inhabitants lived, with the double purpoſe of ſparing the moſt valuable buildings in a city, which, as was expected, was ſoon to belong to the Emperor, and alſo to excite the moſt numerous claſs of the inhabitants againſt the rich, and make them force the commander to deliver up the town. It had no ſuch effect, however, and the enthuſiaſm of the inhabitants increaſed every hour. The courage and alacrity of the inhabitants in ſeizing and removing the hot bullets before they had time to kindle the wood was ſurpriſing. They had iron inſtruments contrived for that purpoſe; and the towns of Armentiers, Bethune, Arras, Dunkirk, Caſſel, Cambray and others ſent their engines for extinguiſhing fire, to Lille, and volunteers from all thoſe cities preſented themſelves in great

I i 4 numbers

numbers for the defence of the place ; which obliged the Auſtrians to retreat from the town, after having beaten down by the bombardment three complete ſtreets in the quarter of St. Sauveur, and many other houſes in different parts of the town, which ſtill remain in ruins. There are few houſes into which ſome bullets have not entered, and they are kept as precious relicks by the inhabitants.

In the hotel de Bourbon, twenty bullets entered during the ſiege ; and the mark of the burning on the floor, occaſioned by one of them in the room where I now write, is very evident : but no perſon was killed belonging to the family, except the chief waiter, as he was croſſing the ſquare to put a letter into the poſt-office.

A poor fellow who is decrotteur to the hotel, told me that it was owing to the watchful care and mercy of Providence, that he happened to be out of the way when that

letter

letter was fent ; for otherwife, as he ufually carried the letters to the poft-office, he *himfelf* might have been killed inftead of the waiter.

I do not know whether it will be confidered as a fign that a fenfe of religion is declining among the French, that the beggars in afking charity no longer add *pour l'amour de Dieu*, but inftead of that, generally cry *Vive la nation* ; but that religious fentiments are becoming every day weaker on the minds of the common people of this country, is moft apparent ; but it never occurred to me, that one order of fociety was gaining in that article, what another was lofing. A friend of mine told me, however, that he was this forenoon in a bookfeller's fhop ; that having obferved the fhelves of one fide entirely filled with books of devotion, he had afked of the bookfeller, if books of that kind were in much requeft at prefent.

" A good

"A good deal," replied the bookfeller, "with the ariftocrates : as for the patriots, they hardly ever look into them."

"The reafon of that," refumed my friend, "perhaps is, that the patriots being the poorer have not money to lay out on books."

"They ufed to purchafe them formerly," faid the bookfeller ; "and it is only fince the ariftocrates became poor, that many of them began to purchafe them at all."

How far the bookfeller's account of this matter is to be depended on I know not; but it is a lamentable truth that a great propor-tion of mankind think very little of the next world, till the prefent becomes infupportable to them. And with regard to the inhabitants of this country, it muft be acknowledged that the revolution has been hitherto fo wretchedly managed, as to render the higher orders of fociety miferable, without making the lower happy.

Although

———————————

Although my Journal is continued until the 14th of December, when I returned to England, I omit the remainder, that I may infert what will be thought more interefting.

Some of the following particulars relative to the King's procefs, and the treatment which he and his family met with in the Temple, I learnt while I was in France; others I have been informed of fince my return in England. I imagine the whole may be placed with propriety at this place, with an account of the King's death.

With whatever irregularity, precipitation and injuftice the procefs againft the King will be thought to have been carried on, it was with much difficulty and perfonal danger, to one party of the Convention, that it was fo long protracted. I have reafon to believe that fome of the Convention regretted

gretted exceedingly the precipitate decree which abolifhed royalty, and were convinced that it would have equally tended to the happinefs and lafting freedom of France, if the Convention had reftored the King and re-eftablifhed the conftitution, with fuch alterations as might have been thought expedient.

I have reafon to believe that there was a ftill greater number of the members who were of opinion, that after the republican form of government was decreed, the moft equitable and moft politic meafure which the Convention could adopt, was to declare that they would make no inquiry whether the King had been in correfpondence with the enemy or not ; becaufe, at any rate, the nation was determined on a republican form of government, and therefore fhould order the whole Royal family to be efcorted to the frontiers, and permitted to go wherever they judged proper, with an

annual penfion of at leaft one hundred thoufand louis, to be regularly paid as long as
they fhould live in tranquillity, without exciting war againft France, or a civil war in
it for their reftoration ; revoking at the fame
time the decree againft Savoy, and renewing their original declaration, againft extending their dominions and offenfive war
of any kind.

That part of the Convention who were
of either of thofe opinions, with all who
were defirous of faving the King, finding
it dangerous to avow their fentiments,
endeavoured by various means to prevent a
trial, until the public mind fhould be fo
much foftened as to admit of a fair trial, or
till the idea of trial fhould diffipate altogether. When this failed, they attempted to
carry the fentence of confinement during
the war, and exile after it : when that failed,
they tried the appeal to the primary affemblies ; and finally, they endeavoured to fave

him

him by voting to poftpone the execution of
the fentence.

Inftead of thofe evafive meafures, the no-
bler part would have been, no doubt, to
have voted him not guilty at the firft nominal appeal.

I do not know that this was the opinion
of any of them ; but I have heard feveral of
them declare, that they thought the King's
life fully protected by the Conftitution, and
that he could not be juftly condemned to
death, although all were proved which was
laid to his charge, which in their opinion
was not the cafe.

The violent party againft the King, on
the other hand, took great pains and ufed
many arts, both within and without the
Affembly, to have all forms of procefs cut
fhort by a bloody and fudden cataftrophe.

Legendre propofed that all thofe who
had publifhed their opinions, or put them in
writing, fhould lay them on the table of the
Affembly ;

Aſſembly ; and that after the intervention of one day, the Convention ſhould pronounce ſentence witnout hearing the King.

Robeſpierre was for ending the whole in twenty-four hours without ſeparating.

St. André declared that the King had been judged and condemned by the people on the 10th of Auguſt, and that the Convention had nothing to do but to order his execution.

It was dreaded by ſome who wiſhed the death of the monarch, that his appearance at the bar of the Convention would ſoften the people, and perhaps move them in his favour; and when they found that others of their own party, who were equally the enemies of the King, were determined that he ſhould be heard, they imagined means of the moſt profligate nature to prevent it.

Papers were cried through the ſtreets to inflame the minds of the populace to ſuch a degree, that they ſhould inſiſt on his immediate execution; and if

that

that was delayed, to execute him themfelves, either in prifon or when he fhould
be carried to the Affembly. It was afferted
that the country never could be happy while
he lived; that all the misfortunes of the
country, all the diftrefs the people fuffered,
and the ftill greater with which they were
threatened, proceeded from the King's
being fuffered to live; that a party in the
Convention, namely, the Gironde and the
friends of Roland and Briffot, were bribed
by the Powers at war with France, to
fave the King, and prolong the diftreffes
of France; and that although they durft
not openly in the Convention deny that
he was criminal, and deferved death,
yet they were endeavouring, under various pretexts, to prolong his procefs, and
delay his execution, till an opportunity occurred to re-eftablifh him on the throne.

The moft abfurd affertions were made in
the Convention itfelf to this tendency. At
one time, a little before I left Paris, when
there

there was a discussion concerning the scarcity of grain, which by different members was imputed to different causes, I heard a voice pronounce, *La véritable cause est dans le Temple.* I was informed that this wise observation came from Legendre.

Hand-bills were distributed with these words : " Républicains, guillotinez moi Louis XVI. et l'Autrichienne si vous voulez avoir du pain." And the printed opinion of Marat was sold at the same time.

When the Royal Family were first lodged in the Temple, they were treated with some degree of respect, and they were allowed the comfort of each other's company, and the liberty of walking in the garden of the Temple ; but the appearance of respect gradually diminished, and at last the treatment they received was in many instances brutal.

A person who was admitted into the Temple by the means of a near relation on duty there about the beginning of December, affured me, that at the hour at which, by a ftanding order from the Council, the prifoners were to be confined to their apartments, he faw the keeper go to the King, who was ftill walking in the garden, and addrefs him in thefe words: "*Allons, monfieur Veto, il faut monter.*"

When the Royal Family dined, a Commiffioner from the Commune of Paris was always prefent. The Queen happened at one time to raife the hand in which fhe held her knife a little fuddenly towards her breaft.——The Commiffioner feemed alarmed, and made a movement as if he dreaded that fhe had an intention againft her life ; which the Queen obferving, faid with emphafis : "Non, Monfieur, je réferve cet honneur aux Francois*."

From the time that the King's procefs was refolved upon, the Royal Family were

---

* I referve that honour to the Convention.

confined

confined more clofely, and watched more ftrictly than ever. The Council ordered that in future two Commiffioners fhould pafs the night in his bed-chamber, inftead of one, which had been the cafe before. All perfons who were admitted into the prefence of any of the Royal Family were previoufly fearched. Orders were given that the razors with which the King was in the ufe of fhaving himfelf fhould be removed: this was done from a fear that he might prefer fuicide to the humiliation of a public trial before the Convention.

Such an idea was remote from the King's way of thinking. When his razors and penknife were demanded from him, " Do you think me fuch a coward as to kill myfelf?" faid he.

The order not only comprehended knives and razors, but alfo fciffars, and all inftruments contondant, tranchant et *piquant*, and it was extended to all the Royal Family.

" Il faudroit auffi nous enlever nos ai-
guilles," faid the Queen when it was read to
her.

When the King, afterwards, repeatedly
applied for a razor, it was at laft granted by
the Council, who directed, however, that he
fhould fhave himfelf under the infpection
of the Commiffioners: and the Queen and
Princefs Elizabeth were allowed fciffars to
pare their nails with the fame reftriction.
This laft feems ridiculous, and the former
abfurd; for if the King had had any intention of ufing a razor in the manner they
fufpected, he could have put it in execution as effectually while the Commiffioners
were prefent as at any other time.

After a long and warm debate, it was decreed by the Convention, that the King fhould
be brought to their bar ; that the act of accufation fhould be read to him ; that the Prefident fhould put certain queftions to him,
which were previoufly drawn up by the
committee,

committee, and approved of by the Aſſembly ; and that after his anſwers had been taken down, a day ſhould be appointed for hearing him finally, and pronouncing judgment. It was alſo decreed that the opinions of the Deputies ſhould be taken by the appel nominal.

This mode was violently inſiſted on by the faction of the Mountain, in the hopes that ſome, whoſe conſciences acquitted him, might, from a terror of the mob, be induced to pronounce againſt him.

Had the opinion of the Convention been taken in the uſual way, it would have been leſs under the influence of fear; but the moſt certain method of getting the unbiaſſed judgment of the deputies, would have been by ballot : had that been adopted, there would probably have been a majority in favour of the King, even on the firſt general queſtion of guilty or, not ; and there is no doubt but it would have been carried by a

K k 3 great

great majority againſt the pains of death, if the firſt queſtion had been loſt.

In the mean time, the King knew nothing of its being decreed that he ſhould appear at the bar of the Convention. In an extract from the report of the Commiſſioners that were on ſervice at the Temple on that day, the following particulars are mentioned :—

The King roſe as uſual at ſeven ; he ſpent only a few minutes in dreſſing, and about three quarters of an hour in prayer. At eight the drums were heard ; he enquired of the Commiſſioners what was the meaning of it, as he had not before heard them ſo early.

The Commiſſioners pretended ignorance. "Do you not think," rejoined the King, "that they beat the general ?" The Commiſſioners replied, they could not diſtinguiſh. The King walked muſing through the room, and ſometimes ſtood liſtening attentively. ". I think

think I hear the found of horfes' feet in the court," faid he. The Commiffioners gave no explanation.

The Royal Family breakfafted together that morning ; they were full of alarm and difquietude at the noife, which increafed every moment, and of which they plainly perceived the caufe was carefully concealed from them.

Uncertainty in fuch circumftances agitates the mind more than a full affurance of the worft ; the Queen and Princeffes went 'to their own apartments after breakfaft; and left the Prince Royal with the King. The Commiffioners at laft informed him, that he was about to receive a vifit from the Mayor of Paris.—" So much the better," faid the King. " But I muft inform you," refumed the Commiffioner, " that he can- not fpeak to you in the prefence of your fon." The King then, after preffing the child to his breaft, defired him to go and embrace

his

his mother in his name. Clery, the valet who attended the King, withdrew with the Prince.

The King afked the Commiffioner, " if he knew what the Mayor's bufinefs with him was," and was anfwered in the nega-tive. He walked about the room for fome time, ftopping at intervals to afk queftions refpecting the perfon and character of the Mayor. The Commiffioner anfwered, " that he was not particularly acquainted with him, but that he was of a good character, and, to the beft of his recollection, of a mid-dle age, thin, and rather tall. The King feated himfelf in a chair, and continued ab-forbed in meditation. Meanwhile the Com-miffioner had moved behind the chair on which the King was feated. When he awaked from his reverie, not feeing any body, he turned fuddenly round, and per-ceiving the Commiffioner clofe behind him, faid with quicknefs, " What do you want, Sir ?"

Sir?" "Nothing," replied the other; "but fearing you were indifpofed, I approached to know what ailed you *."

Monfieur Chambon, the Mayor, entered foon after, and informed the King, that he came to conduct him to the National Convention: the King accompanied him without making any objection. When he came to the court, which was full of troops, horfe as well as foot, he feemed furprifed at feeing fome of them in uniforms with which he was unacquainted.

Before he ftepped into the Mayor's coach, he threw up his eyes to the window of the apartment in which his family were confined, and the tears were obferved to trickle down his cheeks.

---

* Thefe particulars, which fome may think of a nature too trifling and minute, ftrongly paint the ftate of agitation and fufpicion, in which the mind of the unhappy Monarch was at this time.

The

The coach then proceeded to the Convention, attended by the troops.

The Commiffioner afcended to the Queen's apartment, and found the whole family overwhelmed with fear and forrow.

He acquainted them that the Mayor had been with the King: the young Prince had already informed them: " We know that," faid the Queen; " but now—where have they carried the King now ?" " To the Convention," replied the Commiffioner. " You would have faved us much uneafinefs," faid the Princefs Elizabeth, " if you had informed us of this fooner."

What dreadful apprehenfions muft this Princefs have been under, to find any relief in hearing that her brother was carried before an Affembly of men fo prejudiced againft him as fhe knew the Convention to be!

The King was conducted to the Convention

vention by the Boulevards, la rue neuve
des Capucines, la place Vendôme, et la
cour des Feuillans. All the streets which
open to the Boulevards had guards stationed
in them, with orders to prevent a multitude
from assembling; and cannon were placed
at the entrance of all those streets; patrols
were ordered to prevent any kind of ob-
struction by groups, or carriages, along the
whole of the way that the King was to be
conducted. Strong guards were placed at
different posts near the Tuileries and Hall
of the Assembly. It is said there were
near 100,000 men in arms that day in
Paris.

The glasses of the coach were down during the whole way, and there was no dif-
turbance. Great numbers however were
waiting, in all the passages leading to the
Assembly, and the tribunes had been filled
from six in the morning. It was remarked,
that Marat was dressed in a new suit; and
that

that his features announced satisfaction and good humour, which was considered as still a greater rarity.

The act of Accusation having been read, some of the Deputies mentioned circumstances, which they thought of importance, that had been omitted. Drouet, the postmaster, who was the cause of the King's being stopped at Varennes, had been elected a Deputy to the Convention for that service. He thought this a good opportunity to distinguish himself as an orator—" Lewis," said he, " is a *cheat* (fourbe), and wished to impose upon the nation, in saying that he intended to go to Montmedi, for the villain (scelerat) was expected at the Abbaye d'Orvalle; and the traitor knew that a detachment of hussars were waiting for him a few leagues from Varennes: *the monster* then had the intention, &c. &c. &c."

This was more than his audience, prejudiced as it was against the King, could bear; the
post-master

poft-mafter was obliged to ftop in the middle of his abufive career, his voice being
ftifled by an univerfal murmur *.

It was announced by the Prefident, that
from the moment that Lewis fhould appear
at the bar, no petition fhould be heard, no
motion of any kind made, no fign of approbation or difapprobation given, but a
profound filence maintained. When Lewis
appears, exclaimed Legendre, " *il faut qu'il
regne ici le filence des tombeaux.*" This brutal
infinuation had no better fuccefs than the
eloquence of Drouet.

Marat, however, had the fairnefs to declare, that, in his opinion, the King ought
not to be queftioned about any thing
previous to his acceptance of the Conftitution: this is fo evident, that it is won-

---

* When Drouet was in the middle of his harangue,
a gentleman afked one of the Deputies, who he was :
" Monfieur," replied the Deputy, " c'eft un Maître de
Pofte, qui a voulu faire claquer fon fouet bien mal-
à-propos."

derful

derful it was left to Marat to make the obfervation, and more fo that it was difregarded when made.

Other propofals were made by other members, and fome adopted : at about one o'clock the Affembly were informed, that the King was in the Chambre des Conférences ; on which Barrere, the Prefident, having reminded the Affembly and audience of the filence they ought to maintain, defired that he might be conducted to the bar.

An awful filence prevailed ; every eye was fixed on the door at which he entered. The King appeared with a ferene air and undifturbed countenance. The fpectators betrayed great emotion.

After a fhort interval, Barrere addreffed him : " Lewis, the French Nation accufe you of having committed various crimes to re-eftablifh tyranny on the ruins of liberty; the National Convention has decreed

that

that you fhall be tried—and the Members who compofe it are to be your Judges. You will hear the accufation read, after which you will anfwer to the queftions which fhall be propofed."

To this the King made no reply.

The general Act of Accufation was then read, after which the Prefident repeated the firft article of accufation, and added, "Lewis, what have you to anfwer?" On which the King gave his anfwer, and the Prefident proceeded to read the fecond article, and demanded the King's anfwer in the fame words; and fo on, until the whole of the articles were finifhed.

During this examination, fome new queftions occurred to the Committee, which were put in writing, and handed to the Prefident, who put them in the fame manner to the King, and received his anfwers.

The King's behaviour during the whole of his appearance in the Convention was calm,

calm, recollected, and that of a man resign-
ed to the necessity of circumstances, without the consciousness of guilt; his answers
were sensible, pertinent, and prompt. He
never lost his composure, except in one instance, when the President read the following strange accusation: " You distributed
money among the populace for the treacherous purpose of acquiring popularity,
and enslaving the nation."

The perversion of his very benevolence
into a crime, astonished the unfortunate Monarch, and deprived him for a moment of the
power of utterance—he shed tears—but a
consciousness of the purity of his intentions
rendered them tears of comfort. " I always took pleasure," said he, " in relieving
those in want, but never had any treacherous purpose."

Upon the whole, when it is considered
that the questions were deliberately drawn
up by a Select Committee, and afterwards
corrected

corrected and enlarged by the whole Convention, while the King's anfwers were given extempore, and without even a previous knowledge that he was to be examined in that manner, it places his underftanding in a very advantageous point of view.

To keep the King ignorant to the laft of any intention of examining him, and then hurry him unprepared to their bar, was ungenerous and fhameful in the higheft degree—it might have difconcerted him in fuch a manner as to have given fcope to malice; his enemies would have imputed to confcious guilt that diforder in his anfwers and conduct, which furprife or indignation might naturally have produced:—and it is impoffible not to fufpect that the fecrecy was employed for that very purpofe. If fo, all thofe enemies have been difappointed; the malignity by which they attempted to obſcure his character, has only ſerved to put it in a fairer light.

When the King had anſwered all the queſtions, the original papers on which part of the accuſation was founded were laid on the table. Valazé taking them up one by one, and reading the title, ſaid, as he preſented each to the King, " Louis Capet, la reconnoiſſez-vous ?" If the King anſwered that he knew it, Valazé ſaid, " Louis la reconnoit ;" and the Preſident repeated, " La piece eſt reconnue." If the King diſavowed it, they ſaid, " Louis ne la reconnoit pas—La piece n'eſt pas reconnue."

The King diſavowed many of them. When the whole had been inveſtigated in this manner, the Preſident addreſſing the King ſaid, " I have no other queſtions to propoſe—have you any thing more to add in your defence ?" " I deſire to have a copy of the accuſation," replied the King, " and

2   of

of the papers on which it is founded.——I alſo
deſire to have a Counſel of my own nomination." Barrere informed him, that his
two firſt requeſts were already decreed, and
that the determination reſpecting the other
would be made known to him in due time.

After which the King withdrew, and was
conducted back to the Temple in the ſame
carriage, and with the ſame attendants that
he had when he came to the Aſſembly. The
crowd in the ſtreets was greater than in the
morning; the continued cries of " Vive la
Republique!" accompanied the coach from
the Aſſembly Hall to the Temple, and the
cry " A la Guillotine!" was alſo heard more
frequently than in the morning, but leſs ſo
than was expected by thoſe who had taken
ſo much pains to irritate the populace againſt
him.

In the coach, the King aſked Chaumet,
the Procureur Syndic, " if he thought the
Convention would allow him to have Counſel."

fel." This man, by the account which he afterwards gave of what paffed, anfwered fhortly, "that his duty was to conduct him to and from the Affembly, and not to anfwer queftions."

When he arrived at the Temple, and was in his apartment, he fent a meffage, defiring to fpeak to the Mayor, who, being in his carriage and ready to drive away, immediately obeyed the fummons, and afcended to the King's chamber. " I hope," faid he to Chambon, " that you will not delay to let me know, whether I am allowed Counfel." The Mayor replied, " that he might rely upon being informed as foon as poffible ; adding, that he was perfuaded the Convention were too juft to refufe to him what the law allowed to all."

Every member of the Convention was not of the fame way of thinking with the Mayor: about thirty or forty Deputies of the faction called the Mountain were

against

against granting that request, and opposed it by the most indecent clamours; but finding their efforts vain, they next insisted that he should be allowed only one person for Counsel. The great majority on the contrary were for allowing him three: the debate became so tumultuous, that the President was obliged to put on his hat *: the Mountain was at last obliged to relinquish this shameful attempt; and it was decreed that the King should have Counsel, without limiting the number, and that a message should instantly be sent to inform him of this. One of those who had opposed his having any Counsel, proposed that two of the servants of the Assembly (huissiers) should carry this message; but the Convention ordered four of their members for that purpose.

After the Mayor left the Temple, the

---

* This is a signal to order, never given but in cases of great confusion, and is generally obeyed.

King

King immediately examined the *Conſtitution*, of which he had a copy, and ſaid to the Commiſſioner, who was now alone with him, " Yes, I find that the law allows me Counſel; but may I not alſo be allowed the ſatisfaction of having my family with me?" The Commiſſioner anſwered, " that he did not know, but would go and conſult the Committee." He went accordingly, and returned ſoon after; he informed the King that he could not ſee his family.—" That is hard," ſaid the King.—" But my ſon, they will not deny me the comfort of his company at leaſt—he is a child, Sir, of only ſeven years of age."

" The Committee have declared," replied the Commiſſioner, " that you ſhall have no communication with your family—Your ſon is of your family."

The Commiſſioner left the King, and went to the Queen's apartment, where all the Royal family were. The Queen immediately aſked,

afked, if they might not all wait on the
King, who they knew was returned from
the Convention. The Commiffioner gave the
fame anfwer he had given to the King.—
" At leaft," faid the Queen, " let him have
the company of this child ; pray allow his
fon to go to him." The Commiffioner replied, " that as the child could not be with
both, it was beft that the perfon who might
be fuppofed to have the greateft courage
fhould fuffer the privation : befides," he added, " a child of that age has more need
of the care of a mother than of a father."

The following day the four Deputies informed the Convention of their having been
with the King, and that he had named Target and Tronchet as his Counfel.

Tronchet accepted, declaring at the fame
time, that he was aware of the delicacy and
danger of the office, which humanity to a
man, over whofe head the fword of juftice
hung, impofed on him——and for which, in all
events, he would accept of no recompenfe.

Target

Target wrote a letter to the Prefident of the Convention, excufing himfelf on account of his age and infirmities, and defiring that his letter might be fent to the King, that he might choofe another.

This afforded fome Members of the Affembly a frefh opportunity of difplaying their difpofition—they complained of the incidents which continually occurred to retard the final iffue of the procefs. Offelin * faid, that one Counfel might refufe after another, to the lofs of much precious time, and therefore propofed that the Convention fhould name Counfel for the King, whom he muft either accept, or find others within twenty-four hours.

This revolted the greater part of the Affembly ; and when it was afked, how it could be imagined that the King could place confidence in thofe of their nomination, Tallien faid with a rancour that well ac-

* This fame Offelin was Prefident of the Criminal Tribunal of the 17th of Auguft !

corded

corded with his character, " Qu'il s'arrange,
qu'il trouve des Confeils qui acceptent; c'eſt
fon affaire; la nôtre eſt de venger la Ma-
jeſté nationale *."

Fermond and Rabaut de St. Etienne fpoke
againſt this favage precipitation; another
propofed to adjourn : Thuriot, and Benta-
bole, the fame who had accompanied Marat
on his vifit to Dumourier, oppofed the
adjournment. " Do tyrants ever adjourn
their vengeance againſt the people ?" faid
Legendre, " and yet you talk of adjourn-
ing the juſtice of the people againſt a tyrant." This argument was well fuited to
the underſtandings and inclinations of the
audience in the galleries, and met with their
applaufe.

In the mean time, a deputation from the
Council of the Commune of Paris came to
communicate to the Convention a decree
which they had paffed regarding the mea-

* He muſt do the beſt he can, he muſt find thofe who
will accept, that is his bufinefs ; it is ours to avenge the
Majeſty of the Nation.

fures

fures they thought neceffary to follow in the prefent circumftances. By this decree, the King was to have no communication with his family :—his valet de chambre was to be locked up with him, and to have no intercourfe with any body elfe :—his Counfel were to be ftrictly examined (fcrupuleufement examinés, fouillés jufqu'aux endroits les plus fecrets). After having thrown off the clothes in which they entered, they were to be dreffed in others provided for them in the Temple, and under the infpection of the Commiffioners who attended the King, and were not to be allowed to leave the Temple till after fentence was pronounced. It was alfo an article in this Decree, that the Counfel fhould take an oath never to mention any thing they heard while in the Temple."

Decrees have fometimes been propofed, and meafures have been adopted, by thefe men, of fuch a deteftable and atrocious nature, that we are almoft tempted to fufpect that

that fome individual among them is bribed to fuggeft and perfuade them into meafures which muft render them and their caufe for ever odious and deteftable. What could the enemies of civil liberty wifh more, than that thofe who call themfelves her friends fhould act fo as to fhock common decency, and revolt all the feelings of humanity?

This abominable decree was with difficulty heard to the end; it excited the greateft marks of difguft; there was a cry from all parts of the Affembly to annul the decree, and cenfure thofe who made it. Robefpierre had the courage to face this ftorm; he declared that he was convinced that a very laudable fpirit had dictated the decree,— "which," added he, "is perhaps too mild for the occafion." This declaration produced violent murmurs, and many voices were heard exclaiming—"*Hors de la tribune!*"

"I know," refumed he, "that there is a party

party in this Affembly for faving the traitor ; but I am furprifed that thofe who fhew fo much tendernefs and fympathy for an oppreffor, have none for the good people whom he oppreffed."

This gained the galleries in an inftant, and they refounded with applaufe.

Several Members however put the inquifitorial and fhameful Decree of the Commune in a juft light ; and conjured the Affembly, in the name of decency, humanity, and juftice, to annul it; which was carried.

The Convention were afterwards informed, that feveral people had offered to be Counfel for the King ; all of whom he had refufed except-M. Malefherbes and M. Tronchet, who having been at the Temple and admitted into the King's prefence, on the 14th, found that he had not then received any of the papers he had demanded.

Monfieur de Lamoignon-Malefherbes is a man of an amiable and refpectable character;

3

racter ; of diftinguifhed fenfe, probity, and learning ; of one of the chief families of what is called The Robe in France ; he is grandfon of the Chancellor Lamoignon, who was an intimate friend of Boileau, Racine, and other men of genius in the reign of Lewis the Fourteenth.

The prefent Monfieur de Malefherbes diftinguifhed himfelf towards the end of the reign of Lewis XV. by fome very eloquent and courageous remonftrances which he drew up when he was firft Prefident of the *Cour des Aides*, and for which he was banifhed.

In the beginning of the reign of Lewis XVI. he fucceeded Monfieur de St. Florentin in the Miniftry ; but afterwards, for reafons which are varioufly ftated, he defired and obtained leave to retire.

This refpectable man is feventy-two years of age ; his generous offer to be Counfel for the King gains him the applaufe of the public, and forms a contraft greatly in his

favour

favour with the cautious conduct of M. Target, which has been condemned by all parties. —— Even the fishwomen of Paris marked the difference, went in a body and hung garlands of flowers and laurel on the gate of Monsieur de Malesherbes, and afterwards proceeded to the house of Monsieur Target, in the intention to insult him in a manner peculiar to themselves. Fortunately for him, he was advertised of their intention, and made his escape.

It is much to be wished that all the Members of the Convention had been endowed with equal sentiments of justice with these Poissardes. The discrimination displayed on this occasion is a proof that the lowest inhabitants of Paris are not devoid of sentiments of generosity; and that if they were acquainted with the real character of the King, the spirit of rancour which has been perfidiously raised against him would soon be turned against his persecutors.

It

It will not be improper here to infert an anecdote which does honour to the heart of this unfortunate Prince. Two Commiffioners of very oppofite difpofitions were with the King when the fhocking exhibition of the head of Madame de Lamballe was made under his windows, on the third of September. One of thofe men hearing the noife, and recognifing the head, had the brutality to invite the King to come to the window, and he would fee a very curious fight. The King was advancing towards the window, when the other ran and withheld him, faying, the fight was too fhocking for him to fupport.

The perfon to whom the King afterwards related thefe circumftances, afked the names of the two Commiffioners. The King freely told him the name of the latter, but refufed to mention that of the former— "becaufe," faid he, "it can do him no credit at any time; and might poffibly at fome

fome future period bring him to trouble."
As the benevolence of the King's difpofition appeared through the whole of his
reign, his enemies have endeavoured to conceal and mifreprefent every circumftance of
this kind. But notwithftanding all the pains
they have taken, fo many proofs of his candour, moderation and integrity were known,
that thofe who wifhed his death were in
conftant dread of a return of humanity and
affection in the hearts of the people towards
him; and therefore were at great pains to
fill the tribunes with perfons hired to make
an outcry againft him: and they were fo
apprehenfive on this fubject as to fufpect
thofe very agents of relenting.

When the King was indifpofed in the
month of November, and the phyfician Le-
monier ordered to vifit him, fome fymptoms
of concern were manifefted by the people,
which alarmed the King's enemies greatly.
It was reported and believed for one day,
that

that he was dead; I myfelf heard it infinuated in a pretty large company that he was murdered; one perfon exclaimed with indignation—" Les fcelerats l'ont empoifonné * !"

The King's appearance in the Convention, the dignified refignation of his manner, the admirable promptitude and candour of his anfwers, made fuch an evident impreffion on fome of the audience in the galleries, that a determined enemy of Royalty, who had his eye upon them, declared that he was afraid of hearing the cry of Vive le Roi! iffue from the tribunes; and added, that if the King had remained ten minutes longer in their fight, he was convinced it would have happened: for which reafon he was vehemently againft his being brought to the bar a fecond time.

The Commiffioners who do duty at the Temple were cenfured for drawing up their

* The villains have poifoned him!

reports so as to excite compassion, and were required to avoid this for the future. The thing was impossible, unless they had been permitted to falsify; for a bare relation of the facts, in the coldest language, must have produced the effect they wished to prevent.

Terror has acted a principal part since the beginning of this Revolution—Terror first produced the emigrations, to which a great proportion of the miseries which France has suffered are owing—Terror produced that shameful passiveness in the inhabitants of Paris and Versailles during the massacres — Terror prevented sympathy from appearing in the faces of many who felt it in their hearts for the unfortunate monarch, during this process, and Terror at last pronounced the sentence of his death.

Besides the means already mentioned, of inflaming the populace by pamphlets and hand-bills, men were hired to mix with the groups, in the Palais Royal, and on the

terrace

terrace of the Feuillans, to harangue on the
neceffity of condemning the King without
farther form of procefs : and fome of thefe
men went the length of afferting, that if the
Convention did not, the people would take
that bufinefs on themfelves, and afterwards
execute the fame juftice on all the Deputies
who fhould vote for faving him.

All thofe inhuman manœuvres did not
prevent its being ftrongly ftated by fome
members in the Convention, that if the
King's counfel were not allowed fufficient
time to prepare his defence, the decree by
which counfel was granted to him would
be confidered as an infult, and the trial a
mockery.—It was alfo boldly afferted by one
member, that " if rancour and mean felfifh
" views had not hardened the hearts of fome
" prefent, fo plain and obvious a piece of
" juftice never would have afforded a mo-
" ment's debate."—" It has been faid," added
another, " that there are Royalifts in the

" Convention.

" Convention. So there are ; but they con-
" fift of thofe who pufh on the procefs with
" royal fury and precipitation—men who
" are not for trying but butchering Lewis
" XVI, and thereby gratifying all the
" princes at war with the Republic, by
" raifing a general indignation all over
" Europe, at the manifeft cruelty and injuf-
" tice of a Republican Affembly."

Thefe remonftrances feem to have had
fome effect ; for it was decreed, that the King
fhould be allowed till the 26th of December
to prepare his defence.

It was alfo propofed, that during this interval the King fhould have a free intercourfe with his family.——This was no fooner
mentioned than it was affented to by the exclamations of a great majority of the Affembly. " You may decree this as much as
you pleafe," cried Tallien; " but if the Municipality do not choofe it, he will be allowed to fee none of them."

Here

Here this man's malice carried him father than his accomplices approved ; it was moved that he fhould be cenfured, and that the cenfure fhould be inferted in the verbal procefs : he attempted to avert this by a filly explanation, which proved ineffectual.

The Affembly feemed pretty generally difpofed to allow a free communication between the King and all his family, when Reubell afferted, that it would be highly improper to allow him any communication with the Queen and the Princefs Elizabeth, who were involved in the accufation, as there was reafon to believe they had fent their diamonds to their brothers, to help them to make war on the nation. On this defpicable pretext the King was allowed to have intercourfe with his children only, and they were ordered to be kept feparate from their mother and aunt till the end of the procefs.

It had been obferved, that very few of

the

the real Bourgeoifie of Paris could of late get accefs to the tribunes, the places being pre-occupied by a fet of hired vagabonds, generally the fame every day : fo that when the other departments complain of being under the controul of the fingle city of Paris, they do not ftate the grievance in its full magnitude. All the departments of France, including that of Parls, are, in reality, often obliged to fubmit to the clamorous tyranny of a fet of hired ruffians in the tribunes, who ufurp the name and functions of the Peuple Souverain, and, fecretly directed by a few demagogues, govern this unhappy nation.

To remedy this, Manuel propofed, that a certain number of tickets of admiffion fhould be fent every day to the fections to be diftributed among the real citizens.— As this plan would have prevented certain manœuvres of the Mountain, that faction oppofed it with great violence ; the people in the galleries thundered againft it ; fome

of

of them called out, "A l'Abbaye Manuel, à l'Abbaye l'ariftocrate Manuel!" Legendre, the butcher, propofed, that it fhould be decreed, that Manuel had loft his fenfes.—This fally, the fineffe of which will not be apparent to all the world, was thought exquifite by the people in the tribunes. When they had done with their applaufe, Manuel returned his thanks to Legendre, for not having moved that it fhould be decreed that he was an ox ; becaufe, if that had paffed, Legendre might have thought he had a right to flaughter him.

Monfieur Defeize was added to Meffrs. de Malefherbes and Tronchet, as a counfel for the King : the bufinefs they had to go through was too laborious for two perfons only, and the time allowed ftill too fhort.

From the report of one of the Commiffioners we learn the following particulars, which, though minute, ferve to illuftrate the character of the King :—The Commiffioners,

M m 4   who

who were ordered on duty at the Temple, having, according to cuftom, drawn lots for their different pofts, that of the King's apartment fell to a M. Cubieres, who, with another Commiffioner, was introdueed at eleven at night, the King being then afleep. He rofe as ufual at feven, and took a book, which they afterwards found was a breviary;—breakfaft was brought at nine, but the King refufed to eat becaufe it was the faft of Le Quatre Tems.—He fpent fome time in prayer, and afterwards afked Cubieres about the health of the Queen and his fifter.—He walked mufing through the room; and then, raifing his eyes to Heaven, " This day (faid he) my daughter is fourteen years of age." The unhappy Prince repeated the fame expreffion after a paufe, during which the tears flowed from his eyes, and he was greatly agitated.

Monfieur de Malefherbes and the other two counfel came, and he paffed moft of that day and the next with them, and with

four

four deputies from the Convention, who came with papers relative to his trial.

One of the Commissioners said to Malesherbes, in a conversation apart, that he was surprised to observe that he gave the Moniteur and other Journals to Lewis, because he would by it become acquainted with many things very disagreeable, and particularly to what a degree the people were prejudiced against him. Monf. Malesherbes replied, that the King (for he persisted in calling him the King) was of a strong character, and beheld his misfortunes with magnanimity.

The Commissioner hinted to M. de Malesherbes, that, by the free admission he had to the King, he might, if he were not an honest man, furnish him with poison.

"If I should," replied M. de Malesherbes, "the King is too sincere a christian to make use of it."

The resolution of the Convention to try the King and to be themselves his judges,

astonished

aftonifhed Europe, and was heard with forrow and indignation by the unfortunate natives of France, whom the violence of the late meafures, or the fears of affaffination, had driven from their country.

Some of them, diftinguifhed for their talents as well as for the offices they had held in their own country, were in England at this interefting period, and fhewed a ftrong defire of doing every thing in their power, in juftification of a prince of whofe innocence they all feemed fully convinced.

M. Louis de Narbonne, who had been Minifter of War when the hoftilities began between France and the Emperor, and from that circumftance was enabled to throw great light on the fubject, wrote to the Prefident of the Convention, offering to appear at the bar as one of the defenders of the King, provided a protection was fent to make it fafe for him to pafs and repafs through France. The Convention paffed

I

to

to the order of the day on this requeſt, without even allowing the reaſons which M. de
Narbonne gave for its peculiar propriety
to be read.

M. de Narbonne then drew up a declaration in juſtification of his Sovereign, which
he tranſmitted to Meſſrs. Tronchet and Ma-
leſherbes: from the laſt he received the following letter:

Paris, 31 Decembre 1792.

" J'ai reçu, Monſieur, votre lettre et la
déclaration de vos ſentimens.

" Vous ne me mandez pas quel uſage
vous voulez que j'en faſſe. Si c'eſt de la
faire imprimer, ce ne peut pas être moi qui
m'en charge, parce qu'étant le conſeil de
celui qui fut mon Roi, je ne peux faire aucune démarche qui ne ſoit regardée comme
faite par lui. Au reſte, votre déclaration ne
peut avoir aucune influence ſur le jugement
de la Convention Nationale, parce que à
l'heure

l'heure où je vous écris, on procéde au jugement.

" Il est possible que le jugement qu'on rendra, entraîne une autre discussion en présence de la nation. Ce sera alors à vous de voir si vous croyez devoir faire paraître votre déclaration en faveur du plus malheureux et du plus vertueux des hommes.

" Quant à moi, si la cause se plaide devant la nation, je suis très déterminé à la soutenir aussi publiquement que je pourrai, quand même on prononcerait que je ne suis plus le défenseur légal de l'innocent.

Dans ce cas-là, Monsieur, je vous préviens que je me servirai de plusieurs articles de votre lettre sans prétendre me les approprier, parce qu'il ne me serait pas possible de rendre aussi bien que vous, plusieurs grandes vérités, qu'il sera important de mettre sous les yeux de la nation.

" Mais la plus grande partie de votre dé-

7   claration

claration concerne des faits qui vous font
personnels, et que vous seul avez droit de
certifier.

   (Signé) MALESHERBES.

" A Monsieur Louis de
Narbonne, ancien Ministre
de la Guerre de France, à
Londres."

          M. de

 " I have received your letter, and the declaration of
your sentiments. You do not inform me what use
you wish to be made of them. If you desire to have
them printed, I am not the person who can take upon
me to do it ; because, being one of his counsel who was
my King, whatever I do will be considered as done by
him. Beside, your declaration can have no influence
on the decision of the National Convention; because, at
the very time I am writing, they are proceeding to
judgment.

 It is possible that the sentence they will pronounce
may occasion another discussion in presence of the whole
nation. You will then consider whether it will be proper for you to publish your declaration in favour of the
most unfortunate and most virtuous of men. As for
my part, if the cause shall be brought before the nation,
I am resolved to support it as publicly as I can, even
although they should decide that I am no longer the legal defender of the innocent.

              In

M. de Narbonne wrote the following answer to M. Malesherbes:

« En m'annonçant, Monsieur, que vous avez reçu la déclaration que j'ai eu l'honneur de vous addresser, vous semblez désirer que je vous indique l'usage que je souhaite qui en soit faite. Permettez-moi de m'en rapporter sur cela à votre courageuse vertu, et soyez sûr que j'apprendrai avec reconnoissance tout ce qui sera fait par vous. Au moment du jugement de celui que je choisirois avec orgueil et avec transport pour mon roi, je fis proposer aux ministres François, actuellement en Angleterre, de se rendre sur le champ à Paris, pour nous ranger autour de notre malheureux monarque. Ils

In that case, I shall avail myself of several articles in your letter, without alteration, because it is not in my power to express so well as you have done, certain great truths, which it will be of importance to lay before the nation.

But the greatest part of your declaration consists of facts personal to yourself, and which you alone have the right to certify.

(Signed)   MALESHERBES.

crurent

crurent voir dans cette démarche, des incon-
veniens pour fa caufe; ils en trouvèrent
également à écrire une lettre fignée de nous
tous, pour demander un fauf-conduit qui
nous mit à même de reclamer toute notre
refponfabilité. Je fus réduit à faire feul
cette démarche, et ma lettre ne fut pas
même lue par l'Affemblée. Il ne m'eft donc
refté de moyen d'acquitter cette dette de ma
confcience, que par la déclaration à laquelle
vous daignez donner quelque éloge.

"Ah! c'eft vous, Monfieur, et vos re-
fpectables collegues, qui les méritez toutes.

"Un de mes amis, Monfieur d'Arblay*,
retiré avec moi à la campagne, a cru que la
dépofition qu'il vous a envoyée, pourroit
être de quelque utilité dans une difcuffion;
il fe joint à moi pour vous exprimer les
mêmes fentimens.

"J'ai l'honneur, &c. &c.
(Signé)   L. de NARBONNE†."

* This is the fame gallant officer of whom mention is
made vol. i. p. 233.

† In informing me that you have received the declaration

M. de Narbonne afterwards received the letter which follows :

Malefherbes, 29 Janvier, 1793.

" Votre lettre du 10 Janvier m'eft ar-

ration which I had the honour to fend to you, you feem to defire that I fhould acquaint you with the ufe I wifh to be made of it. Allow me to leave it entirely to your intrepid virtue, and be perfuaded that I fhall gratefully approve of what you think moft proper.

At the moment of the trial of him, whom with pride and tranfport I would choofe for my King, I fent a propofal to the French Minifters, who are at prefent in England, that we fhould immediately fet out for Paris, and take our ftand by the fide of our unfortunate King. They thought fuch a meafure would be prejudicial to his caufe, and thought it would be equally fo, to write a letter figned by us all, demanding a fafe-conduct, which fhould enable us to challenge the refponfibility of our refpective offices at the bar of the Convention. I was obliged to adopt this meafure alone, but my letter was not fo much as read in the Affembly; and no other means remained for me by which I could fatisfy my confcience, but the declaration on which you are pleafed to beftow fome commendation. It is to you and your refpectable colleagues that every praife is due. M. d'Arblay, one of my friends, who lives with me in the country, thinks that the depofition which he fends may be of fervice; he joins me in expreffing the fame fentiments.

I have the honour to be, &c.

rivée,

rivée, Monfieur, à la campagne où je fuis
retiré depuis l'evenement.

" Vous favez fûrement que la déclaration
de vos fentimens que vous m'avez envoyée
manufcrite a été imprimée. Je ne fais pas
fur quelle copie a été faite cette impreffion:
je n'y ai eu aucune part. Le feul ufage
que j'ai fait de votre lettre, et de la déclaration qui y était jointe, a été de les lire à
celui que cela intéreffait. Il en fut touché,
et même attendri : il me recommanda de ne
les pas publier par la crainte de vous com-
promettre; car il a eu, fur cela, les attentions
les plus fcrupuleufes jufqu'au dernier foupir.
L'original fut remis par lui à un de mes collegues, qui defira de l'avoir pour le relire à
tête repofée; et il m'a affuré qu'il n'eft pas
forti de fes mains.

" J'ai l'honneur, Monfieur, de vous affurer de tout mon attachement.

(Signé) " MALESHERBES*."

* Your letter of the 10th of January I received in the
country, where I have been ever fince the *event*.

. Le Comte de Lally-Tolendal had as early as the fifth of November addressed a letter to the Convention, requesting to be permitted to plead the cause of the King at their bar, on which they also passed to the order of the day : and hearing afterwards that M. Target had declined to assist Monsieur de Malesherbes in that honourable task, he repeated his request to the Convention ; but before this second application arrived, the associates of Monsieur de Malesherbes were already appointed.

Monsieur de Lally, however, while he had the expectation that his offer would be ac-

You know undoubtedly that the declaration which you sent me in manuscript has been printed. I am ignorant from what copy this has been done ; I had no hand in it. The only use I made of your letter, and of the declaration which came with it, was to read them to the person whom they most concerned. He was very much affected ; he desired me not to publish them, lest it should bring you to trouble ; for on that head he observed the most scrupulous attention until his last moment. The original was delivered by him to one of my colleagues, who wished to read it in more tranquillity. He assured me that it never was out of his possession.

I have the honour, &c.

cepted,

cepted, had prepared a very eloquent defence of the King in the form of an addrefs to the Convention, which he publifhed during the procefs.

M. Cazales, who had been a Member of the Conftituent Affembly, was at that time in London. This gentleman wrote a letter to Lewis XVI. requefting, in cafe he fhould fo far acknowledge the jurifdiction of the Convention as to make a defence before their tribunal, that he would choofe him for his advocate. M. Cazales urges fome particular reafons for this requeft, that feem equally juft and generous.

He addreffed the Prefident of the Convention, that he might be allowed a fafe-conduct to enable him to perform the honourable tafk which he had folicited, and was in hopes of obtaining leave to execute; adding, that he did not make this requeft in the expectation of having his name effaced from the lift of emigrants, for he gloried in parti-

N n 2
cipating

cipating their political opinions and their misfortunes.

M. Cazales enclofed both thefe letters in one to Petion, the Mayor of Paris ; begging him, after he had read them, to deliver the one to the King and the other to the Prefident of the Convention, and requefting an anfwer as foon as poffible from Petion.

This propofal of M. Cazales was treated with the fame neglect with the others. The Convention paffed to the order of the day when it was laid before them.

It will, no doubt, be thought extraordinary that the Convention fhould have made the fmalleft difficulty in admitting any body as the defender of the King who was agreeable to him ; but what is much more extraordinary, and muft be confidered as a piece of ftriking injuftice, was, to intercept papers intended for his juftification from reaching him, or thofe who were charged with his defence. Yet this injuftice, ftriking as it feems, was

was certainly exercised towards this unfortunate Prince.

M. Bertrand de Moleville, late Minister of the Marine, was obliged to conceal himself, and afterwards to fly to England, in consequence of a decree of accusation issued on the 16th of August against all the late Ministers *.

Being at London when the King's process began, and in possession of facts which he thought might be of use for his justification, he transmitted them with the proofs to the Minister of Justice, requiring that they might be delivered to the King.

Afterwards, under cover to the same Minister, he addressed a packet of papers to M.

* This decree was instantly agreed to, on reading in the Assembly the note mentioned in Vol. I. page 278. M. de Bertrand was not acquainted either with M. Barnave or M. Lameth; he knew nothing of the note, which besides was in itself of no importance. Yet it is evident, from what has since happened, that he has had a just notion of the disposition of those he had to deal with, and acted very wisely in taking refuge in England.

de Made Malefherbes, infcribed *Pieces pour la Juf-tification de Louis XVI.* and he wrote at the fame time to M. de Malefherbes, informing him of the two parcels which had been fent.

Nothing can be conceived more facred than this depofit in the hands of a Minifter of Juftice.

One of the abufes complained of in the ancient government was, that the papers fent to prifoners neceffary for their defence, were fometimes intercepted, and not deli-vered to them in time; the Conftituent Affembly therefore had decreed, that accufed perfons fhould freely receive all papers or memorials for their defence within the fpace of twenty-four hours.

M. de Bertrand muft have been greatly furprifed and fhocked when he received the following letter from M. de Malefherbes:

Paris, le 31 Octobre, 1792.

" Le Miniftre de la Juftice a reçu un pa-quet

quet de M. de Bertrand pour être remis à Louis XVI. et contenant des pieces pour sa justification.

" Le Ministre n'ayant point de communication avec le prisonnier, a envoyé ce paquet à la Convention Nationale.

" Le même Ministre a reçu une lettre depuis du même M. Bertrand, adressée à moi, et il y avoit sur l'adresse, Pieces pour la Justification de Louis XVI. Ces mots ont fait penser au Ministre qu'il étoit aussi obligé de renvoyer ce paquet devant la Convention Nationale. C'est ce que ce Ministre m'a dit quand j'ai été le réclamer.

" J'ai su que ces deux paquets avoient été renvoyés par la Convention à un comité; j'ai été à ce comité pour réclamer au nom de celui dont je suis le défenseur, le paquet qui est pour lui, et en mon nom celui qui est pour moi. J'ai vu que les paquets avoient été ouverts : il y avoit des pieces imprimées, et dans un des paquets, qui n'est pas le mien,

des

des pieces manuſcrites qu'on ne m'a pas laiſſé lire, et qu'on m'a dit être des actes.

« On m'a remis ſans difficulté les imprimés que j'avois déjà : pour les manuſcrits, on n'a pas voulu me les remettre ſans avoir un ordre de la Convention Nationale.

« Quelqu'un du comité a été à la Convention, les pieces à la main, pour demander l'ordre. Il eſt revenu, et m'a dit que ſur ſa demande on a paſſé à l'ordre du jour. Mais il n'a point rapporté les pieces, et m'a dit qu'il les avoit laiſſées ſur le bureau. Il ne m'a pas parû qu'il ait fait conſtater, par aucun acte, que ces pieces qui étoient dans ſon depôt en étoient ſorties.

« J'ai demandé à ces M. M. comment je pourrois me pourvoir pour avoir ces pieces. Tout le monde s'eſt regardé, et perſonne ne m'a rien répondu.

« Voila où nous en ſommes. Je n'ai pas crû devoir inſiſter ſur cet objet auprès de la Convention,

Convention, pendant qu'elle est occupée à délibérer sur le jugement de Louis.

(Signé)   " MALESHERBES *."

* The Minister of Justice received a packet from M. de Bertrand, to be delivered to Lewis XVI. containing papers for his justification.

The Minister having no communication with the prisoner, sent the packet to the Convention.

The same Minister has since received a letter from M. de Bertrand addressed to me, with a parcel entitled *Papers for the Justification of Lewis XVI.* These words made the Minister think that it was his duty to deliver this packet also to the Convention. This is what the Minister told me when I waited on him to demand the papers.

Being informed that those two packets had been transmitted by the Convention to a Committee, I attended that Committee to demand in the name of him whose Counsel I am, that which is for him, and in my own name the other which is addressed to me. I perceived that both packets had been opened. Some of the contents were in print; and in that packet which was not addressed to me, there were papers in manuscript, which I was not permitted to read, and which they told me were acts.

They gave me without difficulty the papers which were in print, and which I had already: as for the manuscripts, they did not choose to give me them without an order from the Convention.

A Member of the Committee having gone to the Convention

The language of this letter is very guarded; the writer has not allowed the sentiments he must have felt at such conduct to appear; but a simple detail of the facts is sufficiently expressive.

M. de Bertrand, in a denunciation transmitted from London to the Convention, did not think the same caution necessary; he appeals in terms of just indignation to the reflection of the Convention on such a flagrant breach of their own decrees, and

vention with the papers to obtain the order, returned and informed me, that on this request they had passed to the order of the day; but he did not bring back the papers, telling me he had left them on the table of the Convention. It does not appear that he has ascertained by any act that those papers which were in his possession were taken from him.

I requested of the Members of the Committee to inform me by what means I could recover those papers. They all looked at each other, but none of them made any answer.

This is the present state of things. I thought it would not be prudent to insist on this, while the Convention were deliberating on the sentence to be pronounced on Lewis.

deviation

deviation from every rule of common equity.

The Minister of Justice informed the Convention, on the 14th of January 1793, that he had received this denunciation of M. Bertrand; that he understood it was also published in the Courier de l'Europe, and the minute placed in the hands of the Lord Mayor of London.

One member observed, that Bertrand having emigrated, was dead in law—that a dead person could not be supposed to write or speak. Another said, that if the Convention should bestow attention on what appeared in newspapers, they must neglect the business of their country: and the Minister of Justice declared, that he did not think it became him, as Minister of the Republic, to correspond with a man who was not only an emigrant, but under a decree of accusation: and Valazé, who was of the Committee, said they were teased with the num-

ber

ber of papers fent to them ; and that as for the manufcripts which Bertrand mentions, he knew nothing of them, if they were not in a packet which the Committee had not thought it worth while to break open.

On this candid and fatisfactory ftate of the matter, the Convention paffed to the order of the day; by which means the King's Counfel were precluded from the knowledge of certain facts, which M. de Bertrand thought material in the King's defence ; which feems alfo to have been the opinion of thofe who fo bafely intercepted them.

The day preceding that on which the King was to appear with his Counfel before the Convention, Santerre informed them, that the King, as he believed, might be conducted in fafety to and from the Affembly, provided he returned while there was day-light ; but if he was detained till it was dark, he could not anfwer for what might

might happen; fo great was the fury of the people againft him.

When thofe who exprefs a fear that the populace will deftroy the King, are the very perfons who have been active in exciting the public againft him—it may naturally be thought that the fear is affected, on purpofe to prevent any attempt to refcue him, rather than to prevent his being deftroyed.

The hypocrify that has been difplayed, and the artifices that have been ufed to impofe upon the people, to inflame their minds againft the King, and ftifle every fentiment of humanity and remorfe, are odious and wicked in the extreme.

When the Deputies went on the morning of the 26th of December to the Convention, all thofe who were fufpected to favour the King were infulted by the crowds, who befet the paffages into the Affembly-hall, as Rolandifts, Briffotins and Royalifts: moft of the Deputies were there

5   by

by eight; and notwithſtanding that a decree had paſſed the evening before to clear the galleries, and not to admit any until a cer-tain hour that morning, the galleries were found full of people, who had remained there all night. It was pretended that the guards could not poſſibly put the decree in execution.

Manuel moved, that the galleries ſhould be cleared of thoſe who had ſhewn ſuch contempt to the decree; and that another ſet of citizens ſhould be admitted. This propoſal met with loud murmurs and hoot-ing, from thoſe who were in poſſeſſion of the tribunes, ſupported by all the faction of the Mountain, who exclaimed for the order of the day. Others ſupported the motion of Manuel. The Preſident divided the Aſ-ſembly, whether they ſhould maintain their own decree, or yield to thoſe who openly deſpiſed it: it was carried to paſs to the or-der of the day.

Here

Here the influence of terror is evident.

Some time previous to the King's arrival, one of the Commiſſioners who had been on duty at the Temple preſented a parcel of keys, which the King had given to Clery, his valet.

The Commiſſioner obſerved, that one of theſe keys opened the iron cheſt lately found full of papers in the Palace, and alſo opened other cabinets belonging to the King; and that of courſe he muſt be acquainted with the keys and papers contained in the iron cheſt.

We ſee men every day who are led into the commiſſion of crimes by the influence of their paſſions, although they have the ſame idea of virtue and vice with thoſe who live a more virtuous life ; but the conduct of many actors in this Revolution, particularly of late, tempts us to believe that they have different ideas of the plaineſt caſes of right and wrong, from what have been generally entertained by mankind.

When

When the Council of the Municipality met on the 25th of December, to decide on the manner in which the King fhould be conducted to the Convention, Chaumet, the Procureur Syndic, faid, that as the King could be confidered in no other light than as a condemned criminal foon to be execuied, it would be difhonourable for the Magiftrates of the people to accompany him to the Convention; and that he ought therefore to be conducted by the military only.

This was declaring that the trial was a mere farce, and that it was already determined to put the King to death, whatever proofs might be brought of his innocence, and whatever might be urged in his defence. There is great reafon to think that this was really the cafe; but it is moft extraordinary that it fhould be mentioned as a thing quite reafonable and proper, and it is ftill more extraordinary that it was rejected by only a very fmall majority, who at laft decreed, that the King fhould be accompanied

nied by the Mayor, the Procureur Syndic, and thirty Municipal Officers.

On the 26th of December, his Majesty, with whom his Counsel had been from an early hour, left the Temple a little before nine in the Mayor's coach, and was conducted as formerly to the gate of the Capucins, rue St. Honoré, where the National Guards formed a line, through which he walked to the Chambre des Conferences, where he again met his Counsel.

General Berruyer, Commander in Chief of all the military of the department of Paris, with all the Field Officers then in the capital, who were not otherwise on duty, accompanied the King on horseback from the Temple to the Assembly Hall. Berruyer informed the President, that the King was arrived. The President desired he might be conducted to the bar; which was done in the following order : Berruyer and Santerre walked first, the Mayor of Paris and the Procureur after them, and the King with Meffrs. Malefherbes, Tronchet and Seze followed. The Prefident faid, " Lewis, the Convention has decreed, that you fhould be ultimately heard this day."

His Majefty anfwered, " Monfieur de Seze, one of my Counfel, will read my defence."

M. de Seze then read the defence, which entirely refutes fome of the charges, fhews the conftitutional objections to others, and with equal candour and ingenuity gives a favourable interpretation to all.

During the defence, M. de Seze was obliged to ftop two or three times: at thofe intervals the King was obferved to fpeak to one or other of his Counfel, which he did with a fmiling countenance.

When the defence was finifhed, he arofe, and, holding a paper in his hand, pronounced in a calm manner, and with a firm voice, what follows:— " Citizens, you have

heard

heard my defence; I now fpeak to you perhaps for the laft time, and declare that my
Counfel have afferted nothing to you but
the truth; my confcience reproaches me
with nothing; I never was afraid of having
my conduct inveftigated; but I obferved with
great uneafinefs, that I was accufed of giving
orders for fhedding the blood of the people on
the 10th of Auguft. The proofs I have given
through my whole life of a contrary difpofition, I hoped would have faved me from
fuch an imputation, which I now folemnly
declare is entirely groundlefs." The Prefident ordered the keys to be fhewn to the
King, and afked if he knew them. The
King anfwered, "that he remembered to
have given a parcel of keys to Clery; but
it was fo long fince he had made ufe of them,
that he did not know whether thefe were
the fame."

The Prefident having afked, "Whether
he wifhed to fay any thing farther," and

being

being anfwered in the negative, the King withdrew into the Chamber of Conferences. Obferving that M. de Seze was greatly heated, he exprefled anxiety about his health, and enquired whether he could not find means to change his linen.

On the way from the Temple to the Affembly, fome perfon in the carriage with the King made mention of fome of the Roman hiftorians, which gave him occafion to fay, that he preferred Tacitus to Livy : he accufed the latter of having compofed fpeeches for the Generals, which certainly had never been pronounced. On his return from the Affembly, he preferved the fame ferenity. The Procureur had his hat on, which had not been the cafe when he was in the carriage with the King the firft time he went to and from the Convention. The King took notice of this piece of rudenefs, by faying to him, " You had forgot your hat the laft time you attended me ; but you have been

been more careful of your health on this occasion."

Observing that the Procureur bowed and waved his hand with a look of familiarity to some persons in the streets, the King said, "I suppose these are citizens of your section?" The Procureur answered, "No, they do not belong to my section; but they were members of the General Council of the 10th of August, *whom I always see with pleasure.*"

The Mayor held his snuff-box in his hand: the Secretary of the Municipality looking at a portrait of M. Chambon's wife on the lid, made the usual observation, that the original was handsomer than the portrait. —The King also desired to see it; which having done, he said, that Monf. Chambon was happy in possessing a woman more beautiful than such a portrait.

The King arrived at the Temple in safety, though the cries of the rabble were more noisy and frequent than on the former day.

He

He had no fooner withdrawn from the Affembly, than Manuel propofed that the King's defence fhould be printed, and fent to the eighty-four departments, and that all difcuffion concerning it fhould be adjourned for three days.

The mention of adjournment excited the moft noify murmurs from fome of the members, and all the people in the galleries. Duhem, deputy from the department of the North, diftinguifhed himfelf on this occafion. —He cried, that Lewis had been heard— —that there was no pretext for farther delay—and infifted that the Convention fhould inftantly proceed, by the nominal appeal, to pronounce judgment.—The murmurs were converted into applaufe. Lanjuinais began to fpeak:—" The time is paffed," faid he, " when bloody-minded men could force the Affembly, by threats, to pronounce degrading decrees; do they expect that we fhall difhonour ourfelves by pronouncing judgment, without

out having had time to weigh the defence of the accufed?" He was interrupted by clamours. Some called out to fend him to the Abbaye, on the pretence of his having infinuated a reflexion againft the heroes of the 10th of Auguft : it was with infinite difficulty that he was allowed to explain. After which, Legendre and others recommenced their outcries for pronouncing judgment before they fhould feparate. " Do you intend to act as a judge, or as a *butcher?*" faid Kerfaint?

This farcafm was applauded by many of the Deputies, but hooted by the tribunes.

Raffron, of the department of Paris, always a very zealous, and often a very clamorous Member, attempted to fpeak ; a deaf perfon would have thought, from the violence of his geftures, and his gaping, that he was bellowing very loud : the man

was

was fo hoarfe with a cold, that he could not be heard, which increafed the anger of his heart, and the contortions of his counte-nance, but entirely fuppreffed his voice.——He was advifed, by thofe who were afraid that the violence of his efforts would throw him into convulfions, to put his opinion in writing——which he did; and it was read to the Affembly by the Prefident. The import of it was, that they ought di-rectly to pafs fentence on the King, of whofe guilt, this temperate judge declared, no calm and candid man could have any doubt.

Raffron's opinion was loudly approved of by the galleries, but did not convince the majority of the deputies, fome of whom ventured to exprefs a defire of ftill more time to deliberate on the defence they had juft he ard——The people exclaimed with horror at the idea. Some deputies moved, that they fhould be called to order, which rendered

rendered them more diforderly than ever. It was propofed to adjourn—This made Duhem outrageous : he rufhed into the middle of the hall, followed by a number of the members of the faction of the Mountain, crying " La Mort du Tyran !"—and feeming to appeal to the galleries—and even to threaten Fermond the Prefident.

Had Lewis XVI. really been the bloody tyrant thefe men affected to call him, ftill this behaviour in his judges, on his trial, would have been indecent and odious ; but to fhew fuch an unrelenting fpirit, and fuch fury againft a Prince of fo mild a character —one *who has borne his faculties fo meek*—is not to be accounted for by any of the motives which ufually influence men, whether virtuous or vicious. Some members of this National Convention feem as deaf to the voice of expediency and felf-intereft as of humanity and juftice. Inftead of any ra-

tional

tional principle, they appear to be urged on by brutal and furious inſtinct to the death of the King, like blood-hounds, who never quit the ſcent till they have drunk the blood of their prey.

During this diſgraceful ſcene, Fermond calmly kept his ſeat, allowing the fury of thoſe men to exhauſt itſelf: at length, perceiving that Petion was inclined to ſpeak, he invited him to aſcend the tribune, conceiving, from the ſtrength of his former popularity, that he had a better chance of being heard than any other member who did not belong to the faction of the Mountain: it was with great difficulty, however, that he was allowed to ſpeak.——He endeavoured to convince them of the indecency of proceeding to judgment immediately, and before the members had time to deliberate on the defence which they had juſt heard.

When it appeared that the majority of the

the Convention were not to be driven into the shameful measure of giving judgment directly, the point was given up; and it was decreed that every Member had a right to pronounce his opinion on the whole cause from the tribune, before the day for the nominal appeal was fixed.

Whoever has attended to the conduct and spirit of the Jacobins may have remarked, that however popular any person has been among them—however greatly he may have distinguished himself by promoting their measures with zeal and ability—if he chances to be seized with a qualm of conscience at last, and hesitates to act with them in a single instance, all his past merit is forgotten, and he is execrated by the society as a determined enemy.

The night after the King's defence was made, a Member of the Jacobins gave an account in that society of what had passed at the Convention—particularly that Manuel had

proposed

proposed to adjourn the discussion for no less a period than three days; and that Petion had spoken against pronouncing judgment without separating. This was heard with horror and indignation: it was immediately decreed, that Manuel should be expelled from the society. Petion with difficulty escaped the same fate, which, however, was postponed only for a short time.

For several days after the defence, the time of the Convention was mostly taken up in hearing the opinions of the members: all of them prefaced their discourses, by declaring a conviction of the King's guilt; perhaps they thought this necessary to secure them the liberty of proceeding. They differed however with respect to the penalty he had incurred; many being of opinion that justice and policy forbade the pains of death: all the Rolandists, Brissotins and Girondists were of this number.

ber. Danton's and Robefpierre's party argued for immediate death ; and became fo
impatient at the delay, from hearing fo many difcourfes, that they repealed the decree that had paffed a few days before ; and
inftead of hearing every member from the
tribune, they refolved that the difcourfes
fhould be printed, and laid on the table to be
read by thofe who chofe, and the 14th of
January was appointed for pronouncing ultimately. It was not till the 15th, however,
that the firft appeal was made, owing
to the long and warm difcuffions which
took place in the Convention before it was
determined in what terms, and in what order
the queftions fhould be ftated on which the
Convention was to decide: at laft, it was
decreed that the following queftions fhould
be put to all the members, and decided by
the nominal appeal :

1. Is Lewis Capet, late King of France,
guilty of a confpiracy againft liberty, and
of

of attempts againſt the general ſafety of the
State ? Yes, or No.

2. Shall the judgment to be pronounced
on Lewis, be ſubmitted to the ratification
of the people in the Primary Aſſemblies ?
Yes, or No.

3. What puniſhment has he incurred?

Theſe queſtions were artfully and wick-
edly arranged in this order, to render the
King's condemnation more certain.

Several deputies who thought the appeal
to the Primary Aſſemblies a wrong meaſure
in itſelf, gave their votes againſt it, in the
belief that the King would not be condemned to death——but had the queſtion reſpecting the puniſhment been brought on
in the ſecond place, they would have ſeen
that the appeal to the people was the only
means of ſaving the life of the King, and
would then have voted for that meaſure,
although in general they did not approve
of it.

This accounts for the length and violence of the debates, on a queſtion apparently of ſo little importance as the order in which the propoſitions were to be voted :—for ſome of thoſe who wiſhed to ſave the life of the King ſaw this in the light above ſtated, and ſtrove to have the queſtions other-wiſe arranged :—neither party, however, avowed the real reaſon of their zeal, and the malice of the King's enemies prevailed.

On the firſt queſtion, the Aſſembly voted almoſt unanimouſly in the affirmative.— But many of the deputies declared, that they gave this opinion as citizens and legiſlators, but not as judges; becauſe they neither thought themſelves qualified for that office, nor authoriſed by their Conſtituents to aſ-ſume it.

Moriſſon, of the department of Vendée, refuſed to vote : he ſaid, " he would give his reaſons if the Convention exacted it," which was not done : a very few others declined voting ; among whom was Noel,

of

of the department of Vofges, who faid,
" that his fon having been killed on the
frontiers, fighting againft the enemy, he
confidered the King as the primary caufe of
his fon's death, and felt fo much prejudice
againft him, that he was unqualified for being his judge."

Offelin, who had been one of the Judges
belonging to the Tribunal appointed in Auguft, gave his vote in the affirmative, and at
the fame time ftated, " that one of the accufations againft the King is, that he continued to pay his guards after they were reduced, although many of them had emigrated;
that his Counfel, confcious of the force of
this accufation, had taken great pains to deftroy it, and had afferted that the King had
not paid the guards after the 1ft of January
1792; but that he himfelf, as one of the Adminiftrators of the Commune of Paris, had
had bufinefs to tranfact with M. Laporte,
and that Madame Laporte had made a de-
duction

duction from the revenues of the Civil Lift
of 1,200,000 livres in the month of July
1792, for the payment of the guards, then
well known to have emigrated."

What ftrefs ought to be laid on fuch evidence fo given, I leave to lawyers to decide;
but common juftice might have dictated to
a man, who thus volunteered himfelf as a
witnefs, that he ought not to vote as a
judge.

When the name of M. Egalité was called,
it was imagined that he alfo would have declined voting; and when he pronounced
" *Oui*," a murmur of furprife and indignation was heard.

The fecond queftion was undoubtedly
intended as a means of faving the life of the
King, and would in all probability have had
that effect, if it had not been brought
forward until the fentence of death was
carried.

The meafure of referring the King's fate

to the people themfelves, which from its nature was highly popular, had been rendered the reverfe by the unwearied exertions of thofe who feared that, if carried, it would fave his life.

In giving their votes on this fecond queftion in the affirmative, feveral of the Deputies faid, they were aware of the danger to which they expofed themfelves; but being convinced that their conflituents had elected them as legiflators, and not as judges; and as it was repugnant to their confciences to unite the characters of jury and accufers, they would run every rifk rather than do it.——One Member faid, " As I give my vote for referring this matter to the Primary Affemblies of the people, I expect the worft, and I glory in being of the number of thofe who brave the danger." Another, " that in pronouncing the fame vote, he devoted himfelf to the daggers of affaffins."

The

The speech that Manuel made on giving his vote was remarkable.——" I fee here a Legiflative Affembly, but not an affembly of judges ; for judges do not murmur at the opinions of their brethren, though different from their own : they do not openly abufe and calumniate each other ; they are cold as the law of which they are the organs. If the Convention had been a tribunal of law, a near relation of the King, who has not been reftrained either by a fenfe of fhame or by his confcience, would not have been permitted to vote on this occafion."

The Prefident called Manuel to order, telling him to avoid perfonalities. Manuel then voted for the appeal. Raffron, Panis, Legendre and Marat, who are all of the Department of Paris, and feem of congenial difpofitions, voted againft it.

It was midnight before the Appeal was ended:——there were 424 againft, 283 for the reference ; 10 refufed to vote. The Af-

fembly

fembly adjourned till the 16th, and when it met, incidental bufinefs prevented the appel nominal from being begun till the evening. Many of the members particularifed their reafons for voting as they did. The ceremony lafted through the whole night. The refult was a majority for death. Three hundred and nineteen voted for imprifonment till the end of the war, and then banifhment. Had all who voted for death with reftriction, that the fentence fhould not be executed till the peace, or till the Conftitution was framed and accepted, been fubftracted from the majority, it would have been diminifhed to a furplus of only five or fix votes.

On this occafion, M. Egalité voted for death without reftriction. A murmur of horror was heard. One deputy ftarted from his feat, ftruck his hands together, and exclaimed, " *Ah le fcélérat !*" others repeated the fame expreffion. The terms in which he delivered his vote are remarkable :
" Unique-

"" Uniquement occupé de mon devoir, convaincu que tous ceux qui ont attenté ou at-
tenteront par la fuite à la fouveraineté du
peuple, méritent la mort, je vote pour la
mort*."

· Previous to the fcrutiny, and after every
member had voted, the Prefident informed
the Convention that he had received a letter

---

* Influenced by no confideration but that of performing my duty, convinced that all who have confpired, or fhall hereafter confpire againft the fovereignty
of the people, deferve death, I vote for death.

I have it from good authority, that an acquaintance
of M. Egalité underftanding that he was not to vote on
the favourable fide, advifed him to declare, that on account of the ill treatment which he imagined he had
formerly received from the King, there would be an
impropriety in his voting—that this would be confidered as a good reafon for declining, and would preclude the indignation which muft be the confequence
of his voting againft the King. Egalité promifed either
to follow this plan or to ftay from the Convention on
the day of the appel nominal ; but having the day before that took place been waited on by Robefpierre,
Marat, and others of that party, they urged reafons
which made him act as he did.

from

from the Spanish Minister, and one from the King's Counsel. There was a cry from the Mountain for the order of the day. Garan-Coulon said, that the King's Counsel should be heard, but the Spanish Minister's letter should not be read. " How !" exclaimed Danton, " the Spanish Court have not acknowledged our Republic, and they attempt to influence our deliberations ! If all the members were of my opinion, we should declare war against Spain for this interference alone."

Gensonnet proposed that the King's Counsel should be heard after the result of the scrutiny was known, but that in the mean time the Convention should refuse to hear the letter of the Spanish Minister, and pass to the order of the day. It was unanimously agreed not to hear the letter, and Robespierre declaimed also against hearing the Counsel. In this he failed.

Duchastel,

Duchaftel, Deputy from the department
of Deux-Sèvres, having been indifpofed,
had not been in the Affembly when his
name was called the preceding night. He
now was fupported into the hall, and as the
fcrutiny was not yet clofed, demanded to
give his vote. It was fufpected that he
came to give his vote on the merciful fide ;
and thofe who had during the whole procefs thirfted for the King's blood, and were
now doubtful how the fcrutiny ftood, oppofed his voting. Valazé, one of the fecre-
taries, declaring that the fcrutiny was *not*
clofed, Duchaftel gave his voice for banifhment. A fhameful attempt was next made,
on a frivolous pretext, to erafe his vote——
this was not permitted. The Prefident announced the iffue of the fcrutiny as above
mentioned, and the King's Counfel were admitted to the bar.

Defeze faid, that the law and a decree of

the

the Convention having entrusted them with the defence of Lewis, they came with sorrowful hearts to perform their last duty to their client; he then read what follows from a paper signed by the King: "I owe to my honour, I owe to my family, not to acknowledge the justice of a sentence that declares me guilty of a crime with which I cannot reproach myself. I therefore appeal to the Nation at large from the sentence of its representatives; and I empower my Counsel by these presents, and expressly charge them on their fidelity, to make this appeal known to the National Assembly, and to require that it shall be inserted into the minutes of their fittings.

(Signed) Louis."

Each of the Counsel made a short address to the Convention: Deseze conjured them in the name of humanity and justice, to revise, or leave to the ratification of the People,

ple,

ple, a sentence carried by a majority of only five votes, and against which three hundred and nineteen of the Assembly had declared their opinions.

Tronchet represented that many of those who voted for death, had declared that they founded their opinion on the penal code—yet the penal code requires two thirds of the voices to condemn an accused person. A decree of the Convention, passed only that morning, had pronounced that the majority of a single voice was sufficient. On that decree being objected to, they had simply passed to the order of the day; but in a matter of such immense importance, the appel nominal was necessary: he therefore demanded the repeal of that decree.

M. de Malesherbes said, that he had formerly had occasion to reflect with great attention on the important question of how the votes ought to be taken in criminal cases;

cafes; but that not being in the habit of fpeaking extempore, he begged in the moft earneft and affecting manner, that he might be allowed till the next day to arrange the ideas which he wifhed to fubmit to their confideration.

Robefpierre and others argued on the other fide; and the Convention rejected the appeal made in the name of the King, paffed to the order of the day on the requifition of Malef_herbes, and adjourned till next day the debate on the delay of the execution of the fentence, which was difcuffed at length accordingly.

Two remarkable incidents occurred during this debate, which fhew what an excefs of wanton barbarity and perfevering rancour fome men are capable of upon the moft folemn and affecting occafions. Tallien, with diabolical irony, argued for the King's immediate execution, on what he called motives of humanity. " He knows," faid the wretch,

wretch, " that he is condemned, and that a respite is demanded——to keep him in suspense is prolonging his agony. Let us, in tenderness for his sufferings, decree his immediate execution, and put him out of anguish."

This shocked even Danton, who expressed disapprobation of it.

The other incident occurred when Thomas Paine, who had formerly given his opinion against the death of the King, ascended the tribune: as he was not in the habit of pronouncing French, one of the secretaries read his discourse translated from the original English. His reasoning against the execution of the sentence probably was thought very persuasive, since those who had heard the discourses of Buzot, Condorcet and Brissot to the same purport without interruption, broke out into murmurs while Paine's opinion was reading ; and Marat at length losing all patience, exclaimed that Paine was a Quaker, and insinuated, that

his

his mind being contracted by the narrow principles of his religion, was incapable of the *liberality* requisite for condemning men to death. This shrewd argument not being thought convincing, the Secretary continued to read, " That the execution of the sentence, instead of an act of justice, would appear to all the world, and particularly to their allies the American States, an act of vengeance ; and that if he were sufficiently master of the French language, he would, in the name of his brethren of America, present a petition at their bar against the execution of the sentence."

Marat and his associates cried, that these could not possibly be the sentiments of Thomas Paine, and that the Assembly were imposed on by a false translation.

On comparing it with the original, however, it was found just.

They proceeded to the fourth appel nominal, which was terminated at midnight on Saturday the 19th of January 1793.

The

The voters were reftricted to pronounce a fimple yes or no, without any reafoning; 310 voted for a refpite of the fentence, 380 againft it.

It may be thought, from the refult of this queftion, that the reference to the Primary Affemblies would have been equally rejected, at whatever time that propofal had been voted ; but it fhould be remembered, that it was ftill lefs obnoxious to vote for referring the fentence entirely to the people, than to vote for a refpite of a fentence actually pronounced.

The Executive Council were ordered to notify this to the King the day following, and that the execution was to take place within twenty-four hours of the notification. It was decreed at the fame time, that he fhould be allowed free communication with his family, and to have any ecclefiaftic he pleafed to attend him.

The Executive Council, of which Garat the Minifter of Juftice was Prefident, met

. on

on the morning of the 20th. He, with two other Members of the Council, and the Secretary, fet out for the Temple, where they arrived at two.

Being introduced into the King's apartment, Garat, who was greatly·agitated, faid with a faltering voice—" Lewis, the Executive Council is ordered to notify to you the decree which the National Convention paffed laft night."

The Secretary began to read the decree. In the preamble, the King is charged with having *confpired againft the general fafety of the Nation*—He was fhocked at the idea, and repeated the expreffion with emotion. The Secretary, who had paufed, refumed, and the King heard the reft, including the fentence, with calmnefs.

When the Secretary had finifhed, the King took a paper from his pocket, the contents of which he informed them of, and defired the Minifter of Juftice to prefent it to the Executive Council.

Garat

Garat informed him, that the Council could not decide on the subjects of his demands, but that he would immediately carry them to the Convention, who had already agreed to some of them.

He went accordingly, and read to the Assembly the paper which the King had given him.

It contained a request of a respite of three days, that he might prepare himself for appearing in the presence of God : and for that purpose, that he might be freely visited by a person, whose name he would mention to the Commissioners.

That he might be freed from their inspection during the interval allowed him to live.

That he might have free communication with his family.

That the National Convention would permit his family to withdraw from France to any other country they chose. Finally, he recommended to the generosity of the nation

5   a number

a number of old servants, many of whom had nothing to live on but the pensions he had allowed them.

When the Minister of Justice returned to the Temple, he informed the King, that the Convention acquiesced in most of his demands; he gave a favourable interpretation to the general answer which had been given to that respecting the lot of his family, but added, that *the delay was refused.*

" Allons," said the King, " il faut se soumettre."

There is something infinitely harsh and revolting to humanity in the refusal of this last request; which there is every reason to believe, from the character and conduct of the King, proceeded from the pious motive which he assigned—and not, as his enemies have suggested, from a weak desire of prolonging a wretched existence.

Should it be the fate of any of those men who rejected this request of the unfortunate Monarch,

Monarch, ever to be in similar circumstances, as they will have more need of it
than he had, I sincerely hope that they will
be allowed more than three days to prepare
themselves for eternity.

When the Minister of Justice had retired,
the King gave to one of the Commissioners
a letter addressed to Mr. Edgeworth, who
was the person he wished to attend him in
his last moments.

Mr. Edgeworth's father was originally a
Protestant clergyman of a good family in
Ireland, who was converted to the Roman
Catholic religion, and had established himself in France, where he bred his son as an ec-
clesiastic, in the faith which he himself preferred.—The son recommended himself so
much by his good conduct and excellent
character, that he was chosen by the Princess Elizabeth as her confessor; by which
means he became known to, and highly
esteemed by, the King; of which he gave the

ftrongeft proof, by fending for him on this awful occafion.

The King's letter was carried to Mr. Edgeworth by three foldiers, fent by the Council of the Commune. The contents of the letter were requefting his attendance; but if he found himfelf, from apprehenfion of the confequence, or any other caufe, averfe to come, entreating him to find another prieft who had not the fame reluctance.

Mr. Edgeworth informed the foldiers, that he would attend them directly to the Temple. His mother and fifter were then at a fmall diftance from Paris; he defired Madame d'Argouge, a relation with whom he lived when in town, not to inform them of what had happened, becaufe he faw that lady herfelf greatly alarmed, and feared that fhe might communicate her apprehenfions to them.

Mr. Edgeworth was conducted firft before the Council in the Temple, and then to

the

the King. On his being introduced, he instantly shewed such marks of respect and sensibility as affected the unfortunate Prince so much, that he burst into tears, and was for some moments unable to speak: at length he said—" Excuse me, Mr. Edgeworth, I have not been accustomed of late to the company of men like you."

After passing some time with his confessor, the King thought he had acquired sufficient fortitude to bear an interview with his family. The Queen, Princess Elizabeth, with the Prince and Princess Royal, were conducted to his apartment. They continued near three hours together—No tragic poet has imagined a scene more affecting than what was realized at this interview—The actors, so lately placed in the most brilliant situation that the world can give—hurled from the summit of human splendor to the depth of human misery. A sister, children, and a wife, in a prison, taking their last leave of a

brother,

brother, father, and hufband, rendered more
dear than ever by his paft fufferings, their
common calamity, and the dreadful fate
awaiting him the following day.

The King, though affected at different
times beyond the power of expreffion, retained his recollection to the laft. When
they were to feparate, the Princefs Elizabeth
mentioned their hopes of feeing him again
in the morning. He allowed her to expect
it. The Queen could liften to no words of
comfort. No confideration could prevent
her from pouring forth her indignation in
the moft violent expreffions againft the enemies of her hufband. In the bitternefs of
her foul fhe beat her breaft and tore her
hair ; and her fcreams were heard at intervals, all that night of agony and horror.

After his family had withdrawn, the King
remained for fome time with his eyes fixed
on the ground without fpeaking ; then with
a pro-

a profound figh he pronounced—" Ce moment étoit terrible."

I have it from the beft authority, that after
his family were withdrawn, the mifery of
his own fate did not engrofs his mind fo entirely as to exclude all folicitude for the fate
of others; he enquired in a moft affectionate
manner of Mr. Edgeworth for feveral whom
he confidered as his friends, and particularly
for the ecclefiaftics, who had been perfecuted
with the greateft cruelty; and expreffed fatif-
faction at hearing that many of them had
efcaped to England, where they were received with kindnefs and hofpitality.

Mr. Edgeworth prevailed on him to go to
bed for four hours.

He rofe at five; and expreffing an incli-
nation to hear mafs, Mr. Edgeworth informed the Council who were fitting in the
Temple of the King's requeft. Some difficulties were made, which Mr. Edgeworth removed, faying that the ufual ornaments and

Q q 3   all

all that was requisite for the ceremony could be procured from a neighbouring church.

Mr. Edgeworth shewing great solicitude that the King should be gratified, one of the Commissioners said, he had heard of people who had been poisoned taking the sacrament.

To this horrid insinuation Mr. Edgeworth made no other reply, than by calmly reminding him that the Committee were to procure the host.

What was necessary was provided. Mr. Edgeworth said mass, and administered the sacrament to the King; and then mentioned that his family expected to see him before he left the Temple. The King, fearing that he had not sufficient firmness for a second interview, wished to spare them the agony of such a scene, and therefore declined it.

At half an hour after eight Santerre came

7   and

and informed him that he had received orders to conduct him to the place of execution. After passing three minutes in private with his Confessor, he came to the
outer room where Santerre had remained,
and addressing him, said, " Marchons, je
suis prêt." In descending to the court, he
begged the Commissioners to recommend
certain persons who were in his service to
the Commune; after which, not imagin-
ing that Mr. Edgeworth intended to accompany him any further, he was bid-
ding him adieu. But the other said, his
attendance was not over. " What," said
the King, " do you intend to adhere to me
still ?" " Yes," replied the Confessor, " to
the last."

The King walked through the Court
with a firm step, and entered the Mayor's
coach, followed by Mr. Edgeworth, a Municipal Officer, and two Officers of the National Guards.

Qq 4 The

The King recited the prayers for perfons in the agonies of death during the conveyance from the Temple to the Place de la Révolution, formerly the Place de Louis XV.

When the carriage ftopped at the fcaffold, the King faid—"Nous voici donc arrivé." He pulled off his coat, unbuttoned the neck of his fhirt, afcended the fcaffold with fteadinefs, and furveyed for a few moments the immenfe multitude; then approaching the edge, as there was a good deal of noife, he made a motion with his hand for filence, which inftantly took place *—then fpeaking

* It has been faid that the ferenity which the King fhewed at his death, did not proceed wholly from the fupport he derived from religion, but was partly owing to the hope he entertained to the laft, even when on the fcaffold, that his life would be faved by the people, and that his Confeffor encouraged him in this hope.

Nothing can be more improbable than this ftory. Had the King entertained any fuch hope, it muft ftill have been intermingled with fear; and fuch a ftate of mind, inftead of calmnefs, was more likely to produce agitation.

The

with a raised voice, he said—" Francais, je meurs innocent. Je pardonne à tous mes ennemis, et je souhaite que la France——"

Santerre, who was on horseback near the scaffold, made a signal for the drums to beat, and for the executioners to perform their office. The King's voice was drowned in the noise of the drums.

Three executioners then approached to seize him : at the sight of a cord, with which one of them attempted to tie his arms, the King for the first time shewed signs of indignation, and as if he was going to resist. Mr. Edgeworth put him in mind that the Saviour of Mankind had allowed his arms to

The whole of his behaviour shews a manly and christian resignation to a fate which he thought inevitable, and proves that his hopes were removed from earth to heaven.

The character of Mr. Edgeworth precludes him from the suspicion of having encouraged a hope which would have disturbed that turn of mind which it was his duty to promote and cherish in the King.

be

be .tied : he no fooner pronounced this, than the King became paffive as a lamb. The executioners laid hold of him, and placed him on the guillotine. The Confeffor then kneeling with his face near to that of the King, pronounced aloud—" Enfant de Saint Louis, montez au ciel."—The blow was given—Mr. Edgeworth's face was fprinkled with the King's blood. The executioner walked round the fcaffold, holding up the head to be feen by the people. A few, who had probably been hired for the purpofe, cried—" Vive la Nation! Vive la Republique !"

Thus did the French Nation, who had endured the cruelties of Lewis the Eleventh, the treachery of Charles the Ninth, and the tyranny of Lewis the Fourteenth, condemn and execute for the pretended crimes of cruelty, treachery, and tyranny, the mildeft, moft juft, and leaft
tyrannical

tyrannical Prince that ever fat on their throne.

Let us confider the conduct of the Convention with regard to the King, and decide whether it can be reconciled to good fenfe, juftice, or humanity.

When the Deputies firft met and formed a National Convention, they knew that a moft extraordinary event had happened; that the palace of their King had been attacked; that many citizens had been killed, and almoft all his guards flaughtered; that the King himfelf with all his family had been thrown into prifon, where they ftill remained; and that their duty, as the reprefentatives of the nation, was to inveftigate the caufes of this extraordinary event, and to punifh the guilty.

The Convention were informed by thofe *who had planned and directed* the attack on the palace, " That the citizens had been wantonly fired on by the guards, in confequence

of

of orders from the King; that the King was betraying the country to an invading army, with the leaders of which he was in corre-ſpondence; and that unleſs he had been attacked and impriſoned, the nation would have been enſlaved."

Having heard this accuſation, it was natural to have imagined that the Convention would, in the next place, have wiſhed to know the King's account of theſe tranſactions, that they might be the better able to judge which account was the moſt probable, and the beſt ſupported by known and incontrovertible facts.

One fact they muſt have known, namely, that when the King had reaſon to believe that his palace was to be attacked, he ſent for the Mayor of Paris and other Civil Officers to be near his perſon, and to be witneſſes of his conduct.

From this it was to be preſumed, that the King wiſhed to avoid force, and if he ſhould

be

be driven to the neceffity of ufing it, that it
fhould be under the direction of the Civil
Magiftrate.

The Convention might have recollected,
that although one of the many evils which
are inherent in a *defpotic* government, be,
that there is no door to freedom but through
infurrection; yet the moderate and equitable character of Lewis XVI. had early inclined him to fuch alterations in the old fyftem, as would gradually have united the
prerogatives of limited monarchy with the
rights of free men.

Such confiderations, with a moderate fhare
of candour and gratitude, one would imagine,
would have made them fufpend their belief
in the full extent of the crimes imputed to the
King; and at all events have prevented their
giving a decifion injurious to him, till he
was heard, and till as many of their brother
Deputies as were expected had arrived. Inftead of this, they thought proper, on the
very

very firft day of their meeting, when not above half of their number had arrived, without hearing the King, to pronounce the fevereft fentence againft him which they had a right by the Conftitution to have done, even if all of which he was accufed had been clearly proved *.

They next proceed with more delibera-tion, to determine whether the King may not ftill be tried for his life.

The inviolability with which the Confti-tution had invefted the monarch, was, in the minds of many of the Deputies, an infur-mountable objection to this meafure.

It might have been imagined, that if the terms in which this inviolability was expreff-ed by the Conftitution had been obfcure and fomewhat dubious, ftill it would have been becoming in the legiflators of a great nation to have explained them in the moft

* Abolition of Royalty.

favourable

favourable sense for their unfortunate monarch: there was no room, however, for their exercising their generosity in this manner; for the terms are as clear as language can make them.

This had no effect on a majority of the Deputies, who declared, that they considered the inviolability as a mere chimera, which ought not to be regarded.

The reasoning by which they supported this proposition will appear extraordinary. " The Constitution," say they, " could only render the King inviolable while he was King, but it can have no such effect now that Royalty is abolished; and therefore we may now with propriety try him as a private citizen."

According to the military law and custom of some countries, an officer of the army may be condemned to lose his commission, and to serve in the ranks for certain crimes, for which a common soldier would be condemned

demned to undergo a corporal punishment;
—but nothing so unjust was ever thought of,
as first to make the officer suffer the punishment appointed by the military code for his
crime as an officer, and afterwards, on the
pretence of his being a common soldier, to
inflict a second punishment for the same
crime.

Other Deputies reason in this manner:

The inviolability is very good in ordinary cases, but it is of no use in the present.
The people are sovereign, independent of
the Constitution, and cannot be bound by
any law made by the Constitution.—Louis
XVI. n'étoit Roi que par la Constitution:
La Nation étoit Souverain sans Constitution.
et sans Roi *.

Thus that metaphysical monarch, le Peuple Souverain, is conjured up, on convenient occasions, to answer for every kind of

* Rap. de Mailhe, 7 Nov. 1792.

injustice

injuftice and cruelty:—he was at one time declared to be the author of themaffa-cres of the prifoners, on purpofe to fcreen the real murderers; and in this inftance he is brought forward to annihilate the moft folemn and facred of all obligations.

The Committee who formed the Decree of Accufation againft the King, feem to have been very much perplexed, on account of the force and precifion in which his in-violability is declared by the Conftitution. Mailhe, who prefented it in their name to the Convention, after repeating this em-barraffing article, fays, with fome degree of paffion, " Cela veut-il dire que le Roi, tant qu'il feroit affez adroit pour éluder les cas de la décheance, pourroit impunément s'aban-donner aux paffions les plus féroces, et fe-roit-il quitte pour la perte d'un fceptre qui lui étoit odieux, parce qu'il n'étoit pas de fer ?"

Without taking notice of the falfe and

childish exaggerations which his queftion infinuates, Mailhe may be anfwered, that if
the King had the addrefs to elude all the
cafes to which the Conftitution has affixed
the pain of forfeiture of the crown, he certainly ought not to forfeit it——and if Mailhe
himfelf were on his trial for murder or robbery, and it clearly appeared, that the accufation was falfe, or, to ufe Mailhe's expreffion, that he had had. the addrefs to elude
thofe crimes, I confefs I fhould be for ac-
quitting him; for whatever may be the opinion and practice in France, I adhere to the
old notion, that a man, who has the addrefs
to be innocent, ought not to be punifhed as
guilty.

Nothing can be more unworthy, than for
the legiflators of a nation to attempt to explain away the obvious meaning of a propofition fo clearly expreffed, as that relating
to the King's inviolability is by the French
Conftitution; and the arguments they have
ufed

ufed are as fophiftical as the attempt is unbecoming. For my own part, I do not
think it extravagant to queftion, whether
Lewis XVI would have accepted of the Conftitution, had the inviolability been explained to him *then*, in the manner which it is
now explained. I am convinced he would
not, if he had thought that Danton, Robefpierre, Legendre, and Marat were, in any
prefumable cafe, to be his judges.

But had all objections founded on the
inviolability of the King's perfon been
removed, were it clear that he might have
been tried and dealt with as a private citizen, for crimes laid to his charge as a King;
ftill the Convention, as it was compofed,
could not, with any colour of impartiality,
be confidered as a proper tribunal for his
trial: to have rendered it fuch, it would have
been neceffary to remove all thofe who had
in print, or from the tribune, declared themfelves convinced of his guilt, or in any way

R r 2   manifefted

manifefted a defire that he fhould be executed. What poffibility is there, for example, that the King's innocence fhould be
proved to Saint-Juft, Deputy for the department of l'Aifne, who, in the difcourfe he
read to the Convention, fays, " Le procés
doit être fait au Roi, non point pour le crime
de fon adminiftration, mais pour le crime
d'avoir été Roi: on ne peut point regner in-
nocemment. Tout roi n'eft qu'un rebelle
et un ufurpateur." And Robefpierre, in
the Society of Jacobins, where there were
feveral who had been members of the Legiflative Affembly, and were then of the
Convention, faid, " that if the King were ab-
folved, *they* muft of courfe be confidered and
punifhed as rebels." Were fuch men impartial judges?

And if the objections to particular Deputies were entirely removed, one folid one
remains againft the whole Affembly, namely, that being the King's accufers, they

were

were difqualified from being his jury or judges.

When we next come to confider the nature of the proofs in fupport of the accufation, and the manner in which they were obtained, the force of the objections againft them is obvious and ftriking. The papers found in the King's cabinet on the 10th of Auguft, and thofe afterwards difcovered in the iron cheft in the wall of the Tuileries, are not fair and legal evidence—becaufe papers may have been introduced and mixed with the others by the King's enemies; becaufe papers may have been loft or removed which would have explained and accounted for what appears criminal in others; becaufe a perfon's having criminal papers in his cuftody, is no proof that he approves of, or is even acquainted with their contents; and ftill lefs of his intending to adopt the opinions, or follow the plans or counfels of the writers.

5

Let

Let us farther suppose, that all the papers presented to the Convention are the genuine papers found in the King's closet, without any having been added or subftracted; ftill they do not conftitute a proof of his having formed any fcheme of deftroying the Conftitution, or betraying the country to itse nemies.

Briffot in his writings, Louvet and Barbaroux in their fpeeches in the Convention, affert, that they, and their affociates, brought about the Revolution of the 10th of Auguft, with a view to eftablifh a Republic. They were fo precife and minute on this important point, as even to particularife the place. —It was at Charenton, as they declared, that the meafure of attacking the King in his palace was determined on; it was at firft agreed to be on the 29th of July, but afterwards poftponed to the 10th of Auguft. Danton, Robefpierre, and Chabot, infift that this honour belongs to them. Petion, who
had

had been sent for by the King, who was actually in the palace as a Civil Magistrate, and in the character of a mediator, early that morning, was afterwards very much hurt, because Robespierre insinuated that he had had very little share in the insurrection of the 10th of August. " Les hommes," says he, in his letter to Robespierre, " qui se font attribué la gloire de cette journée, font les hommes à qui elle appartient le moins; elle est due aux braves fédérés, *et à leur directoire secret qui concertait depuis long temps le plan de l'insurrection.*" And in his letter to the Society of Jacobins he claims his own right to part of the glory : " Je n'ai pas peu contribué," says Petion, "à amener la journée du 10 Aout." After this, how could any men of common sense, and common candour, hear with patience the King accused of being the aggressor on that occasion ? Yet this was done in the act of accusation, and repeated by many of the members in their speeches during the procès.

Finally,

' Finally, let it be fuppofed, that the perfon of the King was not rendered inviolable by the Conftitution ; that the Convention was the proper tribunal by which he ought to have been tried ; that the papers were unexceptionable evidence; and that the proof againft him was convincing : after all this has been admitted, ftill it is clear that it was moft inexpedient and unwife in the National Convention to decree his execution, becaufe it would exafperate many of the Princes of Europe ; and if it pleafed any, it would afford even them a pretext for making war with France; thus creating new enemies to their infant Republic, and ftrengthening the hands of the old.

Becaufe the great object of punifhment is to prevent, and not to avenge crimes ; and in a Republic the fame cafe could never again occur.

Becaufe a living and dethroned King would have been lefs interefting to the public,

lic, and therefore lefs formidable to the prefent government of France, than a young Prince, whofe character calumny could not touch, and whofe father had been beheaded.

A French lady, diftinguifhed for wit, having remarked the ingenuity of a footman belonging to a man of high quality, who was as ugly and ftupid as his fervant was the reverfe, faid, " Il faut avouer que la Nature n'eft pas Ariftocrate."—If Nature has been partial to democracy, it muft be confeffed, however, that the Democrates of France have been moft ungrateful to Nature, by violating all her laws, and wounding all her feelings.

The records of mankind exhibit no example of crimes deliberately committed, attended with fo many circumftances of wanton unrelenting cruelty, and fo evidently pernicious to the caufe of the perpetrators.

F I N I S.

EXPLANATION of the MAP.

THE march of the Duke of Brunfwick from Luxembourg to Longwy and Verdun, and from Verdun, by Grand Pré, to the Camp of La Lune, is indicated by a line of a green colour.

The march of General Dumourier from Sedan to Grand Pré and St. Menehould is marked by a red line.

The march of General Dillon from Mouzon to Biefme, red.

The march of General Kellermann from Metz, by Bar le Duc, St. Dizier, and Vitry, red.

The fields where engagements took place, are indicated by fwords croffed.

The rivers are pale green.

The roads yellow.

The Duke of Brunfwick's Camp at La Lune is coloured yellow.

Thofe of Dumourier and Kellermann near St. Menehould, red.

Dillon's Camp at the Côte de Biefme, red.

The Heffian Camp near Dombafle, green.

Check Out More Titles From HardPress Classics Series In this collection we are offering thousands of classic and hard to find books. This series spans a vast array of subjects – so you are bound to find something of interest to enjoy reading and learning about.

Subjects:
Architecture
Art
Biography & Autobiography
Body, Mind &Spirit
Children & Young Adult
Dramas
Education
Fiction
History
Language Arts & Disciplines
Law
Literary Collections
Music
Poetry
Psychology
Science
…and many more.

Visit us at www.hardpress.net

CPSIA information can be obtained
at www.ICGtesting.com
Printed in the USA
BVHW091118270819
556837BV00004B/184/P

9 781314 987782